TWILIGHT ON THE RANGE

Recollections of a Latterday Cowboy

Number Two

THE M. K. BROWN RANGE LIFE SERIES

William Timmons

TWILIGHT ON THE RANGE

Recollections of a Latterday Cowboy

UNIVERSITY OF TEXAS PRESS · AUSTIN

To
my wife,
LORA

and daughters,
LUCILLE   LILLIAN

and granddaughters,
SUSAN   CONNIE

Contents

Illustrations

(following page 146)

TWILIGHT ON THE RANGE

I. CHARLES GOODNIGHT MEETS ME

I WAS FOURTEEN years old when I saw Charles Goodnight for the first time in 1892. Now, almost seventy years later, that October meeting remains one of the most vivid recollections of my life.

In those days Charles Goodnight's name was the best known of any in the cattleman's West, his personality the most striking. Even rival cattlemen and the settlers who were then pouring into the Texas ranch lands were quietly proud of his fame. Young fry like me might grudgingly have admitted that the President of the United States outranked him, but surely nobody else did.

Perhaps I would have been a cowboy anyway, but in the country where I was growing up it looked like the way of life most open to boys my age, though the old-timers who rode the range had mostly come from faraway places.

I first met Mr. Goodnight while I was working for his brother-in-law, Walter Dyer, who gave me my first job on a cattle ranch. It was a womanless place. Walter was at that time unmarried, and Jim Owens, his foreman, was and always remained a bachelor. Dyer and Owens both liked liquor and they made a daily trip to the little town of Claude, twelve miles away. When they'd return, Jim would be jolly and pleasant, but Walter would be harsh and gruff. Before they'd leave the ranch, Jim would tell me what to do, and he was always pleased with the way I did it. Walter never was, but Jim didn't ever let him say much to me.

One day, after I'd been there about two months, Jim told me to take a pair of little Spanish mules, hitch them to a wagon, drive to the corral, and clean out the horse barn. Then he and

3

Walter left for town. About noon I had the wagon loaded and started out to dump it. But those mules had other ideas, and they ran the wagon into a gate post, wedging the post in between the front and back wheels so tight I couldn't back up and I couldn't go forward.

The only solution I could think of was to unload the wagon. I spent two hours trying to loosen that wagon and unloading it. But even empty it was still too much for me to budge. I was wondering how I was going to get out of this when a man drove up in a buckboard. I never had seen Mr. Goodnight before, but there was no mistaking who he was.

He got out of the buckboard, and I saw that he was a big man with great physical strength. Although he was in his middle fifties, his dark hair and beard were hardly touched with gray. Looking at his massive head, those burning eyes of his, his huge shoulders, his bowlegs, and his shuffling gait, I thought of old Sykes, the king of the buffalo herd that grazed behind a high wire fence on the Goodnight ranch.

Mr. Goodnight easily lifted my wagon away from the gate post, and helped me reload. We drove out to the field, and he helped me unload. As we were driving back to the corral and his buckboard, Mr. Goodnight asked me if Walter was good to me.

"No, sir; but Jim is," I replied.

"Well," he said, "you tell Jim he'd better send you over to my ranch tomorrow, and you can go to work for me."

My heart leaped. Here I was getting a job on a big cattle ranch—the Cross J—and a chance to be a cowboy instead of hauling manure. Mr. Goodnight hadn't asked me if I wanted to work for him; he just told me what to do. That was always the Goodnight way. I'm sure my face showed how I felt.

Later I learned more about the man. Charles Goodnight was born in Macoupin County, Illinois, on March 5, 1836, just three days after Texas declared its independence of Mexico. He was nine years old when his family brought him to the state of Texas in 1846. At twenty-one, he formed a partnership with Wes Sheek at Waco, then trailed their herd of cattle up the Brazos River to the Keechi Valley in Palo Pinto County. Soon he had other ranches in Palo Pinto, Parker, and Young counties. Before

4

the Civil War he served as a Texas Ranger and Indian scout and during the war as a scout for a frontier regiment protecting settlers against the Indians. He went back to ranching when the war ended.

Indian raids wiped out his fortune. Then he blazed the Goodnight trail, one of the earliest to carry wiry Texas Longhorns to northern markets and feeding grounds. This trail, long and dusty, ran westward from Fort Belknap, near the Palo Pinto County Goodnight ranch. After crossing the Pecos it turned northward to Fort Bascom in New Mexico, then continued on to Trinidad, Pueblo, and Denver in Colorado. From there it led across the South Platte, to Cheyenne in Wyoming. By 1868, when Goodnight was thirty-two, his fame was no longer confined to Texas. He had given his name to the West.

After that came Goodnight's ranching activities in Colorado, but the panic of 1873 all but wiped him out again. In 1877 he formed a partnership with John George Adair, a native of Rathdair, Ireland, who had come to America and married into the Wadsworth family of New York. Out of the partnership came the JA Ranch, located in the sheltered areas of Palo Duro Canyon, southeast of the present city of Amarillo but then hundreds of miles from any railroad depot.

Before Adair died in 1885 Goodnight had built up the JA Ranch to more than a million acres, made it the most complete and up-to-date ranch in the West, and brought in the imported Hereford cattle which were to drive out the Longhorns and make the Texas Panhandle a white-faced cattle country. But after Adair died, Goodnight broke off his partnership with Adair's widow, left the dream ranch in the Palo Duro, and in 1887 established the one which bore his name, along the new Fort Worth and Denver Railroad. At what was to become the town of Goodnight, he built the substantial headquarters home, planted orchards and shade trees, and made it the show place of the Texas Panhandle. The buffalo herd which he had started because Mrs. Goodnight hoped to save the species from extinction was moved from the JA to the Cross J.

On the day Mr. Goodnight offered me the job, his main ranch had, I think, about 160 sections of land or approximately 103,000 acres. But even more impressive to me were two things that everybody said of Mr. Goodnight: more than any other man, he was responsible for bringing law and order to the Texas Panhandle; and he had no equal as a cattle breeder. He was rightly called the Burbank of the cattle world.

After that first flush of joy over Mr. Goodnight's offer, I soon experienced a change of heart. "What about old Jim?" I asked myself. I'd have to leave him, and my attachment to him was strong. He was kind not only to me, but to everybody. I've never known a man who had so many simple little ways of endearing himself. I made up my mind to tell Jim what Mr. Goodnight had said. Then if he didn't want me to go I'd stay.

That day, Jim and Walter rode in late. As usual, Jim was jolly, Walter huffy. Walter started in on me about something, but Jim stopped him and sent him to the house. Jim was angry, too, by this time at the way Walter acted. It was the only time I ever saw him mad.

We had some calves to feed, and while we were doing that I told him about Mr. Goodnight coming and what he had said. Jim praised Mr. Goodnight but made me no answer. When we were through feeding, he said, "Billie, we'll saddle up and ride over to your father's place and stay tonight. I don't want to go up to the house and see Walter."

I was pleased with that, but I could tell he'd had too much to drink that day and my father and mother were very much against liquor. But we had a few miles to ride to their house, and the weather was rather cool. I had hopes the liquor would wear off by the time we got there. We arrived long after my family's suppertime, but when Mother learned we hadn't eaten she quickly fixed up something for us.

The night was very pleasant for me. Jim didn't show a sign of ever having had a drink. Neither of us said a word about Mr. Goodnight's offer. Next morning we rode back to the ranch, and I thought I'd stay on there until Jim said, "Billie, I think you'd better take Brownie and ride over and tell Mr. Goodnight you'll go to work for him."

"Jim," I replied, "I'd rather stay with you."

"If I could keep you with me I wouldn't let you go. But I'll be away a lot next summer; and I can't take you with me. I've got to go to several different ranches and work with their roundup wagons to get Walter's strays, and I don't want to leave you here with Walter."

So I saddled Brownie. This was a rare privilege, because he was Jim's horse—a fast, rangy, well-trained animal that Jim always rode to town. Then I said good-bye to kindly, lovable Jim Owens. I'll never forget our silent handshake that morning when I mounted Brownie and rode off to become the youngest cowboy Charles Goodnight ever hired. Our parting was so painful to me that I couldn't have uttered a word. And there were times when Jim didn't seem to want to say anything, either.

II. I START AT THE TOP

CHARLES GOODNIGHT intended that every man employed on his Cross J Ranch should learn everything necessary to make him a first-class cattleman. He also meant for every man to learn the Goodnight way, which was quite different from the methods used on other ranches in that vast grazing domain. This Goodnight ranch was a network of separate divisions; Mr. Goodnight had strung many miles of barbed-wire fence so he could keep a close check on his cattle.

In November, when I had just turned fourteen, Mr. Goodnight sent me to the camp of an old Mexican named Juan

Rodríguez. Juan ran the kindergarten class. He had been with Goodnight eleven years and knew his ways inside out. There were alfalfa and corn at his place, and Juan was feeding a few hundred Hereford bulls.

Juan was to teach me the way animals were cared for in wintertime on the Goodnight ranch. My job was to shuck corn, then round up the bulls—confined in a small pasture—and see that all of them were on the feeding ground when Juan put out the feed. While I knew that, as far as the work was concerned, I was starting at the bottom, I felt that from the standpoint of the kind of ranch I was on, I was starting at the top.

Juan's wife was a Bohemian woman named Rosie. She knew how to prepare all of the best American dishes and all of the wonderful cooking of her Czech homeland, too. Whenever Rosie found out there was something I especially liked, she'd fix it for me. I brought in the wood and water for her and often dried the dishes. She taught me a few things about cooking, things I'd need to know when thrown on my own, as I was sure to be some day.

The couple had a little girl named Clara, about three or four years old. I became devoted to all three of them, and it was a pleasant winter. Juan and Rosie remained my friends as long as they lived. I somehow lost track of Clara over the years.

Juan gave Mr. Goodnight a good report on my work, and when the winter ended I was transferred to the home ranch to do little jobs, odds and ends. My foreman then was Walter McLaren, a nephew of Mr. Goodnight, who was a patient, understanding, and kindly man—and a good teacher. As it turned out, of all my friendships formed on the ranch the one with him was to be the longest. (In 1957 he was eighty-seven years old, living in California. To my knowledge he is the only other survivor of the days when I lived on the ranch.)

When the spring roundup of 1893 started I had my first mount of horses cut out for me. I remember them yet, their good points and peculiarities and their colors. Dick was a small dun, Curley a bay with a white stripe down his face. Kid and Coley were black. Happy Jack was a dark bay. For the roundup I was made the horse wrangler. Dolph Andrews, the cook, quickly became my closest friend. He was far behind Rosie Rodríguez, but he fried a steak and made just the kind of black coffee and sourdough biscuits that I liked. His other top items were potatoes, canned corn, and stewed apricots. A horse wrangler spent more time around the chuck wagon than the cowboys did, and I gained weight on Dolph's good fare.

Our boss that spring was Johnny Martin. I think Martin had a better hold on the Goodnight ideas than any man on the ranch, and Mr. Goodnight probably had more confidence in his judgment than in anyone else's on the ranch. Martin taught me to handle those horses like I'd be expected to handle a beef herd. It was my business not to let them scatter so much that I'd have to chase them to get them together, yet to give them plenty of room to graze. It was also my duty to see that they were where they could get water before changing time—morning, noon, and night—and that they were always near the churck wagon.

Usually there were from 100 to 125 horses in the remuda. I came to know all of those horses and their names, and I could pick out each one by the shape of his head or by some other characteristic.

I soon learned my other duties. When the outfit moved, the wrangler followed the chuck wagon close, and wasn't supposed to ever let the cook get too far ahead. The wrangler was the cook's helper, and part of his job was to unharness and turn loose the chuck-wagon team. I also learned that if the cook liked the wrangler, the boss and everybody else did too. Furthermore, if the cook liked you he made it as easy as possible for you. (Later I discovered the benefit of this happy relationship at home and anywhere else. Stand in with the cook.)

We didn't have a nighthawk, so I stayed with the horses through the first guard and got up with the last guard to bring the mounts in for saddling up. That was long hours for a boy getting his growth, but I liked it.

We didn't have a rope corral for saddle horses or remuda, either; I was to see my first one in North Dakota some years later. (They had stake pins driven into the ground, and they stretched rope around them.) At Goodnight we usually tied a thirty-five-foot catch rope to the front wheel of the bed wagon

and fastened another rope to the back wheel. On past the wagons, cowboys lined up thirty-five feet apart, providing anchors
for other ropes, until the enclosure was large enough for the
number of horses we had. Just one strand of rope was enough;
horses respected that single band of stretched hemp.

But we didn't always do this on the Goodnight ranch. I could
usually handle the remuda myself, except when for some reason
it was temporarily big and unwieldy. I had a long rawhide whip
and the help of some good horses. If an undisciplined one broke
away from the bunch, those smart horses and I put the bunch-
quitter back in place. The old ones were trained to stay put,
and the green ones soon got the idea.

There were no stoves or tents on the Texas range at that time;
or if there were, I never heard of them. All we had were Dutch
ovens and a wagon sheet to keep the bedrolls dry. As a horse
wrangler I was especially concerned with the Dutch ovens, for
I had to draw up wood from creeks or wherever I could find it.
I also gathered cow chips from the open prairie, where our outfit usually worked, and always saw that Dolph Andrews had a
plentiful supply of fuel. There was a swing made of cowhides
under the wagon, and I had to keep it full of chips, so there
would be a dry supply if wet weather came.

In return, Dolph rolled cigarettes for me. All cowboys smoked
cigarettes, and most of them considered that a Bull Durham
label showing above their shirt pocket gave the finishing touch
to their wardrobe. They wore it in the same way some fancy
dressers wear a handkerchief in the breast pocket of a coat. The
way cowboys dressed and smoked caught my attention early,
and I found that it never varied on any ranch I was ever connected with.

A cowboy undresses upward: boots off, then socks, pants, and
shirt. He never goes deeper than that. After he has removed the
top layer he takes his hat off and lays his boots on the brim, so
the hat won't blow away during the night. Spurs are never taken
off boots.

In the morning a cowboy begins dressing downward. First he
puts on his hat, then his shirt, and takes out of his shirt pocket
his Bull Durham and cigarette papers and rolls one to start the

day. He finishes dressing by putting on his pants, socks, and boots. This is a habit that usually stays with a cowboy long after his days in the saddle are over.

Several years after my saddle days were over, my friend Alex Greer, a North Dakota cowboy, came to Amarillo to visit me. He got to town by train, late at night, and telephoned me to come to the hotel and spend the night with him.

I went. We had one of those sessions where we talked of things we both remembered—or reminded one another of things one of us had forgotten. Then we went to bed, undressing as usual: boots first, hats last. Alex watched me in a bemused sort of way; then he said, "Billie, what did you say you're doing for a living?" I replied, "I have a stock farm. I'm farming about a thousand acres. I also buy and sell some town property."

"Yet you're just a cowboy," Alex said. "You don't undress or dress like a man should. You undress up and dress down. Just nothing but a cowboy still!"

Dolph tried to make a cigarette smoker out of me but failed. I got a pipe that looked good to me, especially after that first sick spell. After losing my supper that one time I had no more trouble. I was the only man on the ranch besides Mr. Goodnight who didn't smoke cigarettes. He chewed tobacco and smoked a pipe or cigar, but never a cigarette.

In dressing, I varied the routine of the cigarette smoker a little. I waited until I got to my pants; then I took the pipe out of a pocket and lit up. After the smoke I ate a big breakfast, caught and saddled my horse, and went to do a day's work. I learned early in the game that sometimes things happen so a cowboy can't get back to the chuck wagon in the middle of the day. Breakfast is still my big meal.

After that introduction to range life, I spent the winter of 1893 in what was called the rawhide camp on Rawhide Creek. Dolph Andrews, the summertime cook, became a wintertime cowboy along with me. We were to ride a portion of the range, pick up anything that needed feeding, and get the animals to the feeding camp where there were haystacks, cottonseed, and a hay meadow. Whether cottonseed meal or cakes had come into use elsewhere I don't know, but we had none. In the Panhandle

11

then ranchers shipped in carloads of cottonseed just as it came from the gin, with most of the lint removed.

That winter we made many a cold ride and missed many a meal. But that was no hardship, for I was a cowboy. I'd come in very tired, get a late supper, wash the dishes, then fall on the bed and sleep. Dolph didn't follow my routine. He was learning to play the fiddle that winter, and practiced every night without fail, trying to strike a tune. He knew what it was, if he could only hit it. Sometimes way in the night he'd shake me and say, "Billie, wake up! Listen! I believe I've struck a tune."

I'd listen but it was always the same—just sawing. I would, of course, say something like, "That's fine," to encourage him. This didn't work out too well for me, for Dolph began to wake me more often for additional encouragement. I lost a lot of good sleep. By spring, however, Dolph could play "Old Sally Goodin," "Turkey in the Straw," "Arkansas Traveler," and many of those popular frontier tunes.

That winter I came the nearest to freezing to death I ever did. Early in March there had been some nice days, so with the skies clear and the weather pleasant we decided to make our last pickup of the winter, looking for weak animals that we might have missed in earlier searches.

On this particular day spring seemed pleasantly close at hand. Dolph and I were stirring at daybreak; dawn was just far enough along for us to spot the cattle when we rode out. Dolph headed for the rough country down the creek, where most of the cattle would be, and he told me to take the high-country edge of the prairie. About all I'd be expected to find were cattle that might have left the main herd along the creek. We agreed to meet at noon at the Barker place, the former holdings of a small cowman who'd sold out to the Goodnight ranch. It had a good house, sheds, storeroom, and a little field for oats, but it was never used in winter, being out on the bald prairie.

I hit the high divide a little after a beautiful sunrise. Pretty soon I noticed that the sun wasn't so bright, and the north wind got a little cooler. On I rode, but there wasn't a cow in sight. Instinct had told the animals it wasn't spring yet. Man didn't have that instinct, and Dolph and I were many years ahead of

12

the day when cattlemen could make their plans according to radio weather reports.

As I rode on, the wind got colder and colder. A blue norther was upon us, but I was still unaware of it. I was riding Curley, a good horse, and we'd made many miles that morning, going far out on the plains to where there was a windmill. I found it in good order, with plenty of water in the tank. I rode back to rough land, looking down the draws to be sure I missed nothing. By now the temperature had dropped sharply, and the wind had reached storm proportions. You couldn't see the sun anymore at all.

I was near the Barker place, but I didn't want to get there before Dolph did, for I hadn't seen a single cow, and that, I thought, would be a bad report to make in such weather. Although the wind was blowing harder than ever, I no longer felt cold. But a powerful feeling of sleepiness had come over me, so I rode up to the old storeroom, got off Curley, went inside, fell on some sacks, and dropped off to sleep. I had lost all sense of time and had no idea how long I had been there when Dolph arrived.

Dolph was an old-timer who recognized a freezing person when he saw one. He rolled, rubbed, and beat me until I regained consciousness. He continued to rub me for some time; then he took off my boots and massaged my feet—as well as my hands, ears, and nose.

Only my heels were too frozen to yield to his first-aid help. They turned black, and there was nothing in camp to doctor them with except kerosene and a box of axle grease. I used that freely and bandaged my feet with flour sacks. I put on Dolph's socks and my overshoes and gave my boots a rest.

Dolph wanted to know why I didn't have better sense than to let myself get so cold. I told him I hadn't seen a cow and didn't want him to think I just struck the highland, got cold, and rode straight to the Barker place. He replied, "Billie, I knew you wouldn't see a cow when the weather got so heavy. They knew better than to stay in that exposed place."

I got around on my toes pretty well and never lost a day's work. Why complain about a little frostbite on the heel? I was

13

a cowboy and I wanted to follow the example of another cowboy, Joe Cupell, on the Quarter Circle Heart Ranch in Donley County. When he broke a leg, he went to town and had the doctor set it. When Cupell could stand up on it, he saw that it wasn't set straight, so he got down on the frame around the heater in the bunkhouse and, with his weight, broke it over. He then set it himself, and this time it was straight. That was the way a real cowboy acted.

That blizzard delayed spring but little. We rode bogs then, looking for cattle mired down in mud. Sometimes you could keep after them even after they'd given up and they'd work out. Dolph took the toughest places, and I made the easy ones where cattle caught in spongy earth could most likely struggle out if I got after them hard enough. Whenever I found one that was too tough, I rode to get Dolph, for it's a man's job to get a rope on an animal, drag it free, and turn it loose.

The spring rains soon made grass good everywhere. As we shaped up for the summer ranges we were back with our old outfit. We hadn't seen a one of them since we went into winter quarters. Again Dolph was cook, and I was horse wrangler.

But before we got too deep in cattle we decided to tarry a while for a social affair.

MAXINE PRICE

14

III. GAY NINETIES ON A CATTLE RANCH

THE EARLY 1890's was a time of important migration to the Texas Panhandle. In 1890 a strip of land had been opened for settlers between Mr. Goodnight's Cross J Ranch to the south and the N–N (N Bar N) Ranch, which had been established by the Neidringhaus brothers of St. Louis, to the north.

My father had filed on state-owned land there and had built his home near what is now Groom, Texas. The town was named for Col. B. B. Groom, an Englishman who had come to Texas from Kentucky and who was the nearest approach to a plantation-owning, mint-julep-drinking colonel I've ever seen. His physical appearance and the clothes he wore seemed more suited to the bluegrass of Kentucky than to the buffalo grass of northwest Texas, but he did all right as a cattleman.

Colonel Groom was peculiar among cowmen in another respect: he actually encouraged settlers to come in. Mr. Goodnight, at the outset, extended no such hospitality, and I heard him complain that some land being settled ought never to be touched by a plough, that when the grass was gone the land would blow away. Nearly half a century later I was to be reminded of this prediction by the dust storms and the dust bowl.

But the cowboys on the Cross J Ranch weren't interested in practical economics or in the bickering between the cowmen and settlers. The important thing to them was that some of the settlers had very pretty daughters.

One family by the name of Angel had two especially good-looking grown girls. All the boys around thought they'd hit Paradise and wanted an Angel. We'd been talking about a dance ever since Dolph struck his first tune on his fiddle; so why not give one now at the Allen Creek camp where we had wintered? There was a big bunkhouse to dance in, a kitchen, and an extra room for the women to powder their noses and lay their wraps. It also had a bed on which to put the tots. Most of them were babies in arms, for the child industry in the Texas Panhandle was just getting under way. There were haystacks, meadows, and barns to furnish good fare and housing for the four-footed visitors.

Hill Garrison was in charge of this Allen Creek camp, which was run entirely for feeding and haying. Hill was the saving type and was commonly believed to have a tidy nest egg. He was getting up in years, but he wasn't too old to want an Angel. (In after years I was to have it impressed on me that men seldom get too old to want an Angel.) We took our plans to Hill, and he was all for it. It was, he realized, his chance.

The dance was arranged. Windy Bill, of the Matador Ranch, was invited to call. This was the same Windy Bill who was the caller so highly praised in the poem "The Cowboys' Christmas Ball," a dance held at Anson, Texas. I don't know that I ever heard his last name; it was part of his stock-in-trade to have himself referred to only as Windy Bill. There may have been a strong trace of show-off in him, but he could back it up by doing anything there was to do on a cattle ranch as well or better than anybody else: he could perform tricks with a .45 Colt. No bucking horse could get Windy Bill off his back. He knew all the ins and outs of roping and was a past master with a cutting horse. But, most of all, Bill sparkled as a dance caller. Our Gay Nineties social events in the Texas range country were almost exclusively square-dance affairs; hence a caller who could keep everything going in a lively fashion was a prime necessity. Anytime Windy Bill was master of ceremonies the success of the event was just about guaranteed. Our arrangers got two other fiddlers to help Dolph Andrews.

Goodnight's cowboys did nothing by halves. They set about to make this the grand social event of the Texas Panhandle in the year 1894. The bunkhouse was made spick-and-pan. Food was provided for a spread at midnight and a big breakfast at daylight. In addition, they wanted all the little extras they could

16

think of, especially things that would please the girls—and the arrangers had taken a census to see that no pretty girl failed to get an invitation.

The boys made up a pot and everybody chipped in to get lemons for lemonade, oranges, apples, peanuts, popcorn, and candy. Because I had more time, or was less valuable around the place than anyone else at such a time, they sent me to town to spend the money. I don't think I ever knew how much I had, but I bore firm instructions to spend it all. They gave me only a few suggestions about what to buy, but I was to get anything else I saw that looked good.

Before sunup I headed for Clarendon in Donley County. This was one of two towns that stood at opposite poles of morality in the Northwest Texas cattle country then. Tascosa, in Oldham County, was the sin and six-gun capital, with many saloons. But Clarendon, settled by a religious group, was saloonless. It was a sleepy little frontier town with a few houses and stores, but it was a metropolis to me. Actually, small as it was, it was then one of the two or three largest settlements in the Texas Panhandle.

Clarendon had just one little confectionery, and I went to it first. When I began to put in my order, the proprietor listened in disbelief. I had spied his display of wax (later called chewing gum), which I liked. My order was for more than he had. He asked me what I wanted with it: was I going to start a store somewhere? I said No, but told him no more. He would not have been interested in our dance, anyway. He didn't look like he'd ever had on a pair of boots in his life, and he was wearing a little town hat. I settled for half his wax. I didn't think that was enough. But it turned out to be all that was needed, with a lot left over.

I had trouble calculating how to use all the money, and I wasn't going to tell anybody that I had to spend it all. I still had a few dollars left after I'd bought what I felt was ample, but I added enough to my original orders to use up all the money. We got everything packed up in boxes and tow sacks.

I knew I had to get a haircut and a shave, for it was just a night and a day before the dance. I went to the barbershop and

17

got a haircut. The barber thought he was through, but I asked for a shave. He said I didn't need it. I thought I did; I'd never had one, and I was sure the Angels would be at the dance, and I didn't know who else might be. I insisted and got my first shave. It must have been a good one, for I didn't need another for a year or two.

The boys at the Allen Creek camp were well pleased with my selections, especially with the stock of wax. They noticed my haircut, but as they said nothing about the shave, neither did I.

All of the young folks for miles around were at the dance. Even some of the old ranchers who could still ride a horse and had a desire to see a pretty girl were there. I liked pretty girls, too, but I was at a bashful age and had been in men-only cow camps. I spoke to just the ones I had to. Mostly I watched Windy Bill. His flow of wit never slacked off, from the time he called the first set till he waved all of us "adios" after sunup the next morning. Such a thing as a loudspeaker would have been a waste of machinery with Bill. His voice was as strong and clear as any Longhorn bull's. Soon all were listening, between dances, to hear what Bill was saying. He had come to entertain the crowd, and he permitted no dull moment.

Windy Bill looked comical. And the more you looked at him, the funnier he looked, it seemed to me. He had a large mouth, very prominent nose and ears and thick, dark, hair. His teeth protruded just a little. He was dressed not as for a special occasion, but as for a day's work: high-heeled boots with spurs that jingled and rattled, striped California riding trousers, and a checkered wool shirt. He seldom removed his big black Stetson; when he did he held it in his hand. And he never removed his spurs, as others had done. Someone said to him, "Bill, why don't you take off your spurs?"

"My horse is saddled," he answered. "I might make some crack, get run out, and wouldn't have time to look for my hat and spurs. I might need them."

One of his stunts was to catch with his mouth anything thrown across the room at him. He never missed peanut, candy, or apple. He ate his midnight snack talking and walking, and never sat down or missed a dance.

18

I remember that Mr. and Mrs. James, from the settlement, were there, and Mr. and Mrs. Frazier, Mr. and Mrs. Shirley Boydstun. Margaret and Alice Angel were the belles of the ball; everybody had expected that they would be, but not by such a wide margin. My brother Benjamin picked his individual belle, Miss Lora Boydstun. Later they were married. (In 1956 they celebrated their sixtieth wedding anniversary, both hale and hearty.)

I never forgot one pretty young married woman and her husband—Mr. and Mrs. Shirley Boydstun. They observed my standoffishness and recognized it as bashfulness. They took me in hand and made me talk. Their friendly attitude made the night much more pleasant for me. I often thought of Mr. and Mrs. Boydstun after that and knew there could be angels without the name.

Of course, we had such Cross J standbys as Johnny Martin, Hill Garrison, Walter and Robert McLaren, Charley and George Jowell, Bill Evans, Joe Woods, Wayman Brown, Jim Cardwell, and Dolph Andrews. My older brothers, Benjamin and Claiborne (who had some land, horses, cattle, and other enterprises of their own, but often helped out on the Goodnight ranch at its busy season), were there.

Ed Johnson, foreman of the Flying U, whose range just touched our Cross J on the northeast corner, came and brought some of his cowboys. Joe Humphrey was among those representing the Spur Ranch. Will Christian and some others came from the JA, Hiram and Lon Sweeny from the F, Tom Crawford and a cowboy called Jack the Ripper from the N Bar N. Windy Bill brought along with him Jack Lucky from the Matador Ranch. But we had miscalculated the number of young ladies within riding distance, and with fellows from the other ranches coming in generous numbers, the men were more than double the number of women.

After daylight everybody had breakfast: bacon, eggs, flapjacks, and brown-sugar lick. Dolph Andrews and Hill Garrison did the cooking and saw that everyone got plenty, for our guests had a long way to go home in wagons, buckboards, buggies, or on horseback.

Windy Bill was still walking around at sunup, with something to say to everybody. He had endeared himself to all, and when, after breakfast, he went out to mount his horse, everybody went with him and gathered around to watch him as he loped away and waved to us with that big black hat. I'm sure he felt he had done a good job.

We thought our dance had been a big success. As I've said, my brother Ben married Lora Boydstun. And Ed Johnson married Margaret, the oldest Angel girl; Hill Garrison married Alice. The rest of the boys just had to take what they could get, but all I heard of were well satisfied. There was a younger Angel girl, about my age. She was too young then to go to dances, and I couldn't wait for her. Soon I'd be looking for tall grass and green pastures.

After the dance we went back to our routine. For me the year-round schedule on the Goodnight ranch was something like this: as soon as the bog-riding was over in the spring I rode fence, greased windmills, and drove a team with Bill Evans, hauling and putting out salt over the range.

About the first of May the wagon started and the roundups for classifying the cattle began, most of them thrown in summer pastures. We sorted out the two-year-old steers which, as a usual thing, we shipped to whoever they may have been sold to, by June 1.

Next came the tussle with the calves, which we always branded in early June. We went from that to cutting out the yearling steers and heifers, as well as two-year-old heifers, which were put in a pasture to themselves. We turned the bulls in with the cows; then we went back to doing anything we'd had to neglect while the roundups had been goin on.

In the fall we rounded up and shipped old, fat cows and bulls, as well as fat, dry cows. We'd close up the summer and fall schedule by branding the late calves and putting everything in the winter pastures. Then I'd be sent back to headquarters, and that was really a place where there was never a free minute. But I was proud of my job and liked everything I was told to do, even hauling "freight." All the supplies bought for the ranch were shipped to Goodnight. There Walter McLaren would load a wagon and send me with it to the Allen Creek camp or to a fencing or windmill crew, both bossed by Ira Sharp. After that I might be sent to the Angus pasture to ride fences or grease windmills.

One day in June, 1894, after we'd rounded up to brand calves, Mr. Goodnight came to the wagon. During the midday meal he said to Johnny Martin, our foreman: "Do you ever take Billie to the herd?"

"No, I don't, Mr. Goodnight," Johnny replied.

"Well," said Mr. Goodnight, "take him this afternoon. Put him in the herd, cutting cows and calves."

Then he proceeded to instruct me how to cut out cows with their calves. "Don't get in a hurry," he said. "Work them easy until you are out of the herd, so the calf will stay close to its mother. If you try to rush them they'll separate. Then you'll lose time getting them back together. A cow and her calf must be cut from the herd together."

I never tried to be fast cutting anything out of a herd. A good rule on beef steers was to work them easy, until they were near the edge of the herd you were cutting from. That way, you didn't agitate the rest of the herd you were working.

Turning to Johnny, Mr. Goodnight continued discussing me. "I want him to know every phase of this cow work, even if you have to put somebody else with the horses. He won't want to be a horse wrangler all his life."

A cowboy furnished his own saddle and his own bedroll on all ranches. These and his boots were his most expensive equipment. Johnny Martin and Charley Jowell, the boss and straw boss, told me to go to old man Corbett, the bootmaker in Clarendon, to be measured for a pair of boots. They gave these to me as a present, the first shop-made boots I'd ever had.

I guess I did very well in the cow- and calf-cutting job. Next, I had to rope a beef. It was a fat, strong, rollicky two-year-old heifer. I got the rope tied around the horn of my little twenty-five-dollar S. C. Gallup saddle, made in Pueblo, Colorado. But the heifer pulled the horn off.

If that wasn't embarrassing, just getting to be a real cowboy, and having such a mishap! The boys called me "Mulley"—and just as my wages were raised from $15 to $20 per month! Top wages for men were $25 a month, and I was hoping to get into that bracket soon. Now a dehorned saddle and a let-down!

Mr. Goodnight was a great friend of the saddlemaker. Their close relation had begun when Mr. Goodnight was ranching near Pueblo in the early 1870s. So Mr. Goodnight sat down and wrote a letter to Mr. Gallup, telling him never again to be guilty of putting out a saddle with a horn that a two-year-old heifer could pull off without taking the saddle too. Goodnight worked flocks of cowboys; Gallup needed his business, and he must have taken the advice. That was the last and only Gallup saddle I ever saw that was a "mulley." (Mr. Goodnight also showed Gallup how to make a more comfortable sidesaddle. Women always rode sidesaddle; and Mr. Goodnight's idea was to have a third horn with a curve so that female riders could hold their positions with safety and comfort.)

I soon had a thirty-five-dollar Gallup saddle; the forty-five-dollar ones were the top ones. With my new equipment I was fixed to go places.

One of the reasons I liked to be sent to the headquarters place to do odd jobs when the wagon wasn't running was that I adored Mrs. Goodnight. From the first she had always paid me my wages, giving me a lot of good advice along with them. Her graciousness made me feel I was getting double pay. But though she always paid me, I'm sure Mr. Goodnight set the amount of my first wages, although he never mentioned it.

The family needed all of my check I could spare; I took it to them proudly. My father and mother were hard workers, independent and self-sacrificing, and many times they'd try to make me take the check but I left it gladly. I'd tell Mrs. Goodnight what I'd done, and that always pleased her. This was more than pay to me.

Sometimes, when work on the ranch was slack, Mr. Goodnight would let his cowboys do work for neighbors that he particularly liked. These jobs would always be brief. Twice I was loaned out this way. Once was for a month to Jack Scott, a farmer. Money, always a scarce object, had been especially short since the panic of 1893, and Scott paid me with two shoats

—a boar and a sow—delivered to Mr. Goodnight's headquarters place. After they grew, eating the Cross J feed, Mrs. Goodnight gave me twenty-five silver dollars for the sow. The boar went to my father's place.

The other time I was loaned to Joe Miller, an old Goodnight man that I'd already met. Born in Jack County, Texas, he had come to the JA Ranch in 1882 to run a fencing crew there. He had moved to the new ranch when Goodnight left the JA, and filed on a section of land just north of Goodnight. His old employer had helped him buy and stock the little ranch, and finally Mr. Goodnight bought him out. When Joe moved to Greer County, he wanted me to go with him. It hadn't been decided then whether Greer County was in Texas or Oklahoma; there was a court fight for it and Oklahoma won.

Now I told Mr. Goodnight I thought I might like that part of Oklahoma; and I certainly liked Joe. Mr. Goodnight replied, "Well, go help Joe get his stock over there. Joe Miller's a fine fellow. If you want to stay with him, all right. But remember, if you don't, you always have a job here. You've been good to my stock and that's what I make my money out of. Go to the house and tell Molly to give you a check."

Mrs. Goodnight's name was Mary, but he always called her Molly. I went in to get my check. She had a lot to say to me, for I was going away on a trip. Then I told her I might not come back. I got some more good advice, mixed with a few tears. I can't remember just what I did, but I do know I was homesick before I got started.

As soon as I could I went out to my horse and looked back at that house which was home to many an otherwise lonely cowboy. Mrs. Goodnight had a sincere fondness for all of us on the ranch, and she showed her friendliness in a way I can't explain but I know it made something special out of every one of us. Her motherly affection was a bonus every Goodnight cowboy got. I tried to put the pangs of parting out of my mind by reflecting that if a fellow was going to be a cowboy there were other hills to ride over and more creeks to cross. Then I rode on to Joe Miller's, and we talked over our trip.

Joe had been married for just a short time. He had given his bride a nice bedroom suite, but he needed all his wagon space for the move and couldn't take this furniture with him. He said he'd give it to me in payment for my work; then I could have a steady job with him if I wanted it. The compensation was just right, for I knew the bedroom suite would please my mother very much.

In a day or two I was away with Joe Miller on my first trail drive. It wasn't a long one, covering only three or four Texas counties and a part of the Oklahoma Indian Territory. But it was something new, and I enjoyed it. We cut across the RO Ranch and through the Rocking Chair Ranche, with home offices at 25 Piccadilly, London; its principal owners were the Earl of Aberdeen and the Baron of Tweedmouth. There was nothing new about English and Scotch ownership of Texas ranches, but what made this one outstanding was that it was the only *ranche* in Texas. None of the others used an *e*. During the drive I also saw for the first time the immense Arbuckle range.

Joe's new wife was a fine person, and I liked Joe better all the time. I tried to convince myself that I should stay with them, but that old homesickness kept coming back. It would never leave me easy more than a little while at a time. I found that it was a terrible malady. There's nothing to relieve it besides time, and I didn't think I had the time. I knew that some of those old boys at the ranch would tease me about not being able to stay away, and I hated to be a weakling. But I was sick. Why wait on time for something that just a few days' ride would cure?

I went back to the Goodnight headquarters. Some mighty good people lived there. We hear a lot about how close blood relatives are. There's something else: a close friendship. I've seen that it has about the same effect. So I returned, arriving late at night. The next morning I had breakfast with Mr. and Mrs. Goodnight. Mr. Goodnight said he was glad I was back, and Mrs. Goodnight, with her wonderful way of conveying thoughts without many words, made me feel that things hadn't been nearly as joyful around the ranch while I was away.

Then I went home and got the same loving welcome. I told them about my trip to Greer County, the big ranches I had

24

crossed. The trip, brief though it was, had opened up new horizons to me. But this, I was sure, was the place that would always be dearest to me, with my own family and the Goodnights near.

There was work to do, as there always was around that ranch. I was sent out to Johnny Martin's. He was shaping up for cold weather, branding cattle, throwing everything into winter pastures, putting cows and calves on the river until weaning time. We had some hard fall rains that made the task difficult. When my work there ended, Johnny sent me back to headquarters until winter. Then I was in rawhide camp again with Dolph Andrews.

IV. LURE OF THE DUSTY CATTLE TRAIL

IN THE GREAT DAYS when his reputation as the nation's foremost cattleman went unchallenged, Charles Goodnight was no churchman, had no church affiliations. For himself he had a sort of homemade religion based on the Golden Rule. But he gave generously to churches and, in many cases, provided funds for building houses of worship in the Texas Panhandle.

He was even more generous to schools. Shortly after he built his headquarters at the present town of Goodnight, he provided a combined nondenominational church and school building, paying the entire cost himself. Before that there hadn't been any schools in Armstrong County, where most of Mr. Goodnight's

25

ranch lay, because there wasn't any money to build them or to pay teachers. Like most of the new counties, Armstrong had to build a courthouse and a jail first to take care of those who were educated along wrong lines, The jail was so fancy that the county almost went broke building it.

Still, school needs were few. There were only six children in the vicinity who were of school age. For them Mr. Goodnight hired a teacher and paid the teacher's salary.

His own education had been limited to what he could get in two short terms beginning when he was seven years old. It hardly amounted to a second-grade education. Then he had had to go to work to help support his widowed mother and his two younger sisters. After his marriage Mrs. Goodnight, a former schoolteacher, had got him to continue his education. Most of it was the result of her teaching.

The school he built had a nine-month term. On the religious side, he wrote church authorities, inviting them to send traveling preachers. Most of those who came were Methodists or Baptists. But Mr. Goodnight himself hardly ever went to church and few of the cowboys did, either.

Once, while visiting at my home twelve miles north of Goodnight, I mentioned the school. My mother said, "I do wish I could move to Goodnight and be near that school." Seven miles away was the Lone Star School, but that was too far during the rough Panhandle winters. Yet there were six children in the family younger than I, and four of them already were of school age.

A few days later I had a chance to do something about this. Walter McLaren, my foreman, loaded six barrels of salt in a wagon and told me to take them to the black-cattle pasture and roll them out, leaving two barrels at each of the three windmills. If the barrels broke open when they hit the ground I was to leave them like that. If they didn't break open I was to saw them in two for the cattle.

Just as I was ready to start, Mr. Goodnight came by and asked, "Walter, where're you sending Billie?" When Walter told him, Mr. Goodnight said, "He's not strong enough to handle those barrels by himself. I'll go with him."

As we rode along he became more talkative than he'd ever been with me. He told me I'd be running an outfit myself some day—something which, up to that time, never had entered my mind. When I got to be a boss, he said, I'd find my success depended more on what I knew about human beings than what I knew about cattle. I remember one thing in particular that he said:

"Never hire a man for a steady hand unless he's tried to save something and do something for himself. If by the time he's thirty-five, he's abused every opportunity, he's no good for himself, and he'll be no good for you, either. Just work him through a rush season and let him go."

Then Mr. Goodnight began talking to me about going to school, as he'd done several times before. I told him I couldn't do this, that my folks needed what help I could give them just then. But I told him about my mother's wish, though I had no hope that it could be fulfilled since there wasn't any house they could move into.

I underestimated him. He was always a man of action, and his fast mind, as usual, figured a way.

"There's the Joe Miller place," he said. "Nobody lives in the house, and I don't need it. We can move it up here on a block of land. There'll be room for a garden and an orchard. I've bought a big rooming house in Clarendon. Your father can tear that down and use what he wants of it. With the Miller house, it'll give your family plenty of room.

"Your father is a fine builder, and I've got a lot of construction work to do here. Take a horse tomorrow and go tell him to come over here. We'll make a deal."

I've always thought that ride the next day was the most gleeful of my life. My mother's wish would come true. Her children could be in school. There'd be church services once a month. Just watching the train go by every day was something, too, in that part of the country!

A few days later my father came over and made a swap with Mr. Goodnight that was good for both of them. My father traded grazing land for the town block and for some good farm and meadow land near Goodnight. Then with the Miller place, which he moved, and the lumber from the house in Clarendon, he put up a house that met all of our needs. Although my father was a skilled builder and later became a successful contractor in Amarillo, he really liked farming most of all.

Our new home was only a hundred yards from the combined church-and-school, not far from the railroad depot, and little more than half a mile from the Goodnight residence. We thought we were well off despite the depression that followed the panic of 1893. Added to a terrible drought, it made times very hard. I guess my family would have been rated as poor, but we didn't know we were poor.

My mother had a knack every pioneer woman possessed—of making a little money go a long way. The orchard was soon bearing, but even before that time she canned wild plums and grapes and peaches from the orchard at Goodnight headquarters. My father had brought with him from his native Kentucky a way of curing hams and shoulders—and beef was the most plentiful item of all. We always had a good table at our house. It became a haven for many a lonely cowboy, just like the Goodnight home.

Mr. Goodnight always had a great admiration for my father. Although my father had gone away to join the Confederate Army and was riding in the command of General Nathan Bedford Forrest at an age when he should have been in school, he had educated himself well, especially in arithmetic, history, and geography, and he kept up on current topics.

The school at Goodnight got better as the number of children increased. No teacher was hired without the approval of both Mr. Goodnight and my father and both were hard to please. Then, soon after this success, Mr. Goodnight was to put into operation a dream he had nursed for years—an advanced school that all the young men and women of the Texas Panhandle could attend.

He built Goodnight Academy. He made it as nearly self-supporting as possible, so that cowmen who raised three- to five-cent beef could send their children there for a college education at a cost of nine dollars a month. The girls took turns as helpers to the cook, cared for the dormitories, washed dishes, and waited tables. The boys went to the fields to raise feed, cared for hogs, raised chickens, and gathered eggs. The nine dollars never paid the expenses of a student, but Mr. Goodnight went into his own pocket for the balance. My brothers and sister were to go to that school, but by that time I was to be many hundred miles away, cowboying where I could see those beautiful northern lights.

After my family moved to Goodnight I was again in the rawhide camp with Dolph Andrews for a while. But Dolph got a bone felon on his hand and had to go to town. The pioneer doctors, not very skillful, couldn't do much for him. Despite the pain Dolph decided to come back to camp, and soon after that I was sent to help Walter McLaren feed the black cattle and the buffaloes.

In an experiment, Mr. Goodnight was crossing black cows with buffaloes. They were fed well and kept strong on alfalfa hay; yet many of the cows died. I asked Walter the reason for this, and he told me it was because of the hump on the shoulder of the calves. I believed him, and more than fifty years passed before I thought of it again. By that time almost everybody had forgotten about the experiment, for it hadn't been the success that Mr. Goodnight hoped for. He thought it would result in the first new breed of cattle ever developed in the United States —the "cattalo." Not until a quarter of a century later was a new breed distinctive to the United States developed. Then a Brahman bull from India was the sire; the cows were Shorthorns on the King Ranch, near the Rio Grande. The breed is, of course, the Santa Gertrudis.

Fifty years later, when I was no longer the young believer I had been, I recalled the heavy loss of those breeding cows, and I knew that Walter was wrong because there wasn't any hump on any animal until after birth. The cows were usually big, but was the calf too big while the cow carried it? That couldn't have been true in every case, for I saw the living offspring of the first crossing of the buffalo and the cow.

I saw the cow also—a little, slim long-legged, brindle Longhorn. The calf was brindle, had a hump, and sported horns different from the buffalo—longer and straighter, but not as long as her mother's. The buffalo had thus done his part to get rid of the long horns, which no cowman wanted. The wiry, fighting cow had performed her function—her offspring lived for years. But many larger cows died, and the experiment failed. I've seen little, wiry, gritty men do things that looked impossible for them to do, and I've seen robust men fail at easy tasks. It's too late for an autopsy on the cows; so the mystery of why the little fighting Longhorn lived and the healthy black specimens died is something I never have understood.

After helping Walter McLaren feed the black cows and buffaloes, I was sent back to the rawhide camp to help Bill Koogle, who had taken Dolph Andrews' place. No longer able to endure the pain of the bone felon, Dolph had gone back to town. The doctors kept him there for a month, and they finally cut off the end of his finger. Spring of 1895 was approaching, and I helped Bill ride bogs, the same job I had done with Dolph a year earlier.

Then something got wrong with Bill. He told me he had to go to town. He wasn't sick, he said; he just got to thinking he needed a drink of good strong whisky. He knew that Mr. Goodnight wouldn't tolerate liquor nor gambling and that the penalty for breaking this firm rule was instant discharge. But Bill liked his liquor. He went to town anyway, and was gone four days.

Every day while he was gone I rode bogs, my own and his, and found some cattle I couldn't get out. Each day I hoped Bill would return, for I liked him and needed him. By the fourth day I was terribly worried. I was sure two of the mired cows were dead, and others would soon be. If Bill didn't come back that night I'd have a decision to make. I was there to save cattle, and I couldn't do the job alone. If he didn't come back, I reasoned, I'd have to go to the ranch headquarters for help. If I had to make a bad report on Bill he'd get fired. If I didn't, I'd be fired, and I sure didn't want that.

Then Mr. Goodnight drove in unexpectedly, as he had a habit of doing in emergencies. He asked me where Bill was, and I told him I didn't know. He might have heard by the grapevine that Bill wasn't on the job. I knew then the jig was up.

"Which way did he ride this morning?" he asked me.

There wasn't anything to do but tell him that Bill hadn't been there. He wanted to know how long I'd been alone, and I told him four days.

"Well," he said, "we'll turn my team loose, and I'll stay all night with you."

We got supper, and he asked me more questions: Was there anything in the bogs? I told him there were four. I was careful not to tell him the worst, hoping he wouldn't be too hard on Bill.

For a while after that Mr. Goodnight seemed to be in a deep study. He was silent; so was I. I wasn't going to volunteer anything, just answer his questions. Soon his mood became cheerful. He began telling me of his boyhood days. We sat up late while he talked. Just before bedtime Bill came in.

Mr. Goodnight didn't ask Bill a thing about where he'd been. He recalled something funny that had happened before my time and I went to bed feeling fine; it looked like Bill wasn't going to get the ax after all. They were old friends. Bill had once owned a little ranch next to Mr. Goodnight's and sold it to him.

The next morning Mr. Goodnight was still in good humor. He and Bill laughed and talked. After breakfast Mr. Goodnight said to me, "Billie, get your things together. Put them and your saddle in my buggy."

I did, then went back to the house. I saw them sitting at the table. Mr. Goodnight had out his little black book, showing Bill how they stood. Everything was serious now as Mr. Goodnight wrote out a check. Handing it to Bill, he said, "Take a horse and go wherever you want to. Send him back when you get through with him. You can roll up your bed and put it in my buggy. I'll send it to you when and where you want it."

Bill was through, the first and only man I ever saw fired on the Goodnight ranch. Not a harsh word had been said. They parted good friends. Rules were rules on that ranch and no man could neglect his duty. There weren't any exceptions. Mr. Goodnight's long experience with many men had convinced him that this was the best policy for all concerned. As we left the rawhide camp he said to me, "We'll drive to Allen Creek and have Johnny Martin send two men up here to take care of this camp."

That done, we drove to headquarters. Not a word was said about Bill. I'm sure it hurt Mr. Goodnight more than it did me;

and I liked Bill—hated to see him go. Good-hearted, warm-natured Bill! I never saw him again, but I heard about him.

His sprees soon came more often and lasted longer. During one of them he died, still in the very summer of life. But no man ever loved life more than Bill Koogel.

At headquarters I was under Walter McLaren again and found it very pleasant. He was kind to me; there wasn't any cooking or washing dishes. Too, my father and mother lived nearby—and I could also see Mrs. Goodnight every day. While I worked there I met several cowmen who were buying cattle for the northern range, mostly in Wyoming and Montana.

At times I was sent to drive these buyers to a particular herd to look at some stocker steers; other times, I was taken along just to open the gates. It was from these men that I heard of the tall grass and the fine range, and how big and fat those Texas steers grew in the North. What a paradise that faraway land must be, I thought.

At other times I listened to the tales of the cowboys who had been up the trail. Any time two of them got together they vied with each other in telling of the hardships—bucking horses, driving rains, hail, sudden storms, swollen streams, stampeded herds, lost sleep. All this fired me. I longed to go up the trail to Montana. I told Walter McLaren what I was thinking about. He laughed at me, but that didn't change my mind.

About the only way I could find excitement on the Goodnight ranch, where I got only gentle horses to ride, was to take one of my mounts out of sight of everyone, then get him to buck a little by poking him in the shoulder or just behind the saddle. Coley and Kid got to be pretty good—that is, they'd buck with a little coaching. They seemed to like it, and before long, they sort of got carried away. They began to buck right at the wagon, where everybody could see them. They never went at it very hard, for they probably sensed that I wasn't too good a rider. And they never threw me, but Johnny Martin took them away from me because of the sudden, odd change in their behavior. He said he was puzzled why horses as gentle as they had been would ever develop such ornery habits. I never told him how this could have happened.

If I could go up the trail, I thought, I'd have a freer life. If a horse bucked with me they wouldn't take him away till he'd thrown me so many times they became convinced I couldn't ride him. But I wasn't afraid of getting hurt. I thought I knew how to handle broncos, and I'd ridden some pretty wild calves. I broke two colts to ride at Bob Blanton's, where I stayed while I went to Lone Star School, and one at Joe Dickes's. These colts were used to having people around, but they still didn't want anybody on their backs. They had just about as many twists and turns and were just about as unruly as a mustang would have been. And I'd ridden them before anyone else.

I talked to Walter some more about going up the trail. Walter was Mr. Goodnight's nephew. He'd been around the ranch a long time and had heard lots of cowboy talk. He still didn't think I ought to go. Again he tried to impress upon me the hardships and the dangers. He said some of the boys on these drives got killed by lightning; some had horses fall on them during a stampede and were trampled to death; some drowned in flooded streams.

Yes, I told him, I knew, but some of them had come back, too. I'd talked to them, and they wanted to go again. It was in their blood. I reminded him it was common knowledge among the cowboys that the XIT was getting four herds ready to go to Montana, and I told him how much I'd like to go. Walter was beginning to soften up.

"If you really want to go, I don't think one trip would hurt you," he said. "Uncle Charley is a close friend of A. G. Boyce, the manager. If he'll give you a letter, you'll be sure to get a job. Without it there won't be a chance. There'll be one or two hundred cotton pickers there who can ride a horse and tell a good cowboy story, and the drive'll need only forty men. Chances are that there'll be twenty there who went up last year; so only twenty new ones will be needed."

"But Mr. Goodnight won't give me a letter," I replied. "He'll want me to go to school. I couldn't tell my folks either. They wouldn't consent. They'd want me to go to school, too.

"I've already had more schooling than your Uncle Charley did when he was twice my age, and he's made a success—by going up the trail, taking the chances. It's just a hundred miles up to the XIT. I can ride it in two days and find out if they'll take me. Two days up there and two days back. Just one week's layoff is plenty."

Walter repeated that there wasn't a chance for me without the letter but that with it he felt very sure they'd take me. "I'll talk to Uncle Charley myself," Walter declared, "and see what he says. If I can get a letter, when will you want to start?"

"In the morning. And please see Mrs. Goodnight and get my check. I don't want to see her. She'll ask questions that I can't answer."

Walter left and was gone a long time. I waited anxiously. Then he came with the letter sealed. I never knew what was in it. He also had cash for what was due me. He said that his Uncle Charley had given it to him; that he hadn't seen his Aunt. He volunteered not a word about what Mr. Goodnight said.

The next morning after breakfast, when I was saddling up to go, Mr. Goodnight came out and saddled up too.

"I'm going out that way," he said "I'll ride with you."

As we jogged along he talked about school, about how much better off he'd have been with an education. He told me of my advantages: I could stay at home or on the ranch and go to school till I was advanced far enough. Then he would help me to go on. He had sent Walter, his brother Robert, and others to the university at Georgetown, near Austin, and he said I could go there.

After a pause he asked, "Do you want to go on?"

I replied, "Yes, sir."

Without looking in my direction he said, "Well, I turn off here. Good luck. Come back to the ranch any time you want to."

He swung his horse around and rode off in the other direction. Perhaps he was thinking of the time when he, a sixteen-year-old boy on his own, had decided what he was going to do.

I looked back several times, until he went over a hill and was lost to view. Then a lump came in my throat. The skies were cloudless but there was a little moisture on my cheek as I rode on toward Channing, the headquarters of the XIT.

That night I stopped at the Frying Pan Ranch. The wind-burned old cowpokes there told me one story after another about Tascosa, a little farther west, and how tough the town had been. I knew about its reputation. William Bonney (Billy the Kid) was one of its citizens as early as 1878. So was Pat Garrett, the man who finally got Billy.

Tascosa's Boot Hill had been started when a cowboy named Bob Russell met death in a brawl, and of course he went to his last resting place with his boots on. And one night eight years before my visit to the Frying Pan four men had joined Russell, killed by lead out of a .45 Colt. Still others had followed, by ones and twos, until the little burying ground held many pairs of good boots.

But I wasn't impressed by the fact that I might be able to see Boot Hill the following day. Boots buried just go to waste. Furthermore, seasoned riders on the Goodnight ranch, who could be counted on to hold their own with any man, had told me that most such gunfights as these in Tascosa had started for very silly reasons. I didn't stop at Boot Hill the next day.

I didn't see any reason to tarry in Tascosa, either. I gave it a quick look. The rock courthouse, where once was heard the silver voice of Sam Houston's son, Temple, looked deserted. No longer in Tascosa were any of the noted frontier lawyers. Main Street—its stores, restaurants, and saloons—had all but vanished. A year or so earlier, a flood from the Canadian River had washed away the adobe houses where once lived the fancy ladies who had caused some of the gunfights. The most substantial citizens of old Tascosa had moved to Channing, Hartley, and Amarillo.

It was dark when I got to Channing. The little hotel wasn't crowded, and I got a room for the night. The next morning, I rose, looked out across the prairie, and saw that it was covered with campfires. Some "loners" and others in groups were cooking breakfasts over fires from old railroad crossties and cow chips. Fully two hundred men were there looking for a chance to go with the drive, or for any other job the ranch might furnish.

Hard times had caused many boys to roam. I was in this curious competition, having been lured away from a job where I had it good, and from people I was devoted to, by the fascinating stories of adventures on the long trail northward across the big, sparsely settled states between Texas and the Dominion of Canada.

V. A DREAM IS SHATTERED

IN THAT DAY every school child in Texas knew how the XIT Ranch got started. The State of Texas had offered to deed a generous chunk of land to any person or corporation that would provide it with a new capitol. Attracted by the offer were John V. Farwell, the Chicago capitalist who had one time been a partner with Marshall Field, the merchant; his brother, Charles B. Farwell, who was engaged in the wholesale mercantile business in Chicago (and who later became a congressman and United States senator from Illinois); and Abner Taylor, a Chicago building contractor (who also became an Illinois congressman later).

After long negotiations they reached an agreement with the Governor and Legislature of Texas to build the capitol and take in exchange three million acres of land in the most extreme western part of the Texas Panhandle. The tract began where the boundaries of Texas, Oklahoma, and New Mexico joined, and

36

it extended southward through nine counties: Dallam, Hartley, Oldham, Deaf Smith, Parmer, Castro, Bailey, Lamb, and Hockley. Only Oldham, with Tascosa as county seat, was organized at the time.

Less than ten years before I went to work on the Cross J Ranch, in 1892, the XIT had begun the big job of stocking its range. We'd heard various explanations of why it had chosen the big monogram that mutilated so much of the cowhide, the most believable being that it would be hard for a cow thief to change. All cattlemen tried to find brands that were hard to burn out, but they tried to make them as small as possible. Another version about the choice was that the man who devised it thought the ranch was in ten instead of nine counties and used the Roman numeral for ten, followed by the initials for "in Texas." Still another version was related by Ab Blocker in the *Trail Drivers of Texas.* In 1884, he said, he drove a herd of 2,500 cows and heifers from Tom Green County to Buffalo Springs in Dallam County for John Blocker, and he delivered them to B. H. ("Barbecue") Campbell, who was in charge. This herd was the first to reach the new ranch, and Campbell didn't know what brand to put on them. Ab, with the toe of his boot, marked in the sand XIT, saying it was a good brand, easy to put on and hard to burn out. Blocker said they branded the entire herd XIT. Later hundreds of thousands of other cattle also carried the brand.

But the main thing we heard about the XIT was that it wasn't a good place to work. Drifting cowboys told about being let out suddenly and without any reason. There were squabbles among the owners; nobody seemed to know who was in charge. XIT was very impersonal, a syndicate trying mass-production methods without much success. Some of these stories could be taken as just exaggerations of disgruntled cowboys, but others were convincing. (Working conditions probably improved after my one brief XIT visit in the middle 1890s.)

The XIT conditions contrasted sharply with those on our ranch, where everything revolved around Mr. Goodnight, who had a deep loyalty to the men who worked for him. Consequently morale on the Goodnight ranch was high.

Any big, daring operation such as the Farwells and their associates had undertaken could be expected to attract much attention, and they were always in the glare of the spotlight. They had a lot of trouble finding the material for the capitol and satisfying the state committee appointed to see that the contract was carried out the way they thought it ought to be. The cost of the building, plus the outlay in stocking and equipping the ranch, outran even the means of the Farwells and their associates.

To get more money John Farwell had gone to London and there formed the Capitol Freehold Land and Investment Company, Limited. His partners were the usual lords, earls, and other titled people, as well as some English bankers and merchants who had been the financial backers of many Texas ranches. But the millions of dollars for the new capitol didn't end the XIT grief.

The worst of its troubles was the lack of water for cattle in an arid country. They spent a great deal of money and effort trying to remedy this condition. Furthermore, much of the land was four thousand feet and more above sea level, and the cattle, driven up from much lower land, suffered from the cold. There were staggering losses. To this was added losses from cattle thefts, lobo wolves, and an epidemic of blackleg. The first XIT cattle shipped to the Chicago market had looked so ratty that they sold for less than it cost to produce them. And the ranch had suffered from devastating fires. Some of them probably were set, because XIT relations with neighboring ranchmen and settlers weren't good.

Newspapers in Texas and elsewhere in the United States (and even abroad) carried articles about how the English investors were deciding they couldn't reap the huge profits they had expected. At Goodnight it pleased us to read that these investors were wondering why they couldn't get dividends from the biggest ranch undertaking in the world, while Charles Goodnight was making money with much smaller acreage and fewer cattle.

John Farwell saved the situation by some sort of shift in the arrangement with the English investors and by putting A. G. Boyce in charge, with the title of general manager, in 1890.

Boyce put on an economy wave so strict as to be cruel sometimes to both men and animals. But there wasn't any doubt Boyce knew exactly what he wanted to do and how to do it.

One of his first changes was to end shipping by railroad and to go back to the earlier practice of trail driving. Herds were soon going to a finishing ranch the XIT had leased in Montana between the Yellowstone and Missouri Rivers. There the cattle put on weight and were shipped to the Chicago market by rail.

It was because of the lure of these drives that I showed up at XIT headquarters one bright April morning in 1895. I gave my letter to Mr. Boyce, a man about fifty, who wore a mustache and close-cropped beard. He was cordial enough; anybody who had a letter from Charles Goodnight could get a hearing anywhere. But Boyce's manner left me with no doubt that he was the "pusher" I had heard he was.

Boyce was the kind of manager who delegated a lot of authority. He told me that each of his trail bosses hired his own men. Then he scribbled off a note, put it in an envelope, and handed it to me. He told me to take it to the bunkhouse or barn; everybody connected with the drive could be found over there somewhere.

"See if any of them can do anything for you," he said, dismissing me: "They've come in here to get their wagons ready and hire the help they want. Men are on the range now, gathering their herds. They'll soon be ready to start."

I went to the barn first and spoke to everybody I saw. I didn't ask any questions, for I knew the 14,000 cattle to be driven would be divided into four herds of 3,500 each, and I wanted to spot the four bosses. Then I could pick the man I'd try. Boyce hadn't addressed the note to anybody and it was up to me to decide on which man to hand it to.

From the barn I went to the bunkhouse, then to the company store. I had taken a look at everybody, but I couldn't make up my mind who the trail bosses were; too many men were around. Some who looked like they were in authority were with their men, loading wagons. But this wasn't much of a clue, for there were seven divisions on the ranch, and the managers of them came to headquarters for their supplies. There were also fencing crews and well and windmill men. Then, too, it was spring, a season that brings bustling activity to ranches.

By noon my courage had inched up a little. Furthermore, I knew I had to locate the bosses before they had all their men hired. I asked the stableman to point out the four trail bosses. He told me, "There's one over yonder. Stick around, and I'll show you the others. I guess they're all eating now."

They soon finished and came out, and the stableman pointed them out to me. A tall man, weighing 180 or 190 pounds, came along. Earlier he had stopped me to ask where I was from, and he'd seemed very friendly. Now, when I saw him the second time, I knew he was the man to give the note to. I handed it to him and said I'd brought it from Mr. Boyce. He tore it open, read it, gave me the once-over, and grinned. When he read it again and began sizing me up I got scared. I knew he wouldn't hire me on my looks—I was sixteen years old, small for my age, and walked with a distinct limp, as I had since childhood. Nothing about me looked promising, but I did have on a good Stetson hat and the shop-made boots. He didn't ask any questions, but finally said, "Guess you can go with me."

My new boss was Jim McLaren, but he wasn't related to Walter, Mr. Goodnight's nephew at the Cross J. I liked Jim's appearance. He told me to get my horse and put it in the company barn. I'd eat at the mess hall, sleep with him. I stayed close to his heels.

I soon knew what our setup would be. There would, of course, be 3,500 steers. Eleven men would go: wagon boss, cook, horse wrangler, and eight men with the cattle. Of these eight the two in the lead were called right and left pointers, and it was their business to keep the cattle moving in the right direction while grazing or on the trail. Just behind the pointers came the swingers, to keep the herd lined up on the right and the left. Then followed the two flankers. Drag drivers brought up the rear and took care of weak and lazy cattle, which were slow in coming up when the herd halted to graze. Two men stayed on day work if weather and grazing were good; otherwise they were used as needed. In good weather we'd have sixteen hours of day work and two hours of night guard.

40

We'd move along at twelve to fifteen miles a day, each day's drive depending on the weather and distances between water and camping sites, and sometimes other factors. We'd be going only a little west of due north, for the XIT range in Montana was in the eastern part of the state and the XIT headquarters in Texas were in the extreme western part of the state. During the drive we'd cross the North Platte, Powder, and Yellowstone Rivers. The trip would take three or four months.

A year earlier the XIT had brought a string of saddle horses from Colorado. They were well-bred Hamiltons, larger than our Texas horses, proud-looking and durable. All were the same age.

They'd never felt a saddle or bridle till the previous year; then they'd been ridden two or three times and turned loose to get fat. The next step was to put them on alfalfa hay and corn for from thirty to sixty days, so they'd be stout for early spring work. They had just been shipped down. From them the trail bosses were to get most of their horses.

The two hundred men were assembled at the stockyards and told to ride their mounts. If they couldn't do it they didn't get a job—and these young horses had been ridden just enough to buck good. The brave boys, and the ones who thought they could ride, began catching the horses. They were to keep their mounts within the big catch pen till they saw whether they could ride them.

Most of the cotton pickers got no farther than the top of the corral fence. They watched those husky horses leave the ground suddenly, then whirl and twist through the air in a way downright discouraging to anyone except a genuine bronco buster. They wanted no part of horses that put up that kind of a fight; so they bade farewell to the cattle country and turned back to the cotton patches of East Texas.

Tryouts continued for three days. Each day fewer men were around. Then the trail bosses cut their horses; they had their men. I wasn't asked to ride a horse. I was Jim's boy, and I did just what he said.

I never knew exactly how many Colorado horses there were. After our trail horses were selected the others went to various ranches on the seven divisions.

At this point I had a brief but unforgettable look at A. G. Boyce's famous economy methods. He knew how to make money out of cheap cattle and to keep the business close to the break-even point, even though the XIT, a three-million-acre ranch, wasn't a success. (The Englishmen who put their capital into it didn't get their accrued interest and dividends till the land was parceled and sold shortly after the turn of the century.)

It happened one day after the riding tryouts had ended. Boyce stood by at the company store, watching everything requisitioned for the wagons: flour, bacon, beans, potatoes, sourdough, coffee, salt, and pepper. There wasn't any baking powder nor sugar; cowboys couldn't have luxuries like that if Boyce was going to hold expenses down and keep his syndicate employers off his neck.

I was near Jim all the time, observing what he laid out for our wagon. There were to be two teams of four mules each for the wagon, which carried the chuck and bedrolls. Jim put together the harness, consisting of chains, back and belly bands, and collars. He recalled that during the previous year the collars, sweat-soaked and exposed to sun and rain, had rubbed sores on the shoulders of the mules; so now he put out four collar pads, so he could change them.

Seeing the pads, Mr. Boyce asked, "What're you going to do with them?"

"I'm going to protect these mules' shoulders," Jim replied. "I swore last year if I ever drove another herd I'd do something so I wouldn't have sore-shouldered mules."

"Jim, if you drive a herd for me," Mr. Boyce declared, "you'll put those collar pads back and drive just like you did last year."

That got Jim. "Well, then, I won't drive your damned herd," he said.

Boyce replied calmly but with finality. "That's good, Jim. There're a lot of damned good men looking for a job as trail driver."

"Yes," Jim said heatedly, "and there're men looking for a damned good trail driver, and I'm that." He walked out of the store with me at his heels. Out front, he leaned against a hitching post, then said to me, "Well, old kid, I guess we won't go up the trail together. See Mr. Boyce. He might have some place to send you."

"I'm not going to talk to Mr. Boyce any more," I said.

Jim thought for a moment, then said, "If I was sure what I'm going to do I'd take you with me, but I don't know just which way I'm heading."

We walked to the barn, and I saddled my horse. I told Jim good-bye and never saw him again.

I had almost heard the roll and rumble of the cattle trail; then, in one dismal moment, four collar pads had shattered all my dreams. But I'd forget my bitter disappointment and hit the back trail. Men had to mature early in the Grass Empire. The smooth and the rough, happiness and disappointments alternated, especially there. But those experiences helped me learn how to fight the battles of life.

As I rode I recalled hearing my father say he never did like to take the back trail; it was more interesting to go ahead, even though the path is rough. I now knew what he meant. But the back route is rough, too. Why look for easy places? If I went on back, my folks and Mr. Goodnight would bring up that touchy subject of going to school. I didn't want that; I had been far enough in school to read, write, and figure. That was all the education I needed for what I intended to do in life. Once before I had strengthened my determination to pass up further schooling by reminding myself how well Mr. Goodnight had done with his meager education. He'd been up the trail, knew all about the cow business, and now had a big ranch and was doing a great many things.

Furthermore, I yearned to see Miles City, the roaring Yellowstone, the tall grass, the open ranges. Everything in Texas was now fenced in.

All these things went through my mind as I rode the back trail. Finally I decided that when I got to Tascosa I'd turn down the Canadian River to the LIT, LX, and Turkey Track Ranches. Some of them might be driving herds to Montana yet this year. If not, I might get a job, stay until the next spring, then get a trail job with someone.

I was thinking over these possibilities when I saw a rider coming across the prairie in a lope. I was in a fox trot and knew he'd catch me soon if he wanted to. He soon joined me, and I looked him over. He had all the earmarks of an old cowhand. I was eager to talk. I told him how my hopes of going up the trail had ended in disappointment and that I was looking for a job. He said, "When you get to Tascosa you might find some of the foremen around. I often see the LX foreman there. He hangs out at the general store or at the saloon across the street."

Before long he turned off. With a "So long, good luck," he left me. Again, I was alone, thinking. I hoped some of the men I was looking for would be at the general store, not in the saloon. My father and mother wouldn't want me to even go into a saloon.

When I reached Tascosa I inquired at the general store, and the proprietor told me that the LX foreman had just been there, but that he didn't know whether the man had gone back to the ranch or not. He said I might find him at the saloon across the street.

"Well," I thought, "I have to go in. Nobody will ever know it."

I left my horse hitched in front of the general store instead of leading him across the street to the saloon. I didn't want him to get in the habit of standing in front of grog shops. That horse and I had many secrets between us, but we might not be able to keep this one. Someone who recognized him might see him there.

When I got across the street I made for the Tascosa social center. I noticed that several steps led up to its entrance and assumed they were there to raise it above any possible flood from the river. Water would be the last thing that place needed.

As I went up the steps I heard a noisy commotion. I hesitated, knowing the reputation of these places for being tough. Instantly quiet returned, and I heard not a sound. I went in and looked around. Nobody was in sight. Then through a rear door appeared the bartender. When I asked for the LX foreman he only shook his head. He hadn't spoken a word, but now pointed to a dark spot on the floor near the back door and said, "They just got a Mexican."

44

His matter-of-fact tone gave me the impression that this episode wasn't unusual nor particularly regrettable. Maybe I even detected a little note of apology that the incident was so trivial.

The spot looked like blood to me, but I don't know to this day whether it was. I didn't investigate further, because I began heading for the front door. I knew I'd never pass on what the bartender had told me. What if there was a trial? I might have to go as a witness, have to testify that I saw blood on the saloon floor. Then my father and mother would find out I had been in one of those sinful joints.

As I hurried away from that place, I remembered something the cowboys at the Frying Pan Ranch had told me the night I stopped with them only one week earlier. They had said that not all victims of sudden death in Tascosa were fortunate enough to be put away in Boot Hill—or in any other burial ground. Maybe the men who'd been making the noise went out the back door and took the corpse with them. It was just a short distance to the quicksand of the Canadian River, which never gave up its dead and which had never revealed many dark secrets. The stories I had heard in the Frying Pan bunkhouse seemed more believable now.

I rode my horse four miles through gathering darkness to the LIT Ranch. There I pulled up, hoping to spend the night.

VI. LOTS OF EXPERIENCE, QUICK

WHEN I DISMOUNTED at the LIT Ranch, I found Frank Mitchell, the manager, and just four boys who worked for him. Mitchell, a handsome and friendly man, asked me where I was from. I told him from Goodnight, and he asked me to come to his headquarters and spend the night. His wife was away.

Mitchell plied me with questions and was so friendly I was sure I had a job within my grasp. I detailed the work I had done for Mr. Goodnight and the useful range knowledge I had picked up. I made a point of mentioning these things:

Never unsaddle your horse and turn him loose until you've caught your change and are ready to saddle him.

When a youth be ready at all times to do what older men tell you to do. With their experience they usually know best.

When taking cattle off the bat (the man working between the cut and the main herd is "taking them off the bat"), see that they go to the cut. Never lag behind when someone else darts out to get them, for they're yours and you should need no help. (An old adage was, "Never take a cowboy's job away from him until he cannot do it.") Stay with them till they're headed for the cut.

As you grow older and are sent to other wagons, you're under that boss. Do whatever he tells you to do.

These and many other pointers had been given me by Mr. Goodnight. I repeated them now to Mr. Mitchell, hoping to impress him with my competence. He was a good listener. Then he said, "Charley Goodnight is a grand man and the master cowman. I don't think there's any better place for a young fellow to be. Can you go back and work for him?"

"Yes, sir," I said. "He told me to come back any time. But I want to go up the trail to Montana."

"I don't know of anyone except the XIT driving this year, so go back," he said. "I worked for Mr. Goodnight when I was about your age. At twenty-three I was running the outside wagon for him. It was his recommendation that got me this job. You ought to go back."

There wasn't anything more to say to Mr. Mitchell, but I had firmly decided in my own mind that despite his advice I was going down the river to the Turkey Track and LX Ranches.

The next morning he asked me if I was bound for Goodnight. I told him that I'd see the LX and Turkey Track bosses and that if they had nothing for me I'd strike out for Goodnight. As I left, he cautioned, "You'll have to cross the Canadian several times. The quicksand's very bad. Be careful—you might lose your horse."

I did cross the curving river several times on the way to the LX, but had no trouble. They told me there was no chance for employment. I stayed there that night and left the next day. I crossed and recrossed the river so many times I decided it must be the crookedest one in the world. I had almost finished my day's ride without seeing any evidence of the treachery of that river bed when I caught sight of the remains of a cow. Her horns and just a little of her back were still showing. I was convinced now that the Canadian's hazards had not been overstated.

At the Turkey Track I found them rounding up to deliver 2,500 steers to the stockyards at Panhandle City, to be shipped to Wyoming. They said they could use me till delivery was made. I went to work for them.

Cal Merchant was wagon boss; J. M. ("Mac") Sanford, who later became wealthy in oil and gas, was straw boss. Both were likable fellows. Cal had a sense of fun and a pleasant smile at all times; I never saw him mad. But one thing which was not funny to him was cattle stealing. Some years before, when rustlers were preying on the Jinglebob, John Chisum's ranch in New Mexico, Chisum hired Cal to run his outfit, named Jinglebob because the cattle had their ears split down from the top for marking. He missed no more cattle after that. Cal kept smiling, but the thieves scampered for parts unknown.

It was a great opportunity to be able to work for a man I'd

heard so many fine reports about. I soon found that no matter how many capers a horse knew and tried out on his rider Cal Merchant wouldn't take him away from you unless he pitched you off. But despite this pleasant setup I don't think a short drive ever ran into more mishaps than the one we made. The last few miles of our drive to Panhandle City was near the tracks of the Panhandle and Santa Fe Railroad. When we were about a mile and a half from the track the cattle smelled train smoke, carried to us by a south wind. That made the herd uneasy and restless. Then our trouble was topped off by thunder, lightning, and a driving rain. That night we were all out trying to keep them under control, but they stampeded anyway.

We managed to check them; then they ran again. We were with part of them all night, but more than half the herd had broken away in the pitch darkness. We were till late the next afternoon getting them together, and that night they took off again. I found myself separated from the other men, alone with four or five hundred stampeding steers. Finally they quit running, and I rode around them when they had halted. I saw that we were up against the N Bar N pasture fence. By lightning flashes I could see I had quite a bunch of cattle—and nobody to help me.

The rain was coming down in torrents, and the ground was covered with water. But the cattle were standing quietly, and I was tired and sleepy. I rode some distance away from them, got off my horse, lay down, and soon fell asleep. But I was in a low place, and the water rose so rapidly around me that I moved to higher ground and went back to sleep. I had tied my bridle rein to my horse's front foot.

The rain slacked up just as day was breaking. I rode around and started the cattle back toward camp, three miles away. It was level country, and Cal sighted the cattle. He sent men to help me. They told me they'd all lost their herds and returned to camp. The cattle I had in tow were all we had.

At camp Cal asked me if I had been with them all night. I told him I had. He said, "Go in and get something to eat, go to town, get a good, dry bed, and sleep all day." I didn't tell him I'd slept almost all night.

They got everything gathered in that day. Half of us stood guard till midnight, and the other half till morning. Then the cattle were penned and loaded out.

Panhandle City at that time had two grocery stores, a dry goods store, barbershop, restaurant, boot shop, livery stable, newspaper, church, courthouse, bank, two saloons, and some scattered residences. It wasn't exactly a teeming metropolis, but there weren't many larger towns in the Texas Panhandle, and it was an important cattle-shipping point.

Every man, woman, and child in that town liked Cal Merchant. He knew them all, and every time he came to town they threw a dance in the trial room at the courthouse. This time was no exception. Couriers went out to notify the ranchmen, and despite the short notice all of them showed up at that night's event. Jesse Winn, from the N Bar N, was the fiddler. Everybody got togged up for the dance. I bought all new clothing, even a new suit.

Then I went to get a bath. The only bathtub was at the barbershop, where I also got a haircut. I asked for a shave, but old Pete Leithauser, the barber, had a roomful of customers waiting, and he said I didn't need it. So I got no shave, though I hadn't had one since the Allen Creek dance, two years before.

I'd never had as good a time as I had that night. I got acquainted with just about everybody in Panhandle City, including Mr. and Mrs. Jesse Winn. Without any doubt Mrs. Winn was the most friendly and best looking woman there. She showed me how to follow the caller, and guided me through the figures of the quadrille. My earlier shyness was gone, and I danced with others. Everyone treated me royally, and I developed an on-the-spot affection for Panhandle City and its openhanded, big-hearted people, and I have retained it all my life.

After the dance was over, J. E. Southwood and Arthur Jackson, who owned the livery stable, asked Cal and me to come and occupy one bedroom of their little two-bedroom house, and we did. I found that Mr. Southwood knew my folks well. He had bought the lumber to build the school I attended—the first rural school built in the Panhandle, the one-room Lone Star. Mr. Southwood had cattle and other interests. He had bought the stable for Mr. Jackson, who had gone broke in the cattle business when he was nearing his sixties. Mr. Southwood was deeply attached to him, and it was easy to see why. Mr. Jackson, an ex-Confederate soldier, was the most genteel, polished man I ever met, just natural and courteous to everyone.

The day after the dance I stayed around the town. The following morning, as I saddled up to start for Goodnight, I said to Mr. Jackson, "I'm going back to the place I like, but I don't want to go. I wanted to be away four or five years."

He made me a proposition. "If you don't want to go, how would you like to work for me? I have a lot of calls for rigs from people who don't know the country very well—mostly from cattle buyers and traveling men. They usually want someone to drive for them. You seem to know the country pretty well. When you're not out on drives you can help me here."

I accepted happily. While working for Mr. Jackson I became acquainted with many cattlemen from Montana, Wyoming, North Dakota, and South Dakota. Among them were Gus Streeter of the 777 (always called the Three Sevens), J. B. Clark of the 101 in Montana (not the same as the 101 Ranch of circus fame in Oklahoma), and Ed Lemons and Henry Ware of South Dakota.

Some old friends, the Blantons, lived at Panhandle City. I had stayed with them when they lived one mile from Lone Star and had gone to school with Pearl, who was getting prettier every day. With Pearl nearby, I saw much to make me enjoy my work in Panhandle City.

That June I had a memorable experience. The Turkey Track sent out a pool wagon to work the outside country surrounding the big pastures. The purpose was to look for and bring in strayed cattle. The country we worked was inhabited by nesters and small stockmen, for by this time it had been largely settled. But when hard times and dry years hit, many settlers decided to go back and see how their relatives were. Those who had the grit to ride out the hard times accumulated horses and cattle, and their animals sneaked away from home, just like those on the big ranches did. Getting them back was the reason for the pool wagon, a cooperative effort.

This wagon was furnished by the Turkey Track, and Mac Sanford, of that outfit, was the boss. All the big operators, however, shared the expense of the chuck, horse wrangler, and cook. The little men didn't pay any of the expense, but they did their part of the work. One thing I remember about this trip was that the chuck wagon was the best-stocked one I had ever seen up to that time. And there was a big, fat beef every day, and a cook who knew how to prepare steak.

Mr. Southwood sent me along to represent him. The youngest man in the pool, I was dealing on terms of equality with men several times my age, all of them men of substance. Furthermore, we were dealing with property, a very earnest business. At night, however, there was jollity around the chuck wagon. I heard a lot of interesting conversation.

All the big ranches sent two or three men. When they had finished working the country close to their home base, one or two of these men took their recovered cattle and drove them back; the other men went all the way around. We started with twenty-five riders from the big outfits, but with recruits from nesters and small stockmen we sometimes had as many as fifty riders. A small owner would stay with us only a day or two, leaving us as we moved out of his territory.

Our pool wagon operated over an area larger than some states, and we covered it with a fine-tooth comb. I found Mr. Southwood's cattle as far as fifty miles from home. Some of them might have wandered into a herd that a cowboy was driving, and because of laziness or other reasons, he made little effort to cut them out. Perhaps sometimes a driver just thought a cow belonging to someone else would make an inexpensive beef for winter.

All cattle were held in a day herd that moved along with the pool wagon. They were nightguarded till near their home range, then cut out and driven home. Night guards, from two to four men at a time, went on duty at eight o'clock and stayed on until four in the morning. Each guard stood two hours.

I remember well one night when we camped near a lake on the edge of the small town called Amarillo. Some of the men I met on that pool-wagon trip were also memorable. Several of

51

them remained my life-long friends: Billy Carter, who with Tom Crawford represented the N Bar N men, and Marion Hill. Later I was to become well acquainted with his sons, Jess and Grover.

My experiences with that pool wagon made the work I had been doing in Panhandle City seem very tame. It whetted my desire to follow the calling of a cowboy, to eat from Dutch ovens, to sleep where I could always see moon and stars. I knew also to expect rain and hail, hot sun and night guards, but to me that was much better than eating at restaurants and sleeping in beds imprisoned by walls.

At the end of the pool-wagon trip I went back with Mr. Jackson, but I was looking hard for a ranch job. Then in July I heard that Mr. Goodnight had made a deal that would greatly expand his ranch. I figured he'd need me. I told Mr. Jackson I thought I'd better go back to Goodnight. Mr. Jackson was nice about it, as he was about everything. It didn't take my horse much time to cover the distance to the place that was home for both of us.

VII. THE NORTHERN LIGHTS COME CLOSER

AS SOON AS I GOT to ranch headquarters I went directly to the house. Mr. and Mrs. Goodnight both greeted me. I learned that the total of the purchases from the V Bar V and FHC* outfits was 18,000 cattle, and with 10,000 calves thrown in. Three hundred horses also came along in the deal. Price per head for the 18,000 was fourteen dollars; all of them would have to be branded when received.

After supper I told Mr. Goodnight I wanted to spend the night with my father and mother. As I was leaving he said, "I'll pick up you and your saddle there early in the morning. I've leased the strip of land between my pasture and the N Bar N pasture, where your father's old home was. The wagon is over there somewhere. They're receiving the first consignment of cattle."

At home there was a lot of family news and some interesting items about the numerous visitors who were always dropping in. There were stories about the many people who'd come to see the buffaloes and elks on the Goodnight place and about what cowboys were sparking what girls.

I in turn told them my news: meeting so many interesting people in the three months I'd been away—especially A. G. Boyce, the czar of the XIT; Cal Merchant, the dashing Prince of the Prairie; kindly Mr. Jackson; and Mr. Southwood, who gave me quite a thrill by trusting me enough to make me his representative with the pool wagon. The only thing I held back was

* At a distance the brand looked like two letters, but the F and C were connected by an H, and it was sometimes called the FHC Connected.

what I'd heard about the sudden death of the Mexican in that Tascosa saloon.

The next day Mr. Goodnight took me out to the outfit. They'd received about 9,000 head of cattle and 150 saddle horses, or just about half. They had yet to tally and brand.

As we were driving up to the wagon about noon Mr. Goodnight, whose quick eye caught everything, remarked, "That wrangler has quite a scatter on his horses for this time of day."

I was afraid of what was coming, especially after I saw the wrangler gathering the horses in on a run. When my old boss Johnny Martin appeared, Mr. Goodnight told him, "You'd better put Billie with those horses until they're broken in. Then you can get another man to take them."

Here I was a horse wrangler again—and there was a new cook. Dolph Andrews was now Johnny's straw boss, a cowboy. Again we tied ropes to the wheels of the bed wagon and stretched them out to help hold the horses.

Otherwise everything was different around the ranch. Johnny had become a partner of Mr. Goodnight's, and there were several new men I didn't know, including the horse wrangler whose place I had just taken. Under this new order, if my horse did a little earnest bucking nothing was said. The attitude was, "Ride him if you can." No longer was I the kid everyone had been solicitous about. This gave me a feeling of self-reliance.

The V Bar V purchase had been received first. As soon as we were through with them the FHC group started coming. Out of their crew a good horse wrangler was hired. They made me a cowhand.

We entered a period when there was a hard rain almost every day. Tents weren't used then on the open range, and beds got wet, in spite of good tarpaulins. One night there was a real soaker. Nobody could sleep; all the crew, bundled in slickers, hovered around the wagon. Robert McLaren and Dolph Andrews, becoming solicitous again, picked me up and put me in the wagon under the protection of the wagon sheet and said, "Go to sleep, old kid."

I was very tired and went to sleep. Both my boots were just outside the sheet, and they got filled with water, but I didn't know it until I awoke after a good night's sleep. I realized I was still their kid. Cowboys had big hearts; they looked out for the weaklings.

Handling all those cattle offered a wide variety of work: branding, tallying, night guarding—all requiring long hours. Finally the job was done and everything was turned loose. Then the saddle horses were segregated. The old ones—in fact, any not good as cow horses—were turned out to rest up and put on flesh. These culls were to be fat by fall; that winter they were to be shipped to Louisiana. There they could be traded for cattle, cottonseed, sorghum molasses, and anything else useful on the ranch.

With the end of V Bar V and FHC activity came one of those quick switches for which the Goodnight ranch was noted. All cowboys were put on a fencing job, to cut the winter pasture in half. The line ran twenty-five miles, straight as an arrow, through rough country. Goodnight fence-building was something to behold; the mass methods of Detroit assembly lines years later resembled it.

Two miles of fence was completed every day. First the posts distributed. Posthole diggers followed, then post setters. When the posts were in place, the wire wagon came along. A frame on its rear end held six wires intended for the fence. The staplers came last.

Posts had been placed a rod apart—16½ feet. Between each post the staplers put three 1×4 staves, 5 feet long, evenly spaced. The six wires were stapled to each stave.

A stretcher pulled the wires tight. The bottom wire was 12 inches from the ground. The next two wires were 8 inches apart, the next two 10 inches apart, the topmost one 12 inches from the wire below it. Every two miles was a gate. I never found a sagging wire or a bum gate on a Goodnight fence.

This particular fencing job was completed in twelve and a half days. Dolph was the cook for the fence builders; I was the water carrier. I rode up and down the line with two canteens on each side of my saddle horn. When they were empty I went to the creek and filled them again.

When this fencing job was completed, a new cook and wrangler took over. Dolph and I then rode the range as cowboys, getting together a bunch of cattle for shipment. All old cows and bulls were to go, as well as some fat, dry cows and some coming two-year-old steers ordered for feeders. We wound up branding the late arrivals among the Cross J calves, and that was my first experience wrestling calves. They kicked me and tore off my shirt. I didn't have another one; so I made the shipment from Clarendon to Kansas City wearing an undershirt and a necktie.

We then went back to the ranch and rounded up and separated all dry, young cattle. We threw these in one winter pasture, the cows and calves in the other. The bulls we took to a pasture near the old Juan Rodríguez place. Juan had left the ranch, and Robert McLaren had taken his place there. I was to stay with him that winter and feed bulls. In addition to sheds and corrals there was a nice house; so Robert got married to Allie Vaughn, an excellent woman.

My new boss was Walter McLaren's brother. He'd been on the ranch a long time before I got there. There was no finer fellow.

Romance was budding all around. Johnny Martin built a house for himself on the ranch that autumn and married Viola McLaren, a sister of Walter and Robert and of course a niece of Mr. Goodnight. Viola was a charming, lovely, gay-dispositioned girl, always nice and friendly. She had been both a schoolteacher and Mr. Goodnight's secretary. A little later Walter McLaren married Anna Hickok. Dolph Andrews wed a Miss Owens. Dolph's father-in-law gave him a hundred cows for a wedding present.

Dolph and Walter took advantage of a standing offer by Mr. Goodnight, who always encouraged the men who worked for him to save. He ran free their first fifty head of cattle, and after that he agreed with them on a fair charge.

While on the subject of Walter and Dolph and the help Mr. Goodnight gave them, it's a good time to add something else about this remarkable man. I've read everything I could find about Charles Goodnight, but nothing ever has done him full justice. Certainly I don't think I can do so, but a few more stories about the man might help.

I was told one interesting story by A. N. Jefferies, manager of the Long X Ranch the Reynolds Brothers of Fort Worth, Texas, started in North Dakota. The Reynolds people sold Mr. Goodnight a large herd of cattle in the days when all payments were in cash. Mr. Goodnight sat down on a blanket with his bag of money, poured out the contents, and counted out what he thought was the right amount. He pushed the money across to them.

Reynolds didn't count it at once, knowing that Mr. Goodnight was honest. But three or four days later he counted it and found that Mr. Goodnight had paid $3,350 too much. Reynolds went back and told Mr. Goodnight that there'd been a mistake, but that he was sure he'd be willing to correct any error.

"Yes, I am," Mr. Goodnight replied, "but it seems to me I've given you a hell of a lot of money for those damn cattle already."

Reynolds smiled and handed him back the overpayment.

Charles Goodnight took great pride in his cowboys. His sense of concern in them was, to some extent, like that of a father. He wanted them to be honest, solid citizens. The fact that he and Mrs. Goodnight were childless may have had a part in the interest he took in these young men, especially those who followed his doctrine of "work and save."

When they left him to go on their own he kept aloof from their affairs, so they couldn't accuse him of meddling. But when one of them got into a jam and went to him, he always knew just the right string to pull to help them solve their problem. He looked out for his people.

An example was the case of Jim Owens, the same man who had told me I should accept Mr. Goodnight's offer of work.

Jim had led a pretty reckless life in Oklahoma and elsewhere, but he'd never broken the law, other than to wake up certain towns with bursts from his .45 Colt when liquor made him playful. The town officers chased him but couldn't ever catch him because of the fence-jumping ability of his horse Brownie. The territorial marshals told Texas officers about how Jim had eluded them and asked the Texans to help get the culprit. The Texas officers just laughed, and refused to serve papers on him.

The territorial marshals then trumped up a horse-stealing

charge against Jim. A United States marshal came to Claude by railroad, rode out to the ranch at night, and arrested him. They put handcuffs on Jim and took him to the Claude jail to wait for a southbound train to take him to Bowie, Texas, for trial.

There was another job for Brownie now. He carried a messenger to the cowboys at the Goodnight headquarters that Jim was under arrest and would be taken to Bowie in the morning; the train would bring him through Goodnight.

I don't think I'd ever been so sad at heart in all my life as I was when I heard what had happened. A meeting got under way in the bunkhouse soon after the news came. The boys talked about using force to free Jim, though it wasn't the custom on the Goodnight ranch for cowboys to carry guns. Mr. Goodnight had a regular arsenal in his office and knew how to use it—and many of the cowboys did have guns, though they didn't carry them.

One cowboy took the lead. "Jim's no thief," he said, "and Mr. Marshal hasn't got him to Bowie yet. We'll be at the station in the morning and take Jim away from him."

Then Mr. Goodnight got wind of this. He appeared unexpectedly in the door of the bunkhouse. Everybody knew how Charles Goodnight hated thieves. He was a firm believer that the best remedy for a cow or horse thief was a rope swung high from the limb of a cottonwood tree.

"Let him go," Mr. Goodnight said. "I don't think they have anything on Jim. I'll be at that trial with a good lawyer. They'll have to have the evidence, they can't railroad him."

When the trial was called, Mr. Goodnight was there to see that justice was done. The jury quickly acquitted Jim. He'd known nothing about the horse theft. (Fame came to Jim Owens later, when he joined Buffalo Jones on an African safari to capture wild animals. He returned to the United States and went to Arizona, where he hunted for mountain lions, many of which he captured and sent to zoos. In his new Western home, Jim often entertained notables, among them Theodore Roosevelt and Zane Grey.)

Mr. Goodnight liked for the men who left the ranch to write to him once in a while and tell him how they were doing. When

58

he heard from one who had gone far away and made good he was always delighted. I remember that one day he got a letter from a big sheepman in South America, and it set him to reflecting about something that had occurred years earlier:

Once, while he was dictating letters, a boy came by to ask for a job. Engrossed in the letters, he absent-mindedly said to the boy that he didn't need anybody. When he finished dictating, he inquired about the boy and was told that he had gone, walking westward along the railroad tracks.

"That boy might need a job," Mr. Goodnight said. "Telegraph the sheriff at Claude to look for him and bring him back here."

The sheriff, not knowing why Mr. Goodnight wanted the boy, picked him up. The boy had no idea what he had done to cause this. A green German youth, he had come to this country as a stowaway. He knew that if anyone got to poking around into that fact he might be in trouble. He was scared.

When he was returned to Mr. Goodnight he learned to his relief about the job offer. He worked on the ranch for a year, and the cowboys became very fond of him. The big sheepman of South America who wrote Mr. Goodnight many years later was that German boy.

Another boy that Mr. Goodnight hired because he looked like he needed a job and also looked like a promising worker was Wayman Brown, a lanky native of Arkansas who was probably the most unusual person I ever worked with. There's quite a story to Brown himself that rates telling.

Brown had left home at the age of seventeen, headed for Texas and bent on being a cowboy. He worked at odd jobs after he got to Texas, pushing his way westward across the state and saving every dollar he could. Some months later, in 1887, he got to the JA Ranch. Mr. Goodnight told me what happened then.

When Wayman asked for a job, Mr. Goodnight looked him over and noted his almost threadbare clothes—and his clean, long hair and keen eyes that meant to Mr. Goodnight burning ambition. But Mr. Goodnight didn't know just what he ought to have Wayman do, so he said, "You just watch these gates [there were gates in every direction around the ranch] and every time you see anybody coming toward one, be there to open it." With only those instructions, Mr. Goodnight left him on that job for three days and watched him.

Wayman was out at daybreak and watched till dark. Every time he saw anybody going toward a gate he got there first. If somebody else was going to another gate Wayman managed to get to that gate too.

Next Wayman had odd jobs around headquarters. After he'd been there awhile—perhaps two or three months—Wayman went to Mr. Goodnight and said, "I've got a little money here. I wish you'd take care of it for me."

He went down into the pocket of his duck trousers and drew out a wad of bills that had been sweated on and pressed so close together that it was hard to tear them apart. When it was all separated and counted it came to $200.

"I thought he was a broke kid and needed a job," Mr. Goodnight told me, "but I never did regret hiring him. He had integrity, loyalty, and dangerous courage. Beneath that big black hat his keen eyes always shone. He was a lover of horses and was kind to all my livestock."

When Mr. Goodnight left the JA Ranch, Wayman stayed on, but in time he drifted to Clarendon. After a few days he drew his money and lent $1,400, I believe it was, to Hall and Company, a mercantile firm. In a short time the company went broke. The money seemed gone beyond any hope of recovery.

Wayman brooded briefly over his bad luck, thinking of the years of hard work he had put into gathering the money. He couldn't afford to lose this nest egg, he reasoned, and his clever mind went to work. He pretended to be insane and talked about the loss of his money without letup. He called on his debtors and seemed plainly out of his mind but made no direct threat. However, he left a clear impression that they'd live longer if they paid the debt by a certain date.

He rode back to the ranch and wrote a letter to his girl in Arkansas. He told her the next time she heard from him he'd be selling hot tamales, "for I've got two fellows I have to make up into hot tamales and get $1,400 out of them."

Wayman rode back to town to mail the letter. The post office was closed, and he wouldn't drop it in the mail slot. He said he

60

wanted to hand it to the postmaster. A friend came along and somehow got the letter. It never went to his girl in Arkansas, and in some way Hall and Company became aware of its contents.

Wayman rode back to the ranch. He told the cowboys, "Goodnight's paying too much for salt and bran. I'm going to plant some. We might as well raise it." He sowed some salt and bran and harrowed it in. Then he ran and jumped in the water tank. He said heel flies had gotten after him. After that he saddled the old wood heater. He rode the stove, hollered, and with his .45 Colt put holes in the wall, yelling, "I'll show you how to collect bad debts."

On the date he'd set for his debtors to pay, Wayman rode into Clarendon with a hundred yards of colored ribbons streaming behind him. He stopped at Henry Taylor's store, went behind the counter, and helped himself to a box of .45 Colt shells. He didn't say a word, but rode on over to Hall and Company's store.

It was reported that he was paid in full, in cash. He came back to the ranch, and told everybody goodbye, and said, "I'm heading for Wyoming." In three or four months he was back working on the Cross J Ranch, the same old Wayman.

We were always busy at the Goodnight ranch, but nobody was ever forced into a shotgun-marriage with a job he didn't want. When a fellow was hired he knew in advance that he'd work hard there or his stay would be brief. But Mr. Goodnight didn't expect his cowboys to be saints, only honorable men. He expected them to accept responsibility and to attend to their duties. Expecting them to have a normal amount of fun, he encouraged dances and other social activities. He was also good to his animals and demanded that his men be. Good-intentioned but weak-willed Bill Koogle, the only man I ever saw him fire, had violated a Goodnight rule: "Never fail to succor an animal in distress."

Of course the cowboys grumbled at times about how hard they had to work, but I'm sure every one of them was quietly proud of the "Old Man," as some of those farther along in years than I was affectionately called him. We all knew he was the best cowboy on the ranch, and today, wherever there is a Goodnight cowhand who has not yet joined the great roundup, I'm sure there's a glow of pride from the fact that when the National Cowboys Hall of Fame made its initial selection in 1957 Charles Goodnight was the first choice.*

Mr. Goodnight had an inventive mind. I never knew what to call all the little conveniences he was always adding around the ranch until, many years later, the word "gadget" came into my vocabulary.

He was always punctual; his life was orderly. He answered a letter the day he received it. He borrowed money for his operations and paid it when due; he used to say that the quickest way to measure the flight of time was to sign a ninety-day note. He was a just man, and it would never have occurred to him to deal unfairly with anybody.

He had a great store of information about things outside the cattle business. He didn't have any time for idle chatter, but I have heard him carry on conversations with highly educated experts in many fields. Furthermore, he often had his own ideas about their specialties. It was his example that made me decide to get my education from men who were doing things instead of from books, though I later came to realize the value of books, too. But Mr. Goodnight knew the value of a trained mind and tried to get boys to go to college. Often he paid for their schooling himself.

His fame was so widespread that newspapers and magazines sent their writers to his ranch. He was always helpful as long as the talk was about the country, but when they brought the subject around to him he was likely to become irritable. He didn't want any personal publicity. When he became gruff his conversation could be very pungent.

His manner of speech was, in fact, always salty. I remember one time when he was talking to me about the Bible. He said, "I've read it seven times, and if I live long enough I'm going to read it seven more. It's a damned good book." Knowing him as I

* Others chosen among the first five were Will Rogers of Oklahoma, Theodore Roosevelt of New York and the Dakotas, Charles Russell of Montana, and Jake McClure of New Mexico.

did, that didn't seem irreverent to me. My opinion was supported by Charley Taul, a topnotch man on the ranch who was a lot better educated than most cowboys. He said, "Mr. Goodnight doesn't swear between words; he swears between syllables."

Mr. Goodnight was at all times his natural self. I'm sure he must have had his shortcomings, but even if I'd recognized them they undoubtedly would have seemed but minor ones to me. He was strikingly different from any man I ever saw.

His cowboys were superior too. They had so much pride in the ranch that many of them seemed to think that if you were a cowboy on the Goodnight ranch you had some sort of royal blood in your veins.

Still, my longing to follow a herd pointed northward had in no way lessened when I went with Robert McLaren to the Rodríguez place in the autumn of 1895. It was a time of great change in the Texas Panhandle. All the country around was settling up, and the old boys were getting married. People weren't coming into just Texas; they were settling western Oklahoma and Colorado as well. The old trails were being plowed, and it was becoming very difficult to get a herd through from Texas to Montana. An XIT announcement that it wouldn't drive any more herds after 1895 but would instead ship to Orin Junction, Wyoming, cut off my prospect there.

If I was to get to the northern range, I decided, I'd have to find somebody who would hire me and ship me out with cattle. But men like Mr. Streeter and Mr. Clark from North Dakota and others told me that the northern range was not the place to go. They pointed out that in early autumn hundreds of cowboys were let out after the last beef shipment. They either had to come back south or ride the chuck line until grass came about the first of May—resulting in six or seven months of idleness. (This riding the chuck line, or picking up free meals by going from one cow camp to another, was not a situation most fellows wanted to be in; at no time did I ever have to do it.)

Nothing I heard discouraged me. I still wanted to see the open range, tall grass, no fences. With the approach of Christmas came a slack period, and I asked Robert McLaren if I could get off for two weeks.

"Yes," he said. "We won't feed those bulls much until the middle of January. From then on we'll let them have it pretty heavy."

I went to Panhandle City, where Al Jackson, the livery-stable man, was glad to see me. "I want to put you on my payroll," he said. "I have a drive I want you to make for me tomorrow. It's with Mr. Teague, the N Bar N Land and Cattle Company man. He's going over their land and classify it. I don't have anybody to drive him, and I can't go myself. It'll take a few days."

Mr. Teague was a man of wide experience and good at conversation; so the trip was a pleasant one for me. I got back to Panhandle City for Christmas.

Then I learned that Pearl Blanton, my old schoolmate, was getting married to Ebin Holman, an N Bar N cowboy. She was a little young; she'd be only fifteen in April, 1896—four months away. I wasn't pleased about that wedding, but there wasn't anything I could do about it. I made the best of it by going to the breaks and helping gather cedar to decorate the church.

Their wedding was a real social event of the holiday season. (Fifty years later I was invited to their golden anniversary.) After it was over I began to lay a base for a job going north. I saw Sam Lowery and Billy Greenville, who were wintering Three Sevens Ranch steers in the Dickson Creek pasture before shipping them to Orin Junction in the spring. They would then be trailed to the Three Sevens Ranch in North Dakota. But they couldn't promise me a job, as they didn't have any instructions to hire men.

I ended my stay in Panhandle City and went back to spend the winter with Robert and Allie McLaren. Then, sometime in March, a small thing happened which would mean the turning point in my life, though I didn't see any significance in it at the time. I heard that Mr. Goodnight had sold four buffaloes to be shipped to Yellowstone Park. I thought nothing more of it, supposing they'd be shipped immediately to whoever had bought them.

By April we were through feeding bulls. I quit, returned to

Panhandle City, and went back to work for Mr. Jackson, hoping some northern cowmen would send me out with a cattle drive. I saw Sam Lowery, but he still didn't have any orders to hire men. I talked with Mr. Gus Streeter of Dickinson, North Dakota, who had come down to supervise the shipping of the Three Sevens steers that Sam and Billy had looked after. He said he didn't do any hiring; he was the manager, and the foreman handled the employing. He added that he thought they had all the help they needed. Nor was J. B. Clark, manager of the Montana 101, taking on anybody. Ed Lemons from South Dakota was full-handed.

Then, suddenly my chance came to go to Yellowstone Park with the buffaloes. Captain E. G. Waters wanted somebody with them who knew how to handle them. I quickly convinced him that I filled the bill exactly.

We began getting ready at once. Mr. Goodnight, who had just passed his sixtieth birthday, was around a great deal. He made no fuss about my going and, I think, assumed I'd be back soon. My own thought was the same: that I'd return and maybe start my own outfit some day, like Walter McLaren, Dolph Andrews, and others.

At that time Grover Cleveland's second term in the White House was ending, and there was a lot of speculation between Mr. Goodnight, my father, and the cattle buyers about his successor. While we were preparing for the shipment the Republicans met in St. Louis and nominated Governor William McKinley of Ohio. The Democrats were to meet in Chicago two weeks later.

My father, a Democrat, was for ex-Congressman William Jennings Bryan of Nebraska. Nobody thought Bryan had much chance, however. For one thing he was too young. Congressman Richard Bland of Missouri looked like the winner.

Finally everything was ready to load and ship. It would be some years before I saw the Goodnight ranch again, and I never returned to work there.

VIII. LIGHT HOUSEKEEPING WITH FOUR BUFFALOES

FOR NEARLY TWO YEARS I had been planning a northern trip. But all my plans had been to make it in the great outdoors. I had poetical thoughts of silvery beaming moonlight and of star-sprinkled evening skies.

On June 21, 1896, the four buffaloes—two bulls and two cows —were loaded into a boxcar at Goodnight. Each buffalo had a crated stall made of 2 × 6 and 2 × 9 timber spiked solidly to the frame of the boxcar. Each stall had a gate. There were two stalls in each end and each one had a water trough.

Gone the thoughts of silvery moonlight. And there weren't any stars in the boxcar I shared with the four buffaloes, though I might have seen some if anything had gone wrong with one of those stalls.

The boxcar was routed via the Santa Fe Railroad to Chicago, then to Fond du Lac, Wisconsin, which was Captain Waters' home, and from there to Cinnabar, Montana. I hadn't thought of buffaloes as being very adaptable to human comradeship, but after I got the hang of things I began to enjoy being with them, even if this didn't come up to the rapturous experiences I had expected to have on the trail.

In the center of the car were two water barrels and some loose hay. I had a blanket and quilt, and I slept on the hay. I ate wherever the train crews ate. When we got to a water tank they always filled my barrels with water, and I filled the troughs. When I ran short of hay the railroad had more bales of it delivered—at any division point.

At these division points I sometimes had to wait for hours before I could get a through freight train to the next one. I was three days getting to Kansas City, where there was a long delay. Kansas City to Chicago required twenty-four hours, where there was another long wait. At St. Paul came another.

Railroad officials at each division point would tell me when I could expect to leave on the next part of the trip; then I'd shut my door and go sight-seeing, which consisted mostly of riding streetcars. I always left the end doors open to give the buffaloes some air. Of course they'd have been better off if I had stayed and kept all doors open, but I was eighteen years old and had to see things.

At Fond du Lac I left a bull and picked up a buffalo cow. From St. Paul I went via Northern Pacific to Livingston, Montana, where I spent July 4, 1896. On July 5—fourteen days after leaving Goodnight—we were at Cinnabar, a little town about five miles from Gardiner and at the time at the end of the line.

Four wagons were waiting for the buffaloes, which were the first ever taken to Yellowstone Park. I soon found out what the setup was.

Captain Waters was president and principal owner of the Yellowstone Lake Boat Company, which had a concession from the government giving it the privilege of transporting tourists by boat over the lake between two points where its shores were touched by the road system. It was a monopoly which, I think, existed from about 1890 to 1907.

The four wagons that met us had good strong cages built on them, and there were heavy ropes to tie the buffaloes with. But I didn't want to put ropes on my charges. It would make them get on the fight, and from then on it would be mighty hard to do anything with them. Nevertheless, the man in charge of the wagons said, "Those are my orders. I've got to carry them out." I protested that Captain Waters didn't understand about handling buffaloes and suggested, "Let's try a cow without a rope—or I'm going to leave it all to you."

He finally agreed. So we backed a wagon up to the boxcar, leveled it even with car floor, and two men on top pushed down the trap end-gate and turned a cow out of her crated stall. She walked into a wagon, and we got her securely fixed. Then we brought up two other wagons, and got all three cows loaded.

67

Then the foreman said, "I'm taking no chances with that big bull. I'm going to put a rope on him." I answered, "Now's when your trouble starts. I'm going uptown."

The bull's stall was at the end; so it was easy to open the end door a little and lay a rope over his horns. I walked away but couldn't resist stopping to see what happened when he felt the rope. He flew into a rage, fighting in every direction. He tore his stall down, along with the rest of them, and tore holes in the railroad car.

"Now what'll we do?" the foreman wondered. "I guess nothing for a few hours, until he cools down and gets over his mad fit. Then we can handle him the same as we did the cows. Those cages in the wagons are strong; he won't have room to lunge either way."

We moved his wagon into place and put everything in readiness. We put a cow cage on each side, to give him company and to steady his wagon against being turned over. Then we all went to get supper and to give the bull time to quiet down. The foreman was anxious to get started, for it was sixty miles to the Yellowstone Lake Hotel. We couldn't expect any sleep till we got there.

I knew it was going to take a long time and plenty of patience, or we'd spoil everything. At intervals I eased up to the car and listened. Finally everything was tranquil. We opened the door without a sound so as not to disturb him. Then came another wait, for it was now the buffalo's move, and it had to be of his own accord. Anything we might have done would have fouled the deal. After a few moments he smelled the cows and strolled out to them. We had him in the wagon, with no more trouble than we'd had with the cows.

During the first part of our journey we drove the teams three abreast, then single file. We had breakfast at Mammoth Hot Springs, nine miles away. The lake was fifty miles farther; we arrived there in the night, loaded two cages on a barge tied to the passenger steamboat, and went to Dot Island (now Stephens Island), nine miles from the hotel. There corrals for the buffaloes had been built; so we unloaded them and went back for the others. This time I also unloaded myself: bedding, tent, coffee pot, and frying pan. Plenty of good things to eat were brought over from the hotel regularly. I fared well.

Every day the steamboat landed its passengers to see the menagerie, which consisted of the four buffaloes, two mountain sheep, two antelopes, two deer, and two coyotes. My job was to see that everything was well fed. After that I slept and read. I met the boat every day, with my pants legs stuffed in my boots, cowboy style. My instructions were to answer any questions the sightseers asked. Whether I knew the correct answer or not, I was supposed to tell them something.

So for about thirty days I was a cowboy without a horse. But there was a lot of political excitement to interest me. William Jennings Bryan had made his Cross of Gold speech at Chicago and had stampeded the Democrats into nominating him for President.

With so much time on my hands to think of horses and cattle, and especially of Miles City, the cow town I had long wanted to see, I got restless. I told Captain Waters I had to go. He wanted me to stay, and offered to boost my wages of $1.50 a day. I told him I just couldn't stay any longer.

I went out with the stagecoach. The driver talked me into going to Butte, Montana, where, he said, there was big money for anything I might want to work at all year round. He suggested that if I didn't find something to my liking there I could stop in Billings, another good cow town. So I spent three days in Butte and one day in Billings, fast getting separated from the little money I had. With just enough left to get a ticket to Miles City I left Billings.

I landed in Miles City with one thin dime. I roamed around until nine o'clock in the morning, getting hungrier every minute. Then I walked into a little lunch counter. The only person I saw was an old gray-haired woman who was knitting. She looked at me over her eyeglasses and asked, "Son, what can I do for you?"

I put that last dime on the counter and replied, "Lady, give me all to eat that you can for ten cents."

"I have some rhubarb pie here," she said "It's not very good. You can have it and a cup of coffee."

It had a lot of soft dough and hard rhubarb, but I ate it all and drank the hot coffee. It was good then, but for years afterward I didn't like rhubarb pie.

Then, not quite so hungry, I could think about my situation. There I was, in Miles City, the place I had yearned to see, a thousand miles from home, and dead broke! But I was in a town where you met cowboys and cowmen. That gave me a good feeling; so I sauntered into a saddle shop to look around. While I was there my old friend J. B. Clark came in. I walked over and spoke to him. He returned my greeting with warmth and asked where I'd come from. I told him about my trip to Yellowstone Park and how I got to Miles City, where I hoped to get a job on someone's beef roundup. Trying to sound offhanded, I added that I was just looking over the saddles, as I might need one.

"Well," he said, "I don't usually do any hiring. That's left up to our foreman. But he'll be here with a shipment in about ten days, and I'll see him. You can go with him until he makes his last shipment; then you can go with that to Chicago. I'll be in Chicago, and I might be able to get you a railroad pass home.

"I'm stopping at the old Quinman Hotel. Come eat dinner with me, and I'll make arrangements for you to stay there until my outfit gets in."

After dinner we sat around and talked. Finally I said, "Mr. Clark, I don't want to go home this fall. I want to stay in this country four or five years, long enough to take money home with me when I go."

He was discouraging. "There's not a chance here after the last shipment. There're hundreds of cowboys let out, either to go back home or ride the chuck line and lay around these cow camps until about May. It's no place for a boy like you.

"These men are idle and broke. They get to stealing and robbing trains, get into all kinds of trouble. Some of them end up in the penitentiary. I tell you, this is no place for a boy like you. I'd like to see you make up your mind that you're going home with that last shipment."

We walked around, and I thought of my plight. To go home in two months! I knew he'd buy me a saddle and an outfit when he found out I was broke. Then I'd land in Texas, not only penniless but in debt. I just couldn't do it.

We had supper on the veranda, and I told Mr. Clark I was broke. I couldn't face the prospect of going back to Texas no better off than when I left. I told him I'd like to get a job as soon as possible.

He thought for a moment and answered, "There's a train through here in an hour for Dickinson, North Dakota. Tony Day, of the Turkey Track, is shipping out of there tomorrow. We'll get you a ticket, and Tony will put you on tomorrow."

We went to the depot, where he bought a ticket and handed me five dollars just as the train pulled in. I said, "Mr. Clark, give me your address. I'll send you this money just as soon as I can."

"No, old boy," he replied. "The mule is yours till we meet again."* With that he left me, and I boarded the train.

In 1896 the best large herd ranges in the United States were in the western North Dakota counties of Golden Valley, McKenzie, Dunn, Stark, and Billings, and in the eastern Montana counties of Fallon, Prairie, Custer, Wibaux, and maybe one or two others. The ranches extended across state-boundary lines. When I arrived, Montana and North Dakota had been states for less than seven years, both having been admitted in 1889.

I had gone a long way north from Texas, but not far west, as the Goodnight ranch was a considerable distance west of Fargo, North Dakota, and even farther west than Bismarck. Despite the distance it was a common thing to run on to a ranch owner who had come from Texas, and so far as cowboys, horse wranglers, and cooks were concerned, there weren't many outfits that didn't have one or more. Everybody knew of the Goodnight ranch, and it had many admirers.

In North Dakota, much more than Texas, I found wide-open spaces, for Texas had been fencing furiously in the late 1880's and 1890's. Furthermore, North Dakota had the Missouri River, the biggest stream I had seen at that time. It also had badlands, with the best grass in the West, and large Indian reservations.

---

* I met Mr. Clark in Amarillo, Texas, in March, 1901, and gave him his ten dollars for the railroad ticket and the loan. He didn't want to take it, but I insisted. "I can pay you your money back," I told him, "but it still leaves me owing you a debt of gratitude that I can never repay. What you did is worth more than money to me."

71

To me it was a winter paradise. I remembered now the song I had heard cowboys sing:

> Away I'm bound to go
> 'Cross the wide Missouri.

I had heard of the big cattle boom in Montana and the Dakotas in the 1880s, and how young Theodore Roosevelt and others had gone there. But in 1896 Theodore Roosevelt wasn't a national figure and didn't become so until the Spanish-American War two years later.

Like my part of Texas, the area generally was treeless. It was colder, but not much—the Texas Panhandle lacked a lot of being the land of magnolias. The nationality of the settlers was different, though. In Texas they were Scotch-Irish; here were Germans, Russians, Finns, Swedes, Norwegians, Dutch, Irish, English, and Scotch.

Old Texas punchers had been dinning into my ears that this country to the north was the last frontier. But I disagreed, having always thought of the last frontier in terms of Montana rather than North Dakota.

IX. ON THE FENCELESS RANGE

I ARRIVED in Dickinson, North Dakota, early in the morning of August 17, 1896. Although it was to become a hallowed place to me, my start there wasn't notable. In fact, it began in disappointment.

I went from the train to the Villard House. The night clerk and bartender told me that the Turkey Track had loaded out its wagon, left early in the morning, and was camping that night on Cedar Creek, fifty miles south. The men, after putting their cattle on the train, were making a night ride to catch their wagon. It was just daylight, and I didn't see anybody else. I was walking up and down the street, wondering what to do next, as the sun came up.

Then I glanced down a side street and saw a hefty man waddling in my direction. There was something familiar about him. When he came nearer I recognized Mr. Gus Streeter, the Three Sevens manager. I felt better now; I wasn't in a completely strange town. As he came up I put out my hand and greeted him: "How are you, Mr. Streeter?"

"Fine," he said. "You're out early, I see." He hadn't recognized me.

"Yes, sir," I answered. "I'm Billie Timmons from Texas, looking for a job. I got out early."

"We can fix that," he declared. "But how did you get here?"

While we walked down the street I told him of my rounds, from leaving Texas to meeting Mr. Clark in Miles City, of his sending me to catch Tony Day, of how I was a day too late. Then I found out why Mr. Streeter was downtown so early. He and several other old cowmen living in Dickinson came to the butcher shop every morning to get a beefsteak for breakfast. They also stopped for a bracer to start the day with.

"Let's go in and have a little drink," he suggested.

I'd never taken a drink, but I didn't balk, for I was going to be sociable with Mr. Streeter. I ordered the same as he did. It burned awfully but a little water soon cooled it down. He asked, "Do you have a saddle?" When I told him No, he said, "You'll have to have a saddle. You can't ride these horses in this country without one. They aren't like your little Texas cow ponies that you can ride bareback. These mornings are cool, and horses get a hump in their backs. I'll be back downtown after a while; then we'll go to the saddle shop and see what they have.

"The OX are shipping today. We'll drive out there and get them to bring a horse in for you. My outfits are working eighty or a hundred miles south of here toward Grand River. You can just ride out there and find them."

But OX didn't load that day. They threw their beef herd on Ash Coulee and all came to town, except the day herders, cook,

73

and horse wrangler. By eleven o'clock it looked to me like a wild town. All the cowboys had .45 Colts strapped on and were racing up and down the streets, shooting and whooping it up. As time went on they got wilder. They rode into saloons on the north and south sides of town and shots rang out till that afternoon, when an accident happened.

Mrs. Bill Chaloner was sitting in front of her house, holding her baby, when a stray bullet struck her knee and came out through her hip. Everything became quiet, and the OX cowboys left town.

I had looked for Streeter all that morning. Late in the afternoon he drove in. We went to the saddle shop, where I had already been and selected a saddle, bridle, blanket, and spurs. Somehow Mr. Streeter knew I was broke. He said, "I'll go by and tell him I'll pay for it."

Then we drove out to the OX wagon and had supper. A number of cowboys were around. It was the quietest gathering I'd ever seen in a cow camp. Nobody acted like he'd ever had a drink.

I knew the cook—Lausen Thomas, from Panhandle City, Texas. He'd come up with cattle that spring and was going back with the shipment. He offered to sell me his saddle, bridle, blanket, spurs, and slicker for thirty-five dollars, saying I could send him the money when I got it. So I didn't have to take the new outfit Mr. Streeter had offered to pay for, and I was out of debt after the first month. Mr. Streeter asked for Joe Bilyeu to let me have a horse.

I camped with the OX outfit. Sometime during the night the sheriff came out and arrested the boy who had shot Mrs. Chaloner. Her husband, Bill, was out on the range somewhere with the 7 Bar 7 wagon; so they put the boy in jail till Bill could come in and talk to him. Ashamed of himself, he said he'd pay the doctor bill, give up his gun, and never carry another one or take another drink of any kind of liquor. Chaloner agreed not to file charges, and they released the boy so he could work and pay for his wild spree.

Soon after that Dickinson passed an ordinance prohibiting carrying guns within the city limits.

74

Next morning at daybreak everybody began catching horses. When Joe Bilyeu said, "Anybody who has a chance, catch Rain-in-the-Face," I knew there was some hidden meaning because of the way he said it. The namesake of the Indian chief was hard to catch, but we finally got him. He was muscular, agile, and determined. I had a little trouble saddling him.

By the time I got him saddled everybody had gone to the herd except John Clayton, an H T cowboy, who was having trouble with his horse too. I mounted Rain-in-the-Face, and he really put his heart into his effort to dislodge me. But I couldn't afford to fail, being a new man on the Dakota range. By pulling leather whenever I could find it I stayed on till he was through. But he was still about as sociable as a wolf.

I jogged back to Clayton and asked the direction to the Three Sevens wagon. He said their line camp on Cedar Creek was about fifty miles south of where we were. The line rider, he thought, might direct me to one of their wagons. I asked, "Which way is south?" He pointed and said, "Right over that hill, and keep straight ahead." I went over that hill, and not a house nor a fence did I see.

For a while I rode hard, thinking it would be good for my horse's temper. But it didn't seem to help. Every once in a while he'd renew his efforts to throw me, and I used all my knowledge of horses to stay put. I didn't like him; still, I didn't want to part with him. As it had been hard for me to mount and perhaps would have been impossible to get back on him, I thought it best to stay on till I got to line camp.

I reached Cedar Creek along in the afternoon. I didn't so much as glimpse a cedar, but I felt sure the creek there was the right one. I hadn't seen a house or crossed a fence, just a few dim roads. I'd been afraid to follow any of these roads to see where they went, lest they throw me off my course.

There wasn't anything at Cedar Creek to indicate whether I should go up or down it to reach the crew. I decided I'd chance following it down about two miles and, sure enough, I found George Harkins' camp. I was sure this wasn't a line camp. There were too many improvements around. Harkins' house was fenced; so I got down and tied my rope to Rain-in-the-Face's front foot, then to the bottom of the post, leaving all my gear on him. I was certain the rope would hold him. He tried to throw himself two or three times, but looked like he was giving up.

I needed water and something to eat. It had been a hard day. I still had most of the five dollars Mr. Clark gave me, so I could pay for what I ate, if I could find anything. I looked around and found plenty of food and water.

Women's and children's clothes were hanging out, so I waited. About dusk, George Harkins and Phillip Monroe, his brother-in-law, came in. The family was away visiting. They had supper, but I told them I'd already eaten. They asked if I wasn't going to take the bridle and saddle off my horse. I answered, "No, sir. The rougher for him tonight, the easier for me tomorrow. If he'll throw himself enough times tonight, the less chance he'll have to throw me tomorrow. I'm going to be awfully sore in the morning —it's been three months since I was in a saddle."

They told me the line camp was four miles up the creek, but they doubted that anybody was there. They thought that if I headed south I should get on the trail, as they had seen fresh tracks of horses and wagons crossing that road about two days ago, heading west. They guessed that I'd run into them about twenty miles out and that if I followed the tracks I'd be likely to see them working the country somewhere before night.

Next morning Rain-in-the-Face was easy to get on. I located the tracks and followed them about fifteen miles, again not seeing a house or a fence or another road. But I ran into Sam Lowery's Three Sevens wagon. Sam knew my horse and cursed Joe Bilyeu for sending a kid out alone with that kind of animal.

Sam was burning protective fire guards but it was so dry and windy he couldn't do much except at evenings, around five to eleven o'clock. One evening, just about dark, we saw a prairie fire and found out that Tennessee, the Turkey Track foreman, had let a fire get away from him while burning guards. Quickly we loaded the wagon with water, two cases of tomatoes, and a sheet-iron fire drag—that was before the chain drag came in. Then we hitched two slim, keen horses to it and started for the blaze.

A boy from Arkansas named Henry Ward Beecher was driv-

76

ing the wagon, but he couldn't keep up with the riders. Sam got impatient waiting for him and asked me, "Can you keep that team up with us?"

"Yes," I said, "if they can run fast enough."

He told me to try; so I got in the wagon and really turned them loose. They stayed pretty close to the riders. But at some time a tire had run off a back wheel, and every time the wheel struck a hole, felloes and then spokes broke out. It sure made riding rough, but we were keeping close to the others.

Sam dropped back to see how we were doing and remarked, "Say, you've got a broke wheel." I answered, "Yes, we know. But we're keeping up with you."

Soon all the spokes were gone and riding became easier. But when we got to the fire we found that we'd lost the water. We finally got the fire put out about ten o'clock the next day. Sam took no more chances; a prairie fire in tall grass can get mighty hot.

We next went on beef roundup, Bill Follis working part of the range and Sam another part, getting ready for the last shipment. Bill Follis, a friend of Theodore Roosevelt, was one of the last of the picturesque frontiersmen. Few better ropers ever lived. He lived to a very old age, but when I first saw him he was in his early thirties. A native Texan, he had ranched in New Mexico and Montana, then on the Three Sevens, where as foreman he received the then unheard-of sum of one hundred dollars a month. He was sheriff of Billings County for two terms when Billings included also the present counties of Golden Valley and McKenzie. He'd been foreman of the Three Sevens in the terrible winter of 1886, when snow and chinooks caused a loss of 90 per cent of its cattle.

Also during this roundup in the autumn of 1896 I met the first man I ever knew who had a hankering to be a train robber.

One night a man who gave the name of Bill Dalton and said he was a son of Bill Dalton of the notorious gang carrying that name came to our camp. He wanted to speak to two pals, who were in our outfit, about holding up a Northern Pacific express train. I was greatly surprised when I was told of his mission. Though some cowboys openly rode with Satan and some were weak human mavericks, they didn't stay long around outfits like the Three Sevens or on any other ranch I was ever connected with.

Bill's arrival set me to thinking about some things I'd heard about the Daltons. I knew little about the gang, though I shared a sort of anniversary with them. Bob and Grat Dalton had been killed and Emmett Dalton badly wounded in an attempted double robbery of the First National Bank and the Condon Bank in Coffeyville, Kansas, on October 5, 1892—which was just about the date I was starting to work on the Goodnight ranch.

I'd heard that the elder Bill Dalton—supposedly the father of our visitor—hadn't taken part openly in his brothers' outlawry that had ended at Coffeyville. But he was no doubt as evil as they were.

Bob Dalton, leader of the gang, was said to have been the best-dressed badman in the West. I compared the looks of our visitor with what I knew about Bob Dalton. Young Bill Dalton resembled Bob's pictures, was rather good-looking, about five feet ten inches, weighed 150 or 160 pounds. He was well built, agile, light-complexioned—and an accomplished gunslinger. He gave us some demonstrations of how handy he was with a .45 Colt. He preferred live targets, could get a bird's head every time. But I learned afterward that he wasn't as healthy as he looked. In fact, he wanted to go to the resort at Hot Springs, Arkansas, and the train robbing was his method of getting some easy money.

But a series of events temporarily took my mind off the man who called himself Bill Dalton. While in town making its last shipment, the Three Sevens let out all men except regular employees being kept for the winter and a few old men who were staying around to ride chuck line. The men staying were going back to work the summer range, round up their cattle there, and push them into the Little Missouri breaks for winter.

William Ray and D. B. Zimmerman asked Sam Lowery to recommend a man to go on that throwback for them, to get any cattle he might find and take them to their summer camp. Sam recommended me, and we met them at the Villard Hotel.

Mr. Ray and Mr. Zimmerman looked at me, then at each other

and smiled. Sam and I both got the point, and Sam spoke up, "Yes, he's just a kid. But he can ride your horses, read your brands, cut your cattle, and take them where you want them to go. He's a cowhand you can depend on."

Sam's recommendations seemed to satisfy them. Mr. Ray said, "I have a good saddle horse at the feed stable. Get him and go to our summer line camp. We'll give you a letter to Sam Rhodes, our foreman there, to supply you with a mount of horses to do this work." That horse in the feed stable was Buck, who soon became and always remained the horse of horses with me.

Around noon I was on my way down a well-traveled road fifty miles from Cedar Creek. Twelve miles down that creek was the DZ camp. I bought some cheese and crackers at the New England store and kept riding till I got to Cedar Creek late in the night. I turned down the creek, fearing I'd ride by the camp. Then I decided I'd better stop where I was and get along the best I could during the night—it was getting pretty frosty.

I took my saddle off, tied a bridle rein to the horse's front foot, wrapped the saddle blanket around myself, and got a few naps. It was too cold for long ones, and to keep warm I had to get up and walk around now and then. At the first peep of day I loped down the creek and got there just as Sam Rhodes and Alex Baxter were starting on their line ride. I gave Sam the letter concerning the horses. While they cut them out I ate breakfast, then headed for the Three Sevens line camp sixteen miles up the creek.

There I found nobody; so I ran my horses into the corral and hobbled them. Each had a rope around his neck—the only way line riders had of holding their horses, for there were no pasture fences. In fact, line riding was a job restricted to the open ranges; it was the business of these men to keep cattle on their own range, as fences did elsewhere. With my horses hobbled I went to the shack and soon fell fast asleep.

One line rider, Jay Case, got in at noon that day. I had known him in Texas, where in 1893 he had worked on the JJ Ranch after Mr. Goodnight had left it. He had also filed on a section of land some two miles west of my father's place. Case told me that young Bill Dalton, who had worked with him on the JJ, had come to see him a few days earlier and had said that the fellows who were supposed to be in with him on the Northern Pacific train robbery had run out on him.

There had been an agreed-upon plan, Bill told Jay. If the holdup was successful, they'd divide the loot at a certain rendezvous. Then they'd part, each going his own way, no two together. Bill was going to Hot Springs. He'd warned the others that if one of them ever squealed he'd hunt that man down and kill him. But that warning scared his young pals, and they scattered. Bill was on hand for the robbery, but nobody else was. Then, to my surprise, Jay said, "And Bill's here now. Go round and look in that old sod house."

I found Bill lying on the floor, his boots and clothes on, his hat on one side of him and his six-shooter on the other. He was partly covered with sand. Dried spatterings on the side of the old sod-house wall told what had happened.

Jay told me how Bill, acting very morose, had stayed in the camp for three days. Once in a while, he'd go out and shoot off a bird's head. One morning Jay didn't ride line, but stayed home to wash his clothes. He heard a shot and, thinking Bill—who'd gone outside—had shot off another bird's head, hollered: "Did you get him, Bill?"

No answer came, and Jay thought that Bill had walked up the creek. When he didn't show up for dinner Jay looked for him and found his body. He left it where it was till Howard Eaton, the Billings County coroner, could get there. But Eaton couldn't be located; he was out on a horse hunt somewhere. The burial had to wait.

Jay then told me about his first meeting with Bill Dalton. Bill had come to the JJ, and told Jay he was the son of Bill Dalton, and asked that it be kept secret. Jay, taking it that the youngster wanted to go straight and was embarrassed by his family connection, respected his wishes. He had never known of any criminal act by Bill, though he of course knew about the planned train robbery.

Next morning we shoveled out a shallow grave. Howard Eaton got there just as we wrapped Bill in a tarpaulin and loaded him on a sheet-iron fire drag to take him to the grave.

Five persons were there: Bill Moore and Jeff Barber, line riders, Jay, Howard, and I. No words were spoken as we lowered the would-be outlaw.* Howard, in a rich baritone, sang a mournful cowboy song.

The first roundup was estimated at around six thousand head of cattle, which we separated into several herds to work out according to brands and to hold the others. Steers were started towards the Missouri River badlands, and on we worked.

Then I went to the OX wagon to work. There I had a piece of luck. Henry Ward Beecher had gone home to Arkansas and had sent his bed to me by Sam Lowery. With it was a calfskin coat and a message saying he'd wire me later where to send it. He said I'd likely need it for fall work, and he certainly was right.

At the OX we went through the same routine of rounding up, cutting, and starting thousands of head to the badlands, with the weather getting colder all the time. One morning there was such a dense fog we couldn't see any cattle. Still Joe Bilyeu continued the circle. John Clayton and I were sent off to work one part of the range, and after riding for some time John said, "We're not going to be able to find any cattle in this fog, but I believe we can find the wagon. Let's go in."

We located the wagon. When we got there, Dutch Louie, the cook, said dinner was about ready. John proposed that we turn our horses loose, pointing out that our fresh ones were close by. I said that we shouldn't do this, because I knew from my training on the Goodnight ranch that we should catch fresh horses first. But John insisted, so we unsaddled them and turned them loose. Louie told John and me to go ahead and eat, as the other cowboys might be lost in the fog. We filled our plates and sat down in the back of the cook's tent. Then we started eating, cowboy fashion—with legs crossed, plates on legs.

About that time Joe Bilyeu and some of his men came in.

* To my knowledge, Jay Case never doubted the authenticity of Bill Dalton's self-identification on the JJ Ranch. But the age factor was against it. The man we buried in North Dakota was certainly not younger than his middle twenties, and if the brother of Bob, Grat, and Emmett Dalton was his father, he was a very young one.

Seeing our saddles on the ground and no one around, Joe became very angry. He jumped off his horse and strode into the tent, pulled out his six-shooter, and pointed it at John, cursing him for everything he could think of. John just looked up and said, "Joe, you've got the best hand now. You'd better keep it, before I draw mine."

Joe was trembling—and so was I, for I was right by John's side. Joe put his gun up and never said a word to me. When John and I went out to catch our horses Joe came out and apologized. John replied curtly, "I don't want any of your damned apologies. Just watch your step."

The following day I rode a little white horse that bucked with me. It was all I could do to stay aboard. Grabbing for the saddle horn, I struck it so hard that I knocked some skin off my hand. That night Louie saw it and said, "I'll put some soda and vinegar on it, and it won't get sore." While doctoring my hand he said,

"Kid, I've been watching you—you don't say anything, you just listen and tend to your own business. You haven't got a gun?"

"No, sir," I answered. "I don't think I'll need one."

"You may not," he replied. "I hope you won't. But I'd get one. These fellows all carry guns. Dress like they do. Get a gun. A gun carries respect, anyway."

Louie was an old-timer. I soon got the gun.

When my work was done at the OX wagon I went to the 7 Bar 7. John Goodall was the boss, Jesse Wichharm the cook. I ate supper with them on my eighteenth birthday, September 30, 1896. That same day Mr. Goodall was thirty-nine. Al Jackson, George Stapler, and Bill Chaloner were some of the cowboys there.

The fall roundups were over now. I took the cattle and horses back to DZ summer camp and turned them over to Sam Rhodes. Then with saddle and packhorse I went to Dickinson.

Three and a half months had passed since the buffaloes and I left Texas. In that time I had covered considerable ground.

X. A VERY FORTUNATE CONNECTION

FOR MORE THAN SIXTY YEARS I've counted it as a great blessing that I met William Ray in my first summer in North Dakota. I was, in the beginning, employed jointly by him and D. B. Zimmerman. In the years that followed I had numerous dealings with Mr. Zimmerman and have many pleasant recollections of him—and no unpleasant ones.

But the man who took me in as a broke kid, put me in business, let the bank and businessmen know he was back of everything I did, was William Ray. He laid for me a foundation anybody could have built on. He didn't live long enough for me to make even a first payment on my gratitude to him, but there is a warmth in my heart for him that will last as long as I live.

He was forty-four years old when I met him, and he lived to be only forty-eight. In our first meeting he displayed a manner that bespoke a warm and generous heart, but he was strictly business on that occasion. Later, his personality came to typify to me the spirit of the North Dakota of that time.

He was a man of vision, and truly self-made. Canadian-born, he had come to Minnesota to work as a section hand on the Great Northern Railroad. At twenty-four he was a roadmaster. His personality attracted James J. Hill, the empire builder, and the two men became close friends. A little below medium height, he wore a black close-cropped beard that seemed to add to his stature.

He'd come to the new town of Dickinson after transferring to the Northern Pacific, and he'd been a member of the convention that wrote North Dakota's Constitution. He became interested in hotel, real estate, and cattle businesses and soon left the railroad to give his entire attention to these enterprises. In all of them he was successful. Despite his own wealth it wasn't in his nature to be indifferent about the welfare of anyone. Few men ever helped so many others as he did.

Mr. and Mrs. Ray were father and mother to me. (This gracious lady was to outlive her husband by many years.) There was a kindliness and serenity in the Ray home that I have seen in few others. In it they'd gathered many things which made for convenience and comfort. Its hospitality was famous.

Although Mr. Ray's help was beyond any words I can find to describe it, in the beginning he certainly didn't coddle or overpay me. When I went back to Dickinson as cold weather approached in the fall of 1896, Mr. Ray and Mr. Zimmerman had a herd of young cattle that they were selling to little stockmen and settlers coming into the country. I was put to herding these dogies.

Ray and Zimmerman also had some saddle horses they'd shipped down from Oregon. Mr. Zimmerman came out to the stock pens a few miles west of Dickinson, and together we got these horses out of a little pasture, to herd them with the cattle. The horses had been ridden that summer on work with the last shipment.

The horses all showed they'd been put through the mill, except for one fat, sleek dark bay. I said to Mr. Zimmerman, "That's a pretty horse. I'd like to ride him."

"You just ride him all you want to," he replied. There was a generosity and obligingness in his offer that should have made me wary, but it didn't come to me. Then I thought of an Oregon horse I'd heard of, one that had quickly bested Deadwood Dick. I'd seen this buster ride, and I knew he was one of the best. I asked Mr. Zimmerman, "Is that the horse that threw Dick?"

"Yes, it is," he answered; "but you can ride better than Dick.

There's a little wire corral just ahead of us. Catch him and try him."

I did. He bucked up a sandy hill, then switched and bucked down the same hill and threw me high. I landed on my head in the sand. I knew I couldn't do it. His hide would roll like a badger's. Nor did spurs help to hold. Getting me off his back presented no problem to him; I rode him no more.

They took this horse that respected no rider to the ranch. There Alex Baxter, a good rider from Oregon, tried him. The horse threw Alex sixteen times before he gave up and went to bed for two weeks. Sam Rhodes then took him and rode him once, but announced he'd never do it agin. Then they gave him to Bill Chaloner, the best bronco buster who ever hit North Dakota.

Bill stayed on him for a very bumpy ride, but later told me he was the hardest bucker he'd ever known. Bill finally made a work horse out of him. I was glad to see him in harness, for one try on him had been enough for me.

We worked through a cold, snowy October. In November all dogies were sold. Ray and Zimmerman had bought a thousand Oregon steers they were expecting in, to be driven out to the DZ Ranch to winter. I was to go with them. Then Mr. Zimmerman told me the Oregon steers were snowed in and couldn't be shipped till spring; so he let me out and paid me off.

After buying winter clothes I didn't have much money left. I had to have work. I hadn't seen Mr. Ray for some time. I felt sure he'd find something for me, but for days I couldn't find him. I found that he was out of town. By this time I was out of money; in fact, matters were even worse than that. Henry Ward Beecher had written me to ship his bed and fur coat. I'd worn the coat into the hotel one night, hung it on a rack, and somebody had walked off with it. A new calfskin coat cost $22.50; I had to get that amount before I could ship the bed. Everything was looking gloomier, the snow getting deeper every day. I told Milt Lindsey, the restaurant man I'd been eating with, that I wanted him to give me credit, for how much and how long I didn't know.

"Just as long as my doors are open," Milt said, "come in and get what you want. I'm sure you'll pay me some day. I won't worry about that, and don't you."

McKinley had just beaten Bryan, and most people thought things would get better now. But it didn't look like they were going to improve for one cowboy.

I was staying at the livery stable and sleeping on Henry Ward Beecher's bed. Then Mr. Ray returned. He was as usual very friendly, but I couldn't summon up the courage to tell him my financial troubles. I merely told him I wanted a job. He told me he had all the help he needed at the ranch; so I said no more that day. Next day he was just as friendly. We visited a lot. Late in the afternoon I pressed for a job and didn't get an absolute turn-down.

When he started for home I walked along with him. The snow was very deep, and it was still falling. Mr. Ray remarked, "I have to go a few blocks over here and see about Mrs. Chaloner. I heard she was out of coal, and Bill's out of town."

I went with him. Mrs. Chaloner said it was true that she was out of coal. Mr. Ray told her he'd get a load there as early as he could the next morning. Then he asked her how she was fixed for groceries, and she said she was out of about everything. "Send down to Parker's grocery tomorrow and get what you want," he said, "I'll see Parker and tell him I'll take care of it."

Bill Chaloner later told me he owed Mr. Ray $700 at the time.

I walked on with Mr. Ray until we were near his house. When I was leaving him he said, "I'll see you in the morning and we'll try to work out something." I felt my troubles were over.

Next morning when we met he told me, "I'll send you to the ranch tomorrow. The buckskin horse you've been riding is in the livery stable. Get an early start—the snow's deep. You can't get far in one day, and it's sixty miles out there."

"I may not give you the going wage of $35 a month, but I'll pay you something till spring. You won't be under the boss; he doesn't need any help. You just do what you see needs doing."

Then I told him about my financial troubles. He took me to the Dickinson Mercantile Company and told them to let me have anything I wanted and to send him the bill. To me he said, "Get anything you need. It'll be a long time before you're in town

86

again. When you get the coat to send to that fellow, get one for yourself. You'll need it tomorrow." Then he gave me $7.35 to settle my cafe bill with Milt Lindsey.

I bought two calfskin coats and shipped Henry Ward Beecher his bed and one of the new coats. I was happy. I not only had a job; I had that horse, Buck, again.

On Thanksgiving Day I was on my way to the old Bellows Ranch on the Little Missouri River, fifteen miles north of Medora. (Portions of this ranch were later incorporated in Roosevelt Park.) I thanked the Lord for a friend like Mr. Ray.

It took me three days to make the trip. We found deep snow in low places, and it was hard to get through. But Buck had intelligence and resourcefulness, and he went through, roads or not. First we went by Green River Butte, and I spent the night with a Russian farmer. We went by another butte, then to the Little Missouri badlands and the Three Sevens line camp for the second night. From there we went to the ranch.

I was surprised to find that my old friend and Three Sevens boss, Sam Lowery, was foreman. I was certainly going to do anything Sam told me—and any other jobs I could find. The cattle were mostly rustling their living in the badlands; only the calves and a few cows were being fed. Among the more than six hundred horses on the ranch were six extra fine stallions to be fed. Other stallions were with their herd on the range.

All winter Sam turned over to me the job of caring for the stallions, milking a cow, cooking, cleaning house, chopping wood, and keeping the horse barns cleaned out. I wanted a job and had one, wanted to please and hold it, and I did.

I curried and brushed the stallions every day, and every other minute I could find I put in on the woodpile, until the pile of stovewood, all cut up, was big enough to last all winter and summer.

My downfall came when I tried to act as an assistant to Cupid. I came a cropper, and a prized friendship was ended. It happened this way:

In February, 1897, Mr. Ray and his manager, Rassy Deffebach, came to Medora. They traveled down the river with the mail sleigh to the ranch and stayed three days. I took them back to Medora. When I returned, Sam asked me to write a Panhandle City girl we both had taken to a few dances. He'd written to her but hadn't had any answer, and he thought maybe she hadn't received the letter.

I wrote her—Lena Ridley—just what Sam told me to say: He was the foreman of a large ranch with a comfortable house, nice furniture, an excellent team and buggy. I was working for him. Some of the conveniences he mentioned weren't visible to me, but I wished Sam success when he said all he needed now was for her to share this with him. I liked Lena and thought how fine it would be if she'd accept Sam. Maybe he could even get the buggy and nice furniture he said he had.

A long, friendly letter came back from Lena, telling me all about all the young folks I knew in Panhandle City. She said she was glad I'd written, told me to do it often, and said she'd keep me posted on everything there. Her only comment about the man I'd written the letter for was just a reference to "poor Sam."

I felt sorry for him, but there wasn't anything I could do. I certainly didn't want to show him the letter. He knew I'd received it, and became very cranky with me. Thereafter nothing I did pleased him. Then one day Sam said, "You got a letter from Lena, didn't you?"

"Yes, I did," I told him.

"Why didn't you show it to me?"

"It wasn't a very good letter, Sam, and I didn't want to show it to you. But if you want to see it I'll get it."

He read Lena's letter and said bitterly, "You never sent the letter I told you to."

"Yes, I did," I replied, "and you handed it to the mailman yourself. That's the only letter I've written to Lena. I haven't answered this one from her and never will."

I was sorry later that I'd made this hasty and unnecessary promise, for she was a fine girl. For two weeks Sam hardly spoke to me, and I never did hear from Lena again.

Sam wrote Mr. Ray and told him he'd have to move me, saying, "This kid can't do anything and won't do anything." And he had praised me to Mr. Ray less than thirty days before! In

March Mr. Ray wrote Sam to come to Dickinson. In a very friendly manner Sam told me he'd be gone a few days. He gave me instructions what to do, then went to town and never came back.

On the first of April, 1897, Mr. Ray sent Rassy Deffebach out to see how everything was and to instruct me about how to handle the summer work, how to round up the horses, and what kind of mares to put with new stallions. I wasn't to have anything to do with cattle till branding time.

I just said to him, "Mr. Deffebach, I can't do it. I'm just a kid. My judgment might be wrong."

Rassy replied, "Mr. Ray knows how old you are. He knows you might make mistakes. He knows older men make mistakes. But he likes you and is willing to put you on your own judgment, which is a promotion in itself. Now take my advice: Never turn down anything that's a step up the ladder. He'll send out the help you need."

I promised Rassy I'd stay and do the best I could. Shortly afterward Mr. Ray sent out Bill Chaloner, a real horseman, to round up geldings and dry mares and halter-break and drive them so they'd be ready to sell. We also broke every other animal that looked like it might develop into a good saddle horse. Bill was so good that he could look at a horse and tell just what would be made of him.

Bill was there for fifteen days, and we broke twenty-four horses to halter and drive, six to halter and ride. He told me there were certain fundamentals to observe about a horse: A superior animal holds his head up, has a quick step. But one sure way to judge a horse's intelligence, he said, is by watching his ears. When a horse throws one ear back and the other forward, then quickly changes them, he's smart. He's paying attention to what he's doing, and it's easy to get your thoughts over to him. I recalled that was true of the mature horses I'd ridden on the Goodnight ranch, and it was certainly true of Buck, my North Dakota mount.

Bill showed me how that was helpful in selecting your horses for mounts. When breaking them, watch the ears. Slow ear action can mean anything from dull to dumb. Such a horse might be useful for some things, but he's slow to learn and slow to act after he has learned. In working stock, quick action is needed in both horse and man—quickness to see, think, and act.

He also told me how to judge young horses in a corral. The good horses will be the leaders when you run them around the corral; the ones in the rear will be the ones that throw both ears together, whether backward or forward, and they don't pay any attention to you. A wide-awake horse understands what his rider wants to do, does it, and is as proud of doing a good job, I think, as a man is.

In later years I always compared cowboys with horses. If a man moved with ambition and action, if his eyes and ears worked to catch things, if he paid attention, he made a good cowboy and probably would have done well in any other occupation. I learned that I had a great responsibility with both men and horses—to handle them with care or not to handle them at all. Proper handling could make of a smart horse whatever you wanted. Poor handling could make an outlaw. The same holds true for children.

Neighboring ranchers and cowboys who had visited us that winter told us how wild some of the Bellows horses were. Some ranged a hundred miles from the ranch, as far as the Yellowstone River breaks. They talked especially of Silver Tip, a wild Spanish mare that ran with a bunch of twenty-five or thirty horses that hadn't been corralled for several years. She was chestnut sorrel, with a white mane and tail.

Her gang ranged on the PK divide, which drew its name from the PK Ranch—the Three Sevens horse camp. It included the area between the Little Missouri and Beaver Creek breaks, to where they formed their junction.

Where Silver Tip romped, the divide was from two to three miles wide. When this proud queen saw a would-be rider, she'd bolt for the nearest breaks of the Little Missouri or Beaver Creek country and hide. I'd been told how four or five cowboys had taken stands and relayed runs on her to keep her out of rough country, but she'd always eluded them and escaped. They'd run their horses down; so they quit trying to get her into a corral or in a roundup.

Rassy told me just to let Silver Tip and her pals alone. "There's no use running a good horse down for nothing," he said. "You can't get them. And be careful about old Prince, that big black stallion. He'll fight a rider and a saddle horse that tries to come to his bunch—and any mares you run into his bunch, he'll hold them there. If you want to get colts in to brand, take about three men and good horses. If you throw rocks at Prince, you can keep him away and get them in."

I was to work with the W Bar wagon on the horse roundup, which was to collect all horses on the Yellowstone River range, then go to Three Sevens for their horse roundup. We had about a four-thousand-acre tract. The rough breaks had been fenced off—the fence was just the length of the trails—where it was easy for an animal to get out. The rough places, where the horses probably couldn't get out, weren't fenced. It was government land, and law forbade enclosing the area entirely.

I threw all horses into this place as I gathered them. Then Billy Neuens and his wife were sent out to take care of the ranch, fences, and haying, and Mr. Ray wrote me to come to Dickinson on May 1 and bring their buggy horse. He wanted to talk over the summer work with me before the horse roundup started.

I went in and rode up to his barn. Out came his two beautiful daughters, Eleanor and Agnes, fourteen and eighteen, to see their buggy horse. These girls looked so clean and so nice in pretty spring dresses that I was scared of them. They were friendly and perfectly at ease, telling me that supper was just ready and inviting me in to eat with the family. I was trying to find a polite way to get 'out of it when Mr. Ray came out and seconded the invitation. There was nothing else I could do.

I thought of my old checkered wool shirt, my blue ducks stuffed down in boot tops, the long winter crop of hair, long fuzz on my face. I was awfully embarassed, and even the homey friendliness of the whole Ray family couldn't make me forget my miserable self.

They had a large family table. Mr. Ray sat at one end and Mrs. Ray at the other. Mr. Ray's single sister was on my right, Mr. Ray on my left. Donald, four years old, was in a high chair between us; Eleanor and Agnes were across the table in front of me. The hired girl, who was both cook and housekeeper, brought in heaping platters of food to the table.

Everything looked so nice. There was a table full of good things to eat. I hadn't had a bite since breakfast, and I had traveled sixty miles since then. Yet my appetite was poor. There was a beautiful tablecloth and napkins, and I kept using my napkin so much Donald said, "Oh, he's trying to twist his whiskers—and he hasn't got any whiskers to twist." In the lively talk around the table Donald's remark went unnoticed.

What a relief it was to get downtown to the hotel and, the next day, get a haircut, clean shave, good bath, and a new pair of riding pants to replace the travel-weary ones I had. Never again did I wear blue ducks or an old wool shirt to town, and my boots always were blacked and shining when I rode in. I got a razor of my own, and my mode of life was completely revamped. But I was still scared of girls.

Mr. Ray gave me instructions about my work the next day, and I went back to the ranch, then the W Bar and horse work, and on to the Three Sevens. I'd kept Buck up and fed him all winter. He was my top mount, and I preferred him for all my hard rides. He was fast and never seemed to get tired.

XI. BUCK

I RODE HUNDREDS of horses in my days as a cowboy. Some of them were mighty good ones, but, for any and all work and for intelligent companionship, Buck was the best horse I ever threw a leg over. A cowboy loves a horse who helps him do his job and perform the impossible things, thereby helping him establish a name as a good cowboy. Buck did all that. Sometimes I wonder how many persons ever meant more to me than that horse. We had a way of communicating with one another.

I thought when I first saw him that he wasn't an especially attractive horse—this compact, grayish-yellow seven-year-old. Buck had charm in unlimited quantities. He was dependable, a quality which doesn't always accompany charm, and he had all the dignity expected of a king.

I remember the day and the hour I met him. It was on September 20, 1896, at eleven o'clock in the morning. I have already related how I rode him to get the rest of my mount to comb out the Ray and Zimmerman cattle that had mingled with the Three Sevens, OX, and 7 Bar 7 herds.

Buck's color was so light he was almost silver. He had a dark mane and tail, a short back, long hips, and well-muscled legs. His four white feet were trim, and his white stockings ran almost to his knees. His knees and hocks were a shade darker than the rest of his coat.

His wide forehead and short ears indicated intelligence, strength, and alertness. There wasn't any long hair on his fetlocks; nor did it ever grow long. His mane and tail also were short, and stayed that way. He was so thin-skinned that his muscles, veins, and arteries showed. He was sixteen hands tall and weighed 1,050 pounds. He had just one brand—a blacksmith's bellows—on his left shoulder. So the Bellows Ranch must have been his birthplace. When Mr. Ray bought the ranch in 1894 Buck was already broken to ride.

As I rode out on that first sixty-mile trip to the line camp (which Buck, with his strong, easy gait, made before the sun went down), I knew that I'd never known his equal, nor one so easy on his rider for a long journey. His strides were long and smooth, whether he was walking, fox trotting, or loping.

At the outset I'd known nothing about his background or that of his owner, Mr. Ray. My instant opinion of them was that whatever their genealogy both were thoroughbreds, and time bore that out. My first impressions came from Mr. Ray's kindly instructions about how to do my work, and from Buck's looks and actions.

I never found out who broke Buck nor the names of any of his former riders. Apparently nobody had ever seen anything special about him before. But Buck immediately struck my fancy, and I was in love with him at first sight.

Buck was gentle—I should say gently bred. He was never cross with other horses, but he knew his stall in the barn and wanted his privacy. Never did I have to rope Buck out of the remuda. Whenever I called him he'd trot out from the bunch and come straight to me. His temperament was always quiet, and he never fretted or got excited or pranced. I quickly found that he was a good cutting horse and easy to rope from. He'd go up to the side of anything, so I could just lay a rope on what I was after.

I'd learned on the Goodnight ranch that if you wanted a horse to like you, you had to be good to him. A convincing way to show friendship was to offer him a little sugar or biscuit. When we finished the three-day ride from Dickinson to the badlands in November, 1896, in about as bad weather as I'd ever seen up to that time, I knew I wanted Buck to think as much of me as I thought of him. So I made a sugar and biscuit eater out of him in the winter of 1896–1897.

We finished the Three Sevens horse work just south of Sentinel Butte in the early summer of 1897. I singled out my stock horses and penned them in Mr. Gilbraith's corrals at Sentinel

Butte. I was then ready for an early-morning start back to the wagon for the night. Mr. Gus Streeter, who was at Sentinel Butte, told me Mr. Ray had sent word by him for me to come to Dickinson as soon as I could get there.

At daylight, as I was finishing saddling Buck, one of the boys was thrown, and his horse broke away with the saddle on him. I mounted Buck, and together we swept past the others trying to catch the runaway. We quickly came alongside the horse. I caught the reins and tied them to the saddle horn. The runaway went quietly back to camp with us. Everybody noticed Buck that time, and I thought Buck himself looked a little proud-necked.

I then got my stock and saddle horses out of Gilbraith's corrals and drove to the pasture at Bellows Ranch, a distance of forty-five miles. There I turned the horses out to graze and fed Buck. It was eleven o'clock and sixty miles to Dickinson. I went back out and whispered into Buck's ears, "You're the best horse I've got to get me there. I've been favoring you for this day."

I ate lunch, and we started out. Sometimes we loped, sometimes we trotted. Before it was dark we trotted down Villard Street in Dickinson. Mr. Ray, Mr. Streeter, Sheriff Charley Kono, and one or two others were standing in front of the Villard Hotel.

As I pulled up, Mr. Streeter exclaimed, "That's the horse you were riding this morning. Did you take your horses home?" I told him I had.

"Why, you've ridden him more than a hundred miles today," he said.

"Yes, sir," I replied, "and he shows no weakness yet."

The Sheriff turned to Mr. Ray. "I'll give you two hundred dollars for him."

Consternation seized me. As horses were then priced in McKinley sound dollars, that was a large amount. Top saddle horses were selling for a fourth of that.

"He's not for sale at any price," Mr. Ray responded, to my great relief.

The next morning Mr. Ray came to the hotel and told me why he had sent for me. He had a mortgage on two hundred head of horses owned by Charley Murray, who hadn't kept up the interest and had fallen so far behind that if he didn't pay there wasn't anything to do but foreclose. Mr. Ray wanted me to see that none of the horses got away after the papers were served. I stayed three days. A settlement was made; then I went back to the ranch.

Bill Chaloner had taught me the art of breaking horses, and I was anxious to try my hand. The range stallion herds and the new stallions were in the pasture and needed no attention; so I caught up five nice broncos, halter-broke them, and rode. Three of them were buckskins, the other two black. One black bucked so hard and got so good at figuring out quick ways of getting rid of me that I gave him up as a bad job.

The other black and one buckskin broke out good. The other two buckskins gave it all they had every time I got on, and they seemed to get better at bucking each time. I'd ride them in the large herd corral until I found out who could outlast who.

Several old mares got out of the pasture where they'd been put and headed back to where they'd foaled the year before. (Mares always try to get back to the same place to foal each year.) I knew they were up in some part of the Yellowstone River country. There weren't any places for me to stop for a meal going up there.

This was W Bar range, and all camps were deserted in the summertime. All men were with the chuck wagon, working the range somewhere. I wasn't likely to come across them; so I packed a flour sack with enough sour-dough biscuits and beef-steak to last three or four days, wrapped it in my slicker, and tied it behind my saddle. I got on Buck, and we went horse hunting, seventy-five or a hundred miles from our ranch.

Always on such journeys I took a little sugar for Buck and myself. Sometimes I had dried fruit—apples or prunes. They'd be raw but very good for strength, and filling. Buck doted on sugar and biscuits, and I gave him many a treat I'd have liked for myself. But I was wooing that horse and trying to keep his favor in every way I could.

Not a fence or a house did we see on our journey straight north to the Yellowstone River breaks. Then we began the search for our strayed horses. As we crossed the PK Divide, I could see old Silver Tip's bunch far to the west. They caught sight of us, too, and moved around, ready for a run, just like antelopes.

As Buck and I moved on into the Beaver Creek breaks out of sight of Silver Tip, I was thinking of what Rassy Deffebach had told me about how that old mare, wise and with the speed of a prairie fire, knew how to thwart any effort to domesticate her. I said to Buck, "Some day we'll show Mr. Erasmus Deffebach. You're just the horse to give her the run of her life, and she'll go to the ranch just like it was her own idea in the first place."

I had learned that Buck liked to have his virtues mentioned. When I talked to him admiringly, his clean-cut little ears would wiggle, one backward and one forward, just like Bill Chaloner told me a smart horse's ears would always do.

We were out all day. When night came we found water and camped. I ate, gave Buck a little sugar and a biscuit, and talked to him some more:

"Silver Tip may be a thunderbolt, but you're chain lightning. We'll get her off that perch, and we'll see that she stays out of the rough ground. But let's keep this to ourselves."

I was tired and sleepy. I put my catch rope around Buck's neck and tied it to a saddle horn. I gave Buck a little more sugar. Then, using my saddle blanket and slicker for a bed and my saddle for a pillow, I went to sleep. But Buck would graze to the end of the rope, jerk the saddle, and wake me up. Not a very good night's sleep.

A horse doesn't sleep when he's hungry. When he's filled up he sleeps between midnight and daylight. Two or three hours is a good sleep for a horse. Most times he sleeps standing up. In daytime most horses like to stretch out in the sun and nap, but an hour of that is plenty for them. They put in more time grazing than a cow, and crop the grass much closer.

At daylight I ate breakfast: biscuits, beef, dried apples, sugar, and a drink of water. Buck had a little more sugar, then we were on our way.

We found our horses in two bunches. One of them belonged entirely to Bellows; the others included horses belonging to other ranchmen. I knew I had to drive the Bellows bunch near the second one, dig out the Bellows horses from the mixed bunch, then bring all Bellows horses together. All this had to be done on the run, for every animal there was wild. When the horses were cut off and put together they had to be run until they tired.

But now it was nearly night, and both Buck and I needed a rest; so we camped and had supper without any change of menu. Buck got his sweet tidbit as usual. I made my bed the customary way, tying Buck to the saddle horn. I was so tired that when he jerked the saddle the first time and woke me up I said, "Buck, you need more room to graze in, and I need more sleep. You won't leave me, anyway—I've got the biscuits and sugar."

I untied the rope from the saddle and went back to sleep. I awoke at break of day and saw Buck about three hundred yards away. As I stood up he nickered; he was inquiring about that biscuit and sugar. Then we went after our horses and worked them as planned. By working at top speed we brought the Bellows horses together and shunted them off a few miles from the others.

It was the middle of the day before I got everything under control and could give Buck a little rest. It had been very arduous work for him. Some of those wild Bellows horses were plunging tornadoes, but when one of them put on a burst of speed and tried to get away Buck would streak after him, putting every ounce of his strength into the effort. In a battle of wills with another horse Buck always won. I thought to myself, "There isn't a horse on the range that Buck can't run onto so close I can hit it with my quirt."

It was getting dark when I got my bunch to Beaver Creek. I let them stay at the water until I was sure all had drunk enough, then I pushed them across to a good grazing place. When they were all munching the grass I rode back to the creek, ate my food, and drank good creek water.

I took the bridle off Buck and fixed a catch rope around his neck. There would be no unsaddling this night, as I might have to ride at any moment.

I camped on the opposite side of the creek from the horses, so that if they started back to where I'd found them I'd hear them splashing through the water. But at daylight they were all where I'd left them. I proceeded to the ranch.

As I went back across the PK Divide, I again saw Old Silver Tip's bunch in the distance. I patted Buck and said, "Yes, sirree, Buck, you can put her anywhere. We'll show her some day."

Buck nodded his head. Some people would say it was a coincidence. Knowing Buck, I'm not so sure.

I made three similar trips to the Yellowstone River country that summer, looking for horses that had roamed away. I was trying to get them to adopt an area close to the Bellows Ranch. Thus occupied, I had no time for the contest between Buck and Silver Tip. It was further delayed by a bout with a bronco, a date with the dentist, and the unaccustomed role of being host to some young women.

I always favored Buck by riding the rest of my mounts until there was a long, hard ride or something special which required an extra good horse. While at home this time it was necessary to ride my "broncs." The two buckskins among them were hard to stay on; I couldn't grip them and had to ride on my spurs.

Somebody had told me that if I'd wet the inside of my leggings I could get a better grip and wouldn't have to ride on my spurs, and that the broncos wouldn't buck so hard. I decided to give it a try. I went to the water trough and dampened the inside of my leggings; then I got on the horse without my spurs. He lurched forward, arched his back, and put his whole heart into dislodging me. At every jump I worked up and couldn't get down into the saddle. I went so high that my head bobbed over and struck the bronco between the ears. I went hurtling over his head.

I staggered to my feet and realized that my mouth was bleeding. When my head struck the horse, my lip had been cut by the head-stall buckle and my front teeth knocked loose. The lower teeth came back over my tongue, but I pulled them in place and went to the water trough to wash out my mouth. There I found that my lips had holes in them; the water ran out. I caught my bronco, unsaddled him, and turned him loose.

My gums were so torn up I thought I'd better go to Dickinson and let a doctor look at them. To my relief I found a dentist was there for a week. This was lucky, because at that time Dickinson didn't have any resident dentist. He straightened out my teeth, doctored my gums, and told me to eat nothing but milk toast, oatmeal, or some such soft food for two weeks.

About this time Mr. Ray visited me in my room at the St. Charles Hotel. When he asked how I was getting along, I told him I was doing all right except that the doctor had prescribed soft food for two weeks.

"You can't do much riding on soft food," he said. "I've been promising my girls a trip to the ranch ever since I've owned it. So you take them. I have a spring wagon and team.

"Go up to the house and tell them to get ready to start early in the morning. They have a young married friend who wants to go along."

I was scared. I'd never seen two prettier or friendlier girls, but I was scared of my shortcomings. I wouldn't know how to talk or act around them. But I had orders, and it was my job to carry them out, even though I didn't feel up to them. I went to the house and told them. Eleanor and Agnes were delighted.

The next day was enjoyable. The three girls had lots of fun. I did the best I could but I was so timid I can't say I enjoyed the sixty-mile trip. The three of them took turns riding Buck, and I had to drive the team. I felt the need of solid food.

Mrs. Neuens, who kept the house at the ranch, was a good cook. She had a nice meal for the girls, with milk toast and a tasty custard for me. Everybody was tired and went to bed early the first night.

The next day Mrs. Neuens, who was always my good friend, thought I was too backward and wasn't enjoying the company enough. She came up with the idea that if I'd play some trick on the girls it would give us some fun, thereby breaking the ice and ridding me of my shyness. That evening she said, "Billie, go down to the well and get some frogs from around the old watering trough. Try to find three or four little ones. Tonight, put them between the sheets. They'll be very still until the girls kick the cover loose; then the frogs will hop."

That sounded like a harmless prank. I got the frogs in a can after supper, and while everybody else was out on the porch enjoying the beautiful moon I put the frogs under the bed covers. When I came back, Billy Neuens started telling snake stories. I told about rattlesnakes getting in cowboys' beds on roundups, but I said it was practically impossible for one to get in a bed in a house like this. It wasn't out of the question, I added, but I'd never heard of it happening.

The girls were fagged out, so they went to their room. Our conspirators had talked it over. When the girls discovered there was something in their bed, there'd be no laughing; it would be treated very seriously. When the commotion started, I got Billy to go look for the "snakes." He acted so brave. I trusted him to treat it seriously, for I was afraid I couldn't. When he brought out the four little frogs, they all had a big laugh. Finally, it was all blamed on me; and the charge against me was that I hadn't been brave enough to take any part in looking for the "snakes."

Eleanor, who was in her fourteenth year, said to me. "Mamma said you were so nice and polite. I don't think you're either nice or polite."

But we were all soon friends again, and I enjoyed their company till it was time for them to return to Dickinson. It was then pretty lonesome at the ranch, but there remained sweet memories and a longing to go to Dickinson more often. I was never again scared of girls. Eleanor and Agnes have been my friends ever since.

There came a lag in activities around the ranch, and the time seemed ripe for the contest between Buck and old Silver Tip. I knew she was a mare to reckon with, but I wasn't impressed with Rassy Deffebach's belief that she could show her heels to anything on hoofs in that country.

To put our fun on a business basis, I remembered that the colts in Silver Tip's herd hadn't been branded, and I felt sure Buck could bring everything in. I resolved not to tell anyone. Buck and I would just go out and try, early in the morning.

I let Buck canter a little to limber up his muscles. Then we climbed the rough, steep trail leading to the hogback that ran out to the PK Divide and Silver Tip's domain. When we reached the divide I got down and let Buck rest and graze for a while, so he'd be bolstered for the stiff competition ahead. There wasn't a horse in sight, but we had to be ready.

We moved cautiously up the divide, and I spied the bunch near a grassy knoll not far from the Beaver Creek breaks. Silver Tip looked more regal than ever. I rode into the breaks to keep out of sight till I could get on the other side of the grassy knoll.

I left Buck in a coulee out of sight and climbed to a high place to see whether they'd moved. Silver Tip was three or four hundred yards from the grassy knoll. Then I rode out from the breaks, getting close on the Beaver Creek side in order to turn them out on the divide, which was about three miles wide at this point.

It was evident that we'd have to outdo Silver Tip's wiles and artifices. I knew Buck was a stayer; he had a long stride and rugged strength. He wouldn't waste any energy, would make everything count. On the other hand, Silver Tip and her pals were too fat and soft to last long if we could just keep her from pulling one of her crafty tricks and getting away.

The bunch bounced away when they saw us. Buck felt the excitement of the contest and shot forward right after them. Silver Tip wasn't going to outwit Buck, and she wasn't going to outrun any horse as long-winded as he was.

We ran them hard for two miles, and they were getting fagged. I moved around and turned them the other way, then went into the bunch and tapped Silver Tip with my quirt—just to emphasize to her the fact that Buck had taken a human being closer to her than she'd ever expected one to be.

Buck and I were enjoying the chase. We could play with Silver Tip and her bunch like a cat plays with a mouse. Buck slackened long enough to get his wind. He acted like he could run to the Rocky Mountains, and the wild horses were acting more like they'd had it.

Buck and I headed them down the divide to the hogback, for they were still in the rough and hadn't yet decided that they couldn't get away. We crowded them, going into the bunch, with me yelling as we went off the hogback and churned down deep hills, kicking up dust. I couldn't see anything, but I knew Buck was sure-footed. Soon we were on grass. The dust cleared away, and we were coming into a saddle-horse pasture. Now we were in the horse corral. When I shut the gate, Silver Tip and all her chums were in there.

It was just four o'clock. I was proud of Buck, and patted him in congratulation. I'm sure he was proud too, for we talked it over several times. I always had confidence in him and he never failed me. We were tired and hungry, so I watered him and gave him a bundle of sheaf oats. Then I got a lunch and remarked to the others as casually as I could, "I had a pretty hard ride today."

They asked where I'd been.

"I rode out and got Silver Tip—brought her in and corralled her."

There was a buzz of disbelief.

"Just go out and look," I said. "I fastened the gate good, and I'm sure she's still there."

She was. Buck stood munching his oats and pretending to be unconcerned, but I noticed a little twinkle in his eye.

The next morning we had four lockjaw horses to run into the corral and doctor. The method was to forefoot them, tie them down, and bleed them by splitting the end of their tail. Their gums were also cut, as near to the roof of the mouth as possible. Then a board was laid on the jaw and tapped pretty hard with a hammer, loosening the jaws. The bleeding released the over-supply of blood at the brain.

We lost one horse, but the others came out of it all right. We split the bunch and branded three one- and two-year-old colts. For Agnes I broke a coal-black one and for Eleanor a chestnut sorrel with white mane and tail. They made beautiful saddle horses and proved easy to handle—nice, high-spirited horses.

We hog-tied Silver Tip, trimmed her feet, rasped them down till she was so tender-footed she could hardly walk, and tied a horseshoe in her foretop. She was crestfallen for a while, but that didn't last long. We never had any more trouble corralling her.

Summer work was over. Soon snow covered the ground. I went to Dickinson to spend Thanksgiving. I was liking the town better all the time since there wasn't anybody in it to be scared of anymore.

XII. A NORTH DAKOTA SNOWSTORM

MR. RAY WAS OUT OF TOWN when I got to Dickinson. He was in St. Paul, making one of his frequent visits to his friend James J. Hill, the Great Northern Railroad magnate. While waiting for his return I bought two suits, two hats, and a pair of town shoes.

Just why I should have bedecked myself out so in a country where most cowboys considered anything more than one nice suit as evidence of "clothes mania" I don't know. Maybe it was because the Ray girls were becoming very interesting to me. Whatever the reason, I was fixed to go places, and did. Agnes hitched up the old buggy horse to the cutter and took me for my first sleigh ride.

Mr. Ray's visit to St. Paul lasted somewhat longer than had been expected, but I was having a good time in town. When he did return I enjoyed his account of his visit with Jim Hill. Then I found out that he wanted me at the ranch, not living and boarding in town. He made it plain that I surely could find something to do about the place. So I embarked on a cold, lonely ride. I wouldn't have any use for my new town clothes.

There wasn't much of interest at the ranch. It was lonesome, and time dragged till March 1, 1898, when I got a letter from Mr. Ray saying that the horses had been sold to Joe McCoul and were to be delivered by June 1. He'd heard there were some of our Bellow horses northwest of Glendive, Montana, on the Butterman horse range—150 or 200 miles from our ranch. He wanted me to go for them as soon as weather permitted. I was ready to leave, but waited till the twenty-first for the equinox. When the sun crossed the equator, the storm period in North Dakota was supposed to end.

104

The twenty-fourth of March was warm. The snow was mostly gone; only a few drifts remained. Winter must be over, I reasoned. Early on March 25 I started on the trip. It was long before daylight; the stars were shining bright.

It was just forty-five miles to the W Bar Ranch, but I knew there'd be snowdrifts and low places filled with snow that I'd have to ride around. This would take extra time. I had to get an early start if I was going to finish the trip before dark.

Buck was nine that year—an old campaigner. With a hint of spring in the air he was anxious to get started on the year's business. He was tingling with good health.

With a slicker tied behind my saddle, a beefsteak and a few sour-dough biscuits, I was on my way. Soon a few clouds crossed the clear sky, and there was a chill in the breezy wind. The clouds were thickening as I rode up on the hogback at daybreak. When I reached the PK Divide snow was falling, and by the time I got across to the Beaver Creek breaks it was coming down hard and fast. I could see only a little way, but I felt I could keep my course.

The country was a wide-open range, with not a house or fence between the Bellows and W Bar Ranches. I was using landmarks to go by, but soon nothing was visible. I ate my lunch, still certain that we could make it to the W Bar for supper. Buck was a good, strong horse, I told myself. He'd keep our course and bust through those snow drifts. That afternoon progress was slower than I expected. Night was coming, and it would soon be dark. I didn't know how far I was from the ranch.

I rode into a brush thicket in the midst of a few trees. The snow by now was furious, and the wind was playing a shrill tune. I discovered a log, kicked around and found some old dead limbs, and piled them against the log. Soon I had a fire blazing.

I gathered sage-brush tops for Buck, all he could eat, and rubbed him all over. Then I got more limbs to pile on the fire. The log was burning good now, but I was getting hungry and tired.

Unsaddling Buck, I used the saddle blanket and slicker for a bed and the saddle for a pillow. Moving as close to the fire as I could, I went to bed. The brush-thicket protection was meager,

105

and the snow hadn't slacked up any. I got cold and crawled too close to the fire, burning one of my leather leggings to a crisp. But I had a satisfactory sleep—under the circumstances—until daybreak.

Weak from lack of food, I started on my ride, sure I'd soon find Beaver Creek. Up it or down it, I'd find a camp fifteen or twenty miles either way. Above the W Bar on Beaver was the town of Wibaux, Montana. At the mouth of Beaver Creek, on the Little Missouri, was Theodore Roosevelt's Elk Horn Ranch. So Beaver Creek was what I wanted.

Buck undoubtedly realized we were in trouble, but he was showing his usual composure. As the storm buffeted him he put his heart into the job of getting us out of our predicament. I felt his strong muscles under me and felt reassured. But it was still snowing hard, and I couldn't see much. There was no color but the dead-white expanse.

In the deepening, unbroken whiteness I couldn't tell whether I was going up or down a coulee, and I rode all day without finding Beaver Creek. Buck probably could have found it, but he always yielded his judgment to mine. In my anxiety I was depending too much on myself and only guiding him.

Again night was coming on. I began looking for a good place to camp, but couldn't find any. Neither the thicket nor the trees were as satisfactory as those of the night before. But I couldn't go any farther in the darkness; so I gathered some dead limbs and looked in vain for a log. I kicked away the snow, piled up a few limbs and shavings, and hunched down to build my fire.

I found that I had just three matches. The first two didn't catch in the dampness, but the last one did. Thinking I had a good fire started, I got up to gather more limbs for it. But in my weakness I floundered and fell, kicking snow on my fire and snuffing it out.

There was bleakness everywhere now—no fire, and a long night ahead. My hunger pangs had long since left; my whole being was focused on the job of survival. I knew that if I let sleep overcome me I might not wake up. I realized how savage nature could be in North Dakota; I'd heard of what happened to two cowboys the winter before. Their remains had been found during the next June roundup. I hoped to carry my own bones to the spring roundup, but I knew that the night would bring a hard battle that I had to fight alone.

Though I was weak and tired, I never forgot for a moment that if I became too still I might fall asleep; so I gathered all the sage brush I could find to feed Buck, and I rubbed him, talked to him, and sang all the cowboy songs I could think of. I was too weak to walk much in the snow, so I sang loud and was never still.

My thoughts turned back to home in Texas: to my father and mother and the things they'd taught me—that nothing was impossible with the Lord on your side. My parents were Christians, and I was sure they were praying for my safety that night, as they did every night.

I remembered that when I was ten my father had become very sick; his lungs were weak, and he was spitting blood. One night two doctors came to see him, and both said he couldn't get well. Next morning, as I went through his room to go to the kitchen to help Mother set the table for breakfast, he called me over to his bed and said, "Always be good to your mother, Billie. Help her all you can. I might never be well again."

I went on through the kitchen to the old smokehouse. There I fell on my knees and asked the Lord to spare my father, to leave him with us, please. He was still living, and I had faith in prayer.

So now I prayed. I hadn't been very good myself, so I just asked the Lord to answer their prayers, to help me be what they wanted me to be.

I didn't know where I was or which way to start. But at daylight I went to Buck. He greeted me with one of his endearing little mannerisms: he nuzzled my hand with his nose. I knew he was as tired and cold as I was, but when I mounted him he started out as if he had all the freshness and stamina in the world.

We looked for a place to ride out. Most of the coulees lay deep in snow. Everywhere was the same white wilderness. We found one coulee that looked as if it would be fairly easy to get out of.

Buck threaded his way through it with infinite patience. His whole attention, like mine, was focused on getting us out. I was relying on him as I had never before relied on any animal or man.

I didn't know directions anyway; so I knew we'd just have to ride the course the best way we could. The snow had let up; only occasional white flakes fell, but a cold breeze was blowing. Buck stuck doggedly to his task, but we traveled for hours without seeing any progress. About ten o'clock we came to a high ridge, and from there I looked down on a marvelous sight—Beaver Creek and a house and stables about half a mile away.

There was a possibility that the house might be vacant, of course. But when I reached the creek I heard a dog bark. He ran out to meet me. Then I saw smoke rising out of a stovepipe.

Suddenly I gave way, just like I'd been shot. I could hardly hold myself in the saddle. Buck must have understood what had happened; he took charge and went directly to the door of the house.

An old trapper with long white whiskers came out and looked at me. Without asking a question he took me into a spare room where there were a few sacks of feed and, on them, some empty feed sacks and horse blankets. He made a bed and took off my calfskin coat, overshoes, and boots, Next he massaged my face, nose, ears, and feet. He handed me a little coffee, which had been hot on the stove when I arrived.

"I'm all right," I said, "but my horse needs water and feed."

He went out and took care of Buck. Then, after assuring me that my horse was all right, he said, "I can't take you to the fire —heat drives frost in. I don't know where you are frozen. But I've got some beaver oil—it draws out frost. I'll rub you with it."

He did—first face and ears, then hands and feet, till my body had been oiled from head to foot and I went to sleep. In a few hours he woke me; he had killed snowbirds and made a little broth. That and coffee were all he gave me until the next afternoon, when I had a coffee-soaked sour-dough biscuit and sugar. Later he gave me some root tea; he said he always had some to keep his own system in shape.

After I'd been oiled for forty-eight hours he put me in his

room and bed and let me have solid food. For two weeks I stayed with the trapper, who was known as Frenchy—doing as he said. He was an old frontiersman, that doctor, and he knew just what to do. I came out of it without any ill effects, and I was a more steadfast believer in prayer.

Then he said I could go, but he advised me to take a short ride the first day, increasing the distance as I grew stronger. I rode to the W Bar Ranch the first day; the next night I stayed at Parsons Ranch near the Yellowstone River, twenty miles downstream from Glendive, Montana.

In the Parsons family were two bachelor brothers and an old-maid sister. They had lived there for years. Often Indians camped close to their ranch, and after the camp had been abandoned they'd visit it, looking for relics. Twenty years before I visited them they'd gone to a camp just after the Indians left it and had found a new-born baby girl. They took her home and raised her. When I visited the Parsons the girl, a singer and pianist, was away at college. They invited me to come back that way and stop again, as she would be home.

I went on to the Butterman Ranch, scouting the country and making inquiries, but I didn't find or hear of any Bellows horses. I though some of our horses might be on the Butterman range, for Jim McPeat, a man of doubtful honesty, was head man there. I knew him well; he'd made a good many stops at the Bellows Ranch the year before and had ridden with me. Never giving any indication of being in a hurry, he'd spend two or three days at a time. He seemed like a very nice fellow; we all liked him.

But Jim had acquired a bad habit of gathering stock from other ranches, driving them off and selling them, and never saying anything to the owners about the business. Billy Smith, Montana stock inspector, tried to get him to quit, but Jim continued. Two years later I saw Jim in the morgue at Dickinson. Billy Smith had used the only persuader that could break Jim of his habit—hot lead.

On my return trip I again stopped overnight with the Parsons. The young Indian girl was home. She was tall and nice-looking; she sang and played well.

I went on to the ranch to get my mount of horses, then to the W Bar wagon, and went through their work on the lookout for Bellows horses. I repeated this with the Three Sevens wagon and found it very productive. As I gathered Bellows horses I put them in our four-thousand-acre pasture.

While I was out on this horse hunt Buck and I had another memorable experience. Buck's attitude always seemed to be "Something interesting will turn up." Often it did.

This time my making a sugar and biscuit eater out of him really paid off. During a very hard rain Buck and I took shelter for two or three hours under some trees. All the little coulees filled up with water.

The ranch was fifteen miles away, beyond some rough country. We had many coulees to cross. Riding down a cow trail, I came to a coulee that looked very dangerous; it had become a torrential stream. I saw no way of getting around it; so I spoke to Buck:

"I believe you can jump it, boy. We're going to try."

I rode back a short distance, then trotted Buck up to the water's edge four times. The fourth time I did this I said to Buck:

"We're going to get a running start this time, so you can jump to that other bank."

He ran and made the jump, but the bank was soft and began crumbling. I went over his shoulder onto the bank, thinking that with my weight removed he'd have a chance to pull himself out. But he couldn't make it; he slid back into the water and came out on the other side. I called, and he turned and looked at me. I talked to him, urged him to observe my sad plight, and pleaded desperately. I told him about all the sugar and biscuits I'd give him if he'd leap that water and come to me, for I couldn't get to him.

He walked close to the edge of the water, nickered to me, and trotted around with his head to one side so he wouldn't step on his bridle reins. I knew he wanted to come to me, and I kept up my coaxing. For fear he didn't understand that I'd give him sugar and biscuits, I rolled up my gloves and held them toward him until he moved back, trotted to the water's edge, and made

110

the leap to my side. His hind feet slipped a little, but this time he made it.

It was easy for me to be a horse lover—just because of the things Buck did. I have also loved many people not so much for what they said as for what they did.

When this horse roundup was over, most of our horses were in. Joe McCoul sent Jeff Barber out to help bring them in to Dickinson. Mr. Ray sent me a contract to cut a pick of the best eight work horses and sixteen saddle horses to keep on the ranch. I cut them out of the first herd, thinking that if I saw anything more desirable when I looked at the last I could exchange. We then delivered the rest to Mr. McCoul at the Dickinson stockyards.

I was now a little fearful that someone would offer Mr. Ray a big price for Buck and that he might think, now that we had the horses sold, we could get along without him. I said to him, "Mr. Ray, I want Buck. I don't know how much you want for him, but I want him anyway. If I haven't got enough to pay for him, I'll work till I do have."

He replied, "You go on and deliver the rest of your horses. Throw your saddle on Buck and call him your own. I'll give him to you."

He gave me the proudest possession of my life. My happiness from his gift lasted a long time.

Jeff and I rode back to the ranch and gathered in the last of the Bellows horses. Among them I saw a large, trim brown horse, the best prospect for a work horse I'd noticed. Jeff noticed him too and said, "Joe'll get a good price for that one in Canada."

"Joe won't get that horse to Canada," I replied. "He stays here on this ranch."

"I'll take him," Jeff declared. "You've already picked yours."

"I'm picking till the last horse leaves this ranch; then I'll keep just eight work horses and sixteen saddle horses."

The argument went on, hot and heavy, before it ended—and my opponent was stubborn. Jeff was a tall, lanky, dark-haired Texan. He told me once that he had helped start Boot Hill at Tascosa, but his account of the first bloody battle at Tascosa didn't jibe with the story I knew. There might thus have been a

111

little bravado about Jeff at times. He was a highly efficient cow-puncher, though, and he could be obstinate. Like most cowboys, he carried a long businesslike .45 Colt on his hip.

We drove the horses into the herd corral. I rode into the bunch and cut a horse in to replace the brown one. The next morning we were ready to start the remainder of them to Dickinson. I knew Jeff would start up the argument again, but I also knew he wouldn't be deaf to the authority of a .45 Colt, and I had one. I decided on my course of action.

I had a boy open the corral gate so I could cut the brown horse in. As I came on with my horse, Jeff, with his .45 Colt, stepped into the gate and waved his big black Stetson hat. Just then I realized I'd forgotten something at the house. I told the boy to open another gate; then I went back to the house and strapped on my .45.

I rode up and again told the boy to open the gate, for I was coming through and no fool had better get in the way. Jeff was standing with one of our men, and I heard him say, "That's what you have to contend with when you're dealing with a damned kid."

I brought my horse through the gate. Nobody was there. I told the boy to shut the gate and tie it good, then to open the herd-corral gate wide for us. We passed through it and drove along for several hours, I on one side, the boy helper at tail end, and Jeff on the other side, singing cowboy songs.

When we were through the rough badlands I rode around to the front and checked the horses to let them graze a little. Jeff came over and said, "Kid, you got pretty mad. I was just joshing."

"I was just joshing too," I answered, "but I was going to be sure I could see it through."

I remembered what Dutch Louie had said: "These fellows all carry guns. Dress like they do. Get a gun. A gun carries respect anyway."

At the end of May we finished delivering the horses. Though I didn't know it at the time, that was to be the last cow or horse work Buck and I would do together.

The North Dakota cattle country was undergoing a transition

112

just as Texas had earlier. The big Three Sevens outfit had closed out in 1897. More were to follow. I'd been feeling that Mr. Ray wouldn't mind disposing of the Bellows Ranch, and after I'd finished the delivery of horses to Joe McCoul, something he said made this evident.

"I think you've been around these cow camps long enough," he told me. "You ought to find something in town, so you can associate with young people and get something out of life. Choose anything you think you can handle, and I'll put up the money for you to buy it.

"I know of a grocery and meat market. The man who has it isn't doing very well with it—he'll sell it. He has a large family and wants to get into something else. He owes me about all it's worth; so I wouldn't have to put much money in it. Look it over and see what you think you can do with it. If you don't want to give it a whirl, keep on looking till you find something."

I gave the store the once-over. There were too many things to look after there. Many of the customers said, "Charge it"—too complicated for me. I told Mr. Ray how I felt and kept looking.

Soon I found a livery stable for sale, building and all. Numerous ex-cow hands had found their way into this business, and I had had some experience working for Mr. Arthur Jackson in Panhandle City.

The owner, Mr. Farrar, and I had a talk. I proposed buying the horses, buggies, and fixtures and leasing the building. He agreed to that but stipulated that the lease be for a year at a time, that I could renew as long as I wished, and that I'd have the first chance to buy the building at any time.

"All right," I said. "Make a list and a price for everything you have. That will be a bill of sale, and if it isn't too high I'll pay you for it tomorrow when we fix up the lease."

I told Mr. Ray what I had done. From my experience in the livery business I knew that the buggies were old and in some cases worn out, and I'd want to fix them up for sale or trade. Furthermore, Farrar had only one decent horse I'd keep. Mr. Ray said, "Buy it if you want it, and fix everything up like you want it."

I suggested that we go look at it together.

"No," Mr. Ray said, "this is all up to you. When you get through I'll give you a check for what you need."

I bought it and went to Mr. Ray.

"Here's the bill of sale for what I have," I told him. "I'll give you a mortgage on it for your money."

He declared, "No sirree. If I didn't think you were honest I wouldn't give you the scratch of a pen."

"But if something should happen to me," I said, "I have people in Texas who might think I owned it all."

His answer was characteristic of him: "If you have any people in Texas who aren't as honest as you are and want it, they can have it."

Now I was in business and through with cowboying for the rest of my life, I thought. I'd enjoyed my years on the ranches, the hardships and the free life on the open range, and I said to myself, "Now that I've quit, I'll buckle on my .45 Colt, put on my boots, saddle Buck, and go have our picture taken together, to keep in remembrance of those days."

That was the first picture I ever had taken. It never has been far from me for very long. Buck never looked better than at that time, and when I look at it now a spool of happy recollections unwinds for me.

I liked to ride Buck up and down Villard Street, the only business thoroughfare in Dickinson. Agnes Ray had a nice sorrel horse she was fond of riding, and we'd go along at a lively clip when we hit that street. There were six saloons and several gamblers in town at the time, and the latter were impressed by the way Buck moved.

Some races were scheduled for July 4; so one day the king of the gamblers, Buck Taylor, came down to the barn and asked me if I'd enter Buck in the races. That sounded good, and I jumped at the offer.

"Well," said Taylor, "I'll pay you to take care of him just like I say. We won't let anybody know what we're doing. You'll ride him out to the track at night, and we'll time him. Nobody else will ride him, and you'll also be up on him in the race. I'm handling all our betting money; you don't put up a cent. I'll pay for his keep and your time riding on the track to clock him and

114

to get him used to the course. You get 25 per cent of all he wins."

That appealed to me. I wasn't gambling, they were. They were just going to pay me for what my horse did. For three evenings we went to the race track. I never knew what time Buck made, but the gamblers seemed well pleased and assured me I'd be handsomely paid for my time.

Then Mr. Ray came to the barn and said, "Billie, as soon as you have time, go up to the house. Mother wants to see you."

I couldn't imagine what she wanted to see me about. I was up there often, but hadn't been for the last few days. I wondered what it was so special that Mr. Ray couldn't tell me about it. I was curious to learn, so I lost no time in going. Just Mrs. Ray and the hired girl were there. She greeted me warmly, calling me "William" as she always did.

"You haven't been up for a few days, William. How do you like your new business?" she asked disarmingly.

Fine, I told her. I'd been real busy getting buggies and harness ready to trade off.

"Where've you been spending your evenings?" she asked.

Then I thought of where I had been and tried to think of a way of getting out of answering. I said lamely, "Oh, around the barn somewhere—just one place and another." Mrs. Ray could be very direct when she wanted to be.

"Haven't you been out at the race track with some gamblers, running your horse?"

I told her that was true.

"Don't you know that's bad company for you to be in?"

I admitted it was. Then I told her the glowing tale of my deal with them, how they were paying me $2.00 a day to take care of Buck. They had had him shod with racer plates and they gave me $2.50 every time we went to the track. I wasn't betting a cent, I said, and they'd give me 25 per cent of all Buck won. I'd ride him; nobody else.

I added, "I'm sure he'll win."

"And that would be the worst thing that could happen to you," she said. "We gave you that horse because you thought so much of him. Now he'll be your ruin."

I felt like two cents and blurted out, "Mrs. Ray, I'll never let

115

Buck run in a race. I'll give Buck Taylor back the money he's paid me. I thank you for making me see it this way. I won't go to that race track any more."

I told Taylor that I couldn't let my horse run in the race, that Mrs. Ray didn't approve. "I'll give you back all the money you've been out," I said. Taylor gave a little wave of his hand and answered, "Just forget it. I'm glad you're doing what Mrs. Ray wants you to do. You have the respect of these people; keep it. It's worth more than anything money can buy. I've got money but the respect of nobody—and I was raised by good, religious parents. If you ever need money let me know, and I'll let you have it in cash. Nobody'll know where it came from."

This episode set me to doing some pretty deep thinking about people.

Buck had a cozy stall but little to do now. I knew so much about his likes and dislikes that I could see he wasn't altogether happy. He had always loved to work, and this half retirement seemed to irk him. The old sparkle was missing.

He'd never been sick in his life, but in April, 1899, I noticed he was getting thin on good hay and oats. Finally we discovered a little blood on his feed, then a red dripping from his nose. The only veterinarian I knew of was the state man, Mr. Tracy, at Bismarck.

I wrote to Mr. Tracy, and he replied that I should try soaking Buck's oats in water and to be sure there wasn't any dust in his hay. He also advised me to put him in a fenced-in stall so he wouldn't have to be tied up, to give him plenty of room, to keep a blanket on him, and to be sure he stayed out of drafts. He promised to come and see Buck.

We took all the buggies out of the shed and turned it over to Buck. We washed and dried hay and soaked oats. But when Mr. Tracy got there in May Buck was getting poorer, and blood was still dripping from his nose.

The weather was warm, and grass was getting good. Mr. Tracy said the best thing to do was to turn him out on the grass. His trouble then might clear up.

I took Buck out two miles east, on Heart River, where the grass was excellent. Every day I rode out with oats to feed him.

116

The last time I saw him he was very poor and weak. Then I missed him.

I thought he had simply gone somewhere and died, but we combed the country in vain for his body. Later I heard what had happened. Displaying his old indomitable spirit, Buck had struggled sixty miles back to the Bellows Ranch. There in those hills he loved, amid the scenes of his triumphs, he took leave of these earthly pastures.

Gallant, courageous Buck! Just the unvarnished story of his life is his epitaph. I wouldn't tarnish it by attributing to him one virtue he did not possess.

It's been sixty years since he died; yet I add nothing new to what I said then about this intelligent, lovable horse when they brought me the news that he'd gone on his last long ride. It's the simple tribute of a cowpuncher, paid to one who had carried him through snow and bitter cold, through stampedes and other dangers, and through happy days, too:

"He was the *most* horse I ever knew."

XIII. A COWBOY IN BUSINESS

I ENTERED THE LIVERY BUSINESS at the very peak of the horse-and-buggy era. My optimism was even higher.

My choice of an assistant was a fortunate one. I hired Jim Owens,* the Three Sevens horse wrangler, to be hostler. Jim

* Not the same Jim Owens who urged me to go to work for Charles Goodnight.

was raised at Belle Fourche, South Dakota. He had lived in the West all his life. His whole world was horses, cows, cowboys, and Indians. He was two years older than I and a good worker.

All our spare time went into washing, greasing, and dressing old harness and cleaning, sandpapering, and painting old buggies so I could sell or trade them.

Near town there was a Russian farming settlement. When a buggy and harness were ready I'd drive out there and sell them —or trade them for hay, oats, pigs, chickens, or a good note. They could make a swap with me any way they proposed—all or any part of the outfit I had along. I was out to complete a transaction, realizing that harness dressing and buggy paint soon faded and looked dull, that I had to dispose of them quickly. They were worth the most when they were the shiniest.

Out of the catalogue from a factory in Elkhart, Indiana, I ordered two buggies, two surreys, and one large hack to haul drummers—traveling salesmen. I continued to clean out all the old things in the barn, the idea being to get it in such condition that the livery stable at the other end of town would be no competition.

At this time there wasn't any pleasure-driving trade at Dickinson livery stables. I wanted to develop the idea of people getting out in the country on pleasure trips—an idea that came to Henry Ford later. I was ahead of Henry with the thought, but for the long pull he had a better vehicle.

In 1899 there were more than eighteen million horses and more than three million mules in the country, and their numbers were increasing. The streets and country roads of the nation were uncluttered by automobiles. According to newspapers, a few "cranks" like Ford in Detroit and Duryea in Cleveland were fooling with horseless carriages, but it never entered my mind that they'd be a menace to the horse industry. How was I to know that I'd live to see the day when there'd be eighty million motorized vehicles and less than three million horses and only a million mules?

My idea for pleasure driving hit pay dirt. Vividly do I remember the first fellow who came to hire a horse and buggy to

118

take his girl out riding. He was Billy Herring, who clerked in the drugstore. Just my age, Billy had been a cowboy on the Three Sevens wagon during my first work in North Dakota. But he wanted to be a town boy, and the only job he could hook on to yielded him just enough to eat and wear a clean shirt.

I had Prince, a gentle white horse for which I paid the large sum of $100. Horses were cheap then, and teams were selling for no more than that. But I'd put out the extra money because of this white horse's looks and disposition. Then I'd made an inaugural drive with a girl up and down Villard Street. I was proud of the horse, of the rig, and especially of the young lady.

The combination attracted Billy Herring, who said to me, "I'll give you $1.50 for that layout for one hour."

My heart leaped with joy—something was starting. I replied, "Give me your $1.50. Don't say anything to anybody. Just drive up and down every street in this town and out in the country a little way. You can have him all afternoon."

I needed the $1.50 for feeding Prince; the free time was for advertising. In the future I intended to charge $1.50 for one hour, $2.00 for two hours, and $1.00 for every hour after that.

It wasn't long before Prince had reimbursed me for the premium I'd paid for him. I got more calls than he could fill, and much of the time he was hitched up in front of somebody's house, drawing a dollar an hour.

Mr. Hilliard, the banker, came in one day at noon and wanted Prince and the buggy for his wife at 2 o'clock. I'd rented them out but thought they'd surely be in by that time; so I said, "All right, I'll be there at 1:30."

At 1:30 Prince still wasn't in, and I didn't know when he would be. I wanted to fill Mr. Hilliard's order, for he was a good customer. I decided to go up and borrow Mrs. Ray's horse and buggy, which were just as good. But as I walked up to the Ray house I saw that she and her young son Donald were just driving out for a pleasure ride. She asked, "William, what are you doing walking up here this time of day?"

Under the circumstances I didn't want to tell her my purpose; so I tried to pass off her question by replying, "I just had a little spare time and thought I'd come up for a visit."

119

"No, you didn't come up for a visit this time of day," she said. "You came for something, and I know what it is." With that she stepped out of her buggy and helped Donald down. "You need my horse and buggy. Take them. I can go riding when you don't have the opportunity of making a dollar."

Nothing I could say would make any difference. She was just the kind of woman who was happiest when she could give up her own enjoyment for others. I was on time at Mr. Hilliard's house.

When all the old buggies and harness had been traded off and new harness and buggies had been acquired, Jim and I had reason to be proud of our stock and the increase in business. Because we'd both been cowboys, we were getting the big end of the cowmen's trade. Dickinson was an important shipping point for cattlemen of both North and South Dakota, and we catered to their wishes.

One afternoon Tony Day, manager of the Hank Creswell and Tony Day Turkey Track Cattle Company of South Dakota, drove in with a perfectly matched bay team and an excellent heavy-rubber-tired Concord buggy. He sang out:

"Well, old man, what do you do here—feed horses or just keep them?"

"We feed them, all right," I answered.

"I'm leaving this team with you for three days, and then I'll be back and see what you've done to them," Tony said.

After he'd walked away I said to Jim, "You heard what that fellow told us. Undoubtedly he knows I've heard it said that nobody in the West knows a horse or cow better than Tony Day. We won't miss a feed or watering. The stall will be cleaned night and morning, and his team will be curried and brushed every day. Let's clean and grease that buggy, and I'll bet that all Turkey Track horses ridden to town will find our barn—and they'll lead others to us."

Tony and Ben Garland, owner of the Lake Towne Cattle Company and L 7, were back the third day. Tony inspected his team and remarked, "Well, Billie, you know how to take care of them. They're yours till the last shipment this fall. Any time you want to take your girl riding behind a good team, drive them."

120

I did.

Shipping was going strong at this season, and I hired another helper, Harry Casper, who lived at home with his folks. He was just a youngster but good help. We were busy early and late.

One Saturday evening Billy Greenville, whom I'd known in Texas and who was now foreman for one of Ben Garland's wagons, rode in, along with four cowboys, with a wagon. In it was his half-brother, who'd been struck by lightning and killed the day before while riding around the herd near Grand River, eighty miles from Dickinson.

Greenville and his companions had traveled all the night before and all that day. It was raining, and they were wet and tired. Billy asked my advice about what to do; I took them to the undertaker.

"I'd ship the body home," Billy told me, "but my mother is old and in bad health. It would be too hard on her. I think it would be better to give him a good burial here and let her know he was well taken care of."

"We'll do all we can," I assured him. "I'll ask the undertaker to be ready for burial at eleven o'clock. I'll have a preacher to conduct the funeral service and the newspaper editor to take down everything. I'll get some boys I know to go and sing. And my rigs will carry all who want to go to the cemetery."

We had a good-sized crowd of men—but no ladies. It was still raining when the services were held. M. L. Ayers, the editor, wrote up a good account of it. Billy Greenville was greatly pleased; he had everything he wanted to send home to comfort his mother.

When all this happened Ben Garland, for whom Billy worked, was away marketing his cattle. He was a big man with a big heart. When he got back he came down to the barn and shook my hand. Without a word he sat down at my desk and started writing. As he left my desk, I glanced down to see what he had done and saw that he had made out a check for fifty dollars.

"Mr. Garland, I don't want this," I said.

"Keep it, my boy, as a token from me," he replied. "And remember—there's a just God; as long as you help others in time of trouble, He'll repay you."

121

Finally the last shipment was made. Most of the boys still were in town when Tony Day got his team from our barn and started to his home at Spearfish, South Dakota. As he drove to Grand River and beyond he met with many ranchers coming to Dickinson with four-horse teams to get winter supplies. He stopped all he met and told them to come to my barn, and they came. When I had reached capacity I told them: "We're full. There's another livery barn down the street just across town. They might have room."

Usually I got this reply: "This is where Tony told us to stop. Can't we put our wagon on this vacant lot and tie our horses to the wagon? You feed and water them. We've all got feed bags for grain."

I would respond, "If that's what you want we'll do the best we can—and we'll always have feed in front of them."

I booked them all by name and number, according to the way I placed their wagons. We worked night and day with our own horses besides the 170 other animals—more than twice the number we should have had. That was our reward for so carefully grooming Tony's team.

Sam Carroll, the livery man at the other side of town, came to see us about that time, but I was busy and didn't have much time to talk. Jim Owens told me, "Billie, stop and talk to Sam. He's got something on his mind. We'll do the work."

Sam opened the conversation by saying, "I hear you're cutting prices below what we agreed on. That's why you've got all these horses."

"Sam," I answered, "I don't know where you get your information. But whenever you can get proof that I've broken that agreement, bring it around and I'll give you today's receipts. They'll be pretty good, because I have several teams hired out also."

When Sam went home, Jim said to me, "You've got a good business and we're proud of it. You're treating us okay and working with us. Now we want you to take a little layoff and go visit Sam. Walk through his barn. See how many horses he has."

I didn't want to go, but they insisted and I finally agreed to visit Sam and ask him if he had found any proof of the price-cutting. I walked through his barn, looking for him, and counted 35 horses. I found Sam in his office, asleep on a cot. I had no competition.

With shipping over, business got dull. I'd been paying Jim Owens a sizable wage. He was good but I thought I could do with a cheaper man. When I told Jim, he didn't seem disturbed by my decision.

"Yes, I believe you can," he said. "I'll just keep my bed here for a few days and loaf around town."

I hired another man. That night at suppertime I went over to the hotel. When the meal was over I met my friend Jim Henderson, a little rancher six years older than I, in the lobby. His father had staked him to four hundred head of cattle so he could be a cowman.

"Billie," he said, "I just rode in and put my horse in your barn. That man you have fought him because the horse shied from him—he jerked the horse back on a sleigh and broke it. I took my horse and tied him in a stall myself."

"Go down to the barn and stay till I get there," I replied. "I want to find Jim Owens."

I soon located him and said, "Jim, I just found out I wasn't paying you too much money. If you'll be on the job in the morning your time will start today—and you can stay on as long as I have a barn."

"I'll be down there in an hour or two," he laughed. "I didn't think you'd get anybody to take my place, so I decided just to loaf around and see. You can't run a business like yours and pay cheap."

The new man was paid for one day, and I learned a lesson I never forgot: it isn't what a good man costs but what he's worth. But to pay expenses through the winter some close calculating was necessary. I decided to take all the horses we could do without to Mr. Ray's Bellows Ranch. There they could graze their own living without any feed.

I got Jim Henderson to go with me, for I had an idea Mr. Ray wanted to sell the ranch—and I knew Jim was getting crowded at his location on the Cannon Ball River. I was confident that by spring Jim would buy it, and he did.

After returning to town I was still trying to hit upon other ways to make the livery business pay in winter. Some special inducement had to be offered to sell pleasure driving. All the young people, I reflected, liked to dance. I went to see Mr. Turner, who had charge of the Woodmen of the World hall at Gladstone, twelve miles away. It was a good place to dance.

Mr. Turner said I could have the hall any time I wanted it for two dollars a night. That was my expense. All Mr. Turner wanted was enough to cover the cost of the coal we burned and the coal oil we used in the lamps. We also had to sweep it clean afterward.

Another site for dances was a country schoolhouse seven or eight miles out on Green River. Mr. Fisher, head of the school board, said we could use it any time we wished, if we swept it and put the benches and desks back in place. That provided a change of scenery for the dances.

My horses thus had a place to go to earn a few dollars. The young people liked the trips. I was young also and enjoyed them as much as anybody else.

Spring brought a lively business. I went out to the Bellows Ranch and brought my horses back in. I had Jim Owens and Harry Casper to take care of the business, and I hired Robert Lyons to do any extra driving. I kept a splendid team of black horses belonging to Mrs. Ray in the barn all the time and used them any time I needed them. One day when I was out on some business Bob Lyons took a traveling man to Gladstone with this team. On his return trip he drove on the still-frozen surface of Green River. The weight of the horses and buggy was too much; the team went crashing through. The buggy tongue went under the ice, holding the horses down on their sides in the icy water. They couldn't get up to paw and break their way loose.

Bob was an old man. He got excited and didn't unhitch the team. Instead, he left the horses and walked two miles to Gladstone for help. The rescuers got the horses and buggy out, but the horses had already frozen to death.

That was my first hard luck, and I felt sorrier for the poor animals than for myself. I went to Mrs. Ray and told her I'd pay

124

for them. She said, "You can't afford to pay for them, and I wouldn't take it if you could." I still thought maybe I could do it later, for business looked promising. The outfits were all coming in for supplies.

George Woodman, manager of the HT, was a good friend and customer, as were others: Jim Converse of the Converse Cattle Company; Dock Blaylock and Wilse Richards, foreman and manager of the Crosby Cattle Company; A. N. Jefferies, who'd been manager of the Reynolds Cattle Company the year before, had sold to Converse, and now was on his own; Gus Streeter, manager of the Three Sevens; Sam Rhodes, foreman of the DZ for D. Z. Zimmerman. In fact, all the large stock companies as well as many small ranchmen in our trade territory were giving me their business. The hotels that Mr. Ray owned (the St. Charles was then run by a manager) helped me with the traveling public.

For all this I give credit to Mr. Ray. Everybody knew he was backing me. He told the banks and business houses to let me have whatever I wanted, and he would stand good for it. It is not given to many men to have the kind of friend he was. He often came to see me and often asked how I was getting along, but never once did he suggest that I do one thing different from what I was doing. It was all mine to do with as I wished, to pay out as I wished.

In May Mr. Farrar wrote me that he wouldn't give another lease on his barn, as it was for sale, and he quoted a selling price that was far too high. He probably thought Mr. Ray would buy it. I didn't want it, for it wasn't large enough—and not a good building for putting on an addition. Mr. Ray told me to decide on the kind of building I wanted and where I wanted it located, and to tell him how much the ground would cost.

I drew a sketch of what I wanted. Mr. Ray gave it to Billy Walton and Johnnie Davis, lumber people. They furnished us with an estimate on the barn and the lots, but they told Mr. Ray it was ahead of the town. Somebody would be in trouble, they said, with the two old barns splitting the trade. They advised him not to build another barn.

I had no desire to continue in this business, knowing I could

125

be put out any month. I'd built up a bustling business, but it all went: improved methods for the livery business, good will, everything.

But I wasn't through with giving business a whirl. Next I bought a restaurant; we called it a cafe.

XIV. A WESTERN CATERER

The restaurant I bought in Dickinson was the only one in town, except for one run by a Chinese fellow at the railroad depot. When I took possession I realized what a run-down place it was. Only men ate there; mostly they were workers for the railroad and other firms, cowboys, and a sprinkling of gamblers. This crowd was too rough for women, but my idea was to make the cafe nice enough for anybody.

I locked the door and for five days I cleaned, papered, painted, threw away all the junk and replaced it with new things. I employed anybody I could get to scrub, clean, and make ready for the painters.

M. L. Ayers, editor of the weekly paper, came by to see what we were doing. I was too busy to see him, but one of my hired hands named Stubbs talked to him and told him what "he" and I were doing. I never saw the account until it was reprinted fifty years later. It said Stubbs and I were partners—and I'd never seen Stubbs before or after the five days he had worked for me.

When the building was cleaned, painted, and papered from front to back I was proud of it. Everything looked new. Then I opened the doors for business, and Mr. Ray was the first to visit us. He remarked, "It looks nice. But I didn't know you were buying this cafe or I wouldn't have let you do it. There's little, if any, money to be made in it, and it's too confining for a boy like you who's been raised in the open. You like stock, but here you're completely away from them. You won't like it. I'll be dropping in to see you. If you need anything, let me know."

The cafe never looked good to me again. That was the first and only time Mr. Ray had ever disapproved of anything I'd done. It was in a quiet, kind way, but how it hurt! Why hadn't I asked his advice?

I'd worked every hour I could for five days and nights to open for business as soon as possible. Exhausted, I left everything to the help and went to my room to rest. But a troubled mind allows no rest. I thought how much Mr. Ray had meant to me since I'd known him. Because of my connection with him, and through his influence, I had a favorable acquaintance with the businessmen and cowmen of western North Dakota. I held him in the highest esteem.

I realized I had to carry on, try to rectify my mistakes. I knew I needed a partner now; I couldn't be confined all the time—and the cafe had to run day and night if it was to succeed at all. I went to Billy Herring, the drugstore clerk, and told him I wanted a partner. "I'd be glad to join you," he said, "but I have exactly twenty dollars; that won't buy much."

"If you'll take half interest as soon as you can get away from here," I replied, "go to the cafe and put your twenty dollars in the cash register. I'll figure up what I have invested and you'll owe me half that, less twenty dollars."

"I'll be there in the morning," he answered.

Business seemed good, but the profits were small. Most night cooks were men I got from an employment office at St. Paul,

Minnesota. They gave me trouble, mostly from drinking. They were drunk at a bad time. My day cook was an Irish woman, Maggie Reagan. Every morning at 7 A.M. she was there; at 7 P.M. she was gone.

We served special Sunday dinner. First to come was Andy Thompson, the postmaster, and his wife—then businessmen and their wives. About twice a month there was a dance in the opera house; this gave us night business.

One night cook we got from St. Paul was Sing, an excellent pastry cook. His specialty was baking cakes. One day he made a wedding cake, topped by a bride and groom. It was a beauty. But the ingredients had cost eleven dollars and nobody in town was getting married. So we told Sing to bake no cakes other than those we ordered. That didn't set well with him.

One day when there was a dance scheduled I said to Sing, "We'll have a big midnight crowd tonight. Get ready for them. We need pies and doughnuts. There'll also be orders for oyster stew and fried oysters." Sing, looking peeved, said, "Cake." I answered, "Sing, we don't need any cake."

In about an hour Sing came in with his long, keen carving knife, laid it on the end of the counter, and said, "I make cake."

I was at the other end of the counter near the cash register. I reached under the counter for my .45, laid it on the counter, and said, "Sing, if you make a cake tonight you'll never get back to your country or even hear from your people again. Now get back in that kitchen and do what I told you to do."

Back he went. All was quiet; for half an hour I couldn't hear anything he was doing. Then Sing came out wearing his coat and hat and carrying his long knife. I said quietly, "Sing, lay that knife over there on a table; then step up here and I'll pay you off." He did.

I figured his time and said, "You signed a statement at the employment office in St. Paul that you'd obey my orders, and that if you wanted to quit any time you'd give me ten days' notice. But if you'll leave without any any trouble I'll just dock you five days' pay. Will you do that?"

Sing said, "I go."

I went to the hotel to see if I could find anybody to cook for the crowd I was sure would be there by midnight. I found John Clayton, an HT cowboy friend. He said, "I'm the man you're looking for. I can cook anything they'll order."

"All right, John," I said, "Come on and bring your six-shooter."

He arrived wearing high-heeled boots, a big black hat, and a .45. We had a full house, and they were all taken care of without a bobble. As my customers left that night, each one commented on how good the food was and the quick service. Finally I said, "Well, for this good quick service I give credit to the cook, and I'd like to introduce him to you." John stepped out, still wearing hat, boots, and Colt—and now a white apron. He was a big hit.

During the winter months I saw Mr. Ray every few days. He'd told me he wasn't feeling well, and I made it a point to see him. As spring neared, he told me he was going to Brainerd, Minnesota, for a checkup. That was the medical center for our part of the country.

When he returned, I asked him what the doctors thought. He said, "I'll be all right if I just carry out their orders." I visited with him often after that, and thought he was doing fine. One day I heard he was worse, and next day the word came that he was gone. Numbness came over me. I went to my room utterly depressed, not wanting to see anybody. How much that man had meant to me! My own father couldn't have been better. How could I bear to meet the family?

That I could not do. I stayed alone in my room with grief such as I'd never known before. In the morning I went to the cafe. Will Ray, his oldest son, came and asked me if I didn't want to go see his father. I went and saw him and the grief-stricken family, but I didn't speak to anybody. I returned to my room and saw no more of the family until Will came back and said his mother wanted me to go to the funeral with the family and drive the carriage for them. The depression began to ease a little; tears are a relief to grief. The family was so close I felt it was my own.

After that, days seemed to drag in the cafe business. Billy Herring liked it, but I longed to be on the range again—to punch cows, do battle with storm and hail.

At this point I had a break. Wilse Norrad, a Texas cowboy

and a good friend of mine, had been to Moorcroft, Wyoming, as trail boss to receive a herd of 3,500 Texas steers for Jim Converse, owner of the Long X Ranch. When Wilse's outfit reached Dickinson some of his boys got drunk. Frank Owens, who was riding on the right point, had had a fight with a Mexican boy with the herd, and the law was after Frank. He left the herd and went to the Long X Ranch; so Wilse asked me if I'd help him out. He still had a hundred miles to go to the ranch. I went gladly, leaving Billy Herring to run our business.

The weather was fine. It was just a lark to do fifteen to twenty miles a day. Norman was cook; Sam Paine, horse wrangler; Wilse Norrad, boss; Frank Partridge, left point; Billie Timmons, right point; Bill Evans and Walter Phillips, on swing; Pet Lockett and the Mexican, flankers; Frank Jackson, one of the drag drivers.

At noon on the fourth day out, we camped on Rock Creek, which had good water, trees, fine grass. Norrad, who liked to scuffle, began wrestling with us. He was big and rough; Pet Lockett and I were small. He could handle us easily, and if he skinned us up and a little blood came, that was the best part of the sport for him. Pet and I hadn't got our heads together to team up on him right, and he had the best of it.

After this horseplay, we finished off the midday meal. Then we saw the smoke of a prairie fire about twenty-five miles to the east of us, on Knife River. The lark was at its end.

In that big, open range it was everybody's business to protect the free grass, to go to a fire wherever you saw it—no matter how far—to stay with it day and night till it was out. Wilse left four men with the herd, and the rest of us went to the fire. Norman, the cook, started first with the chuck wagon, firefighting equipment, and a little chuck. We caught good horses to ride.

Just as I mounted I saw Norrad doing the same thing, and I thought it offered a good chance to get even for the little hide he'd knocked off me. I popped my quirt over his head. Then, applying my quirt and spurs, I had my horse running for all he was worth. Wilse was right after me, but my horse was just fast enough that he couldn't catch me. As we passed the chuck

130

wagon, Wilse grabbed Norman's four-horse whip and popped that at me for several miles, but my horse was the best, just a little faster and longer-winded. I kept my distance till we got to the fire, then play was really over. We fought fire all night and until about ten o'clock the next morning.

We knew Norman was up Knife River with the wagon and chuck. Tired, sleepy, and hungry, we rode up the river and found the wagon. Norrad rode back to make sure all the fire was out; from atop hills he looked for smoke. The rest of us ate, then lay down to sleep. I told Pet, "Now, you lie close to me. I'm going to need your help. When Wilse gets here he's going to get in my middle and skin me up. Let's double up on him. If we can get the best of it he'll give us a rest."

I unbuckled my cartridge belt, dropped it beside me, and soon fell asleep. Sure enough, when Wilse got there he came after me. I got my legs up around his neck, my spurs at his throat. Pet grabbed my cartridge belt and laid it on till Wilse gave in, "Enough! You kids have got the best of it." He didn't bother us after that.

Back with the herd, we found that the cattle had been frightened by some ducks flying up in their midst while they were watering. They'd run enough to get worked up, and all four boys were with them to hold them. We could tell it was going to be a rough night. Then a cloud came up and by ten o'clock we had wind, lightning, hail, and rain. The cattle stampeded. All hands were with the herd, and we soon circled it. The frightened animals milled around, keeping us almost as much on edge as they were.

As soon as day broke, we threw the herd on the trail down the Little Missouri badlands to the river itself, which was bank-full. We decided on swimming across despite the quicksand. Rolling in, we pointed the leaders. They tried to turn back. We pointers pushed the leaders on, turning and twisting our horses, but our mounts soon gave up.

Dock Blaylock, range foreman, and Henry Linthicum, another trail boss whose herd was ahead of us, had come out from the Long X Ranch to see us cross and were watching from the opposite bank. When Frank Partridge's horse quit him, Linthicum swam his horse out, tossed his rope to Frank, and pulled him out on the opposite side. But the horse, with Frank's saddle and all his clothes except the underwear and hat he was wearing, came back to the side they started from.

Now my horse let himself down until my head went under water. He came up fighting, so I knew I had to get as far from him as I could. I had never swum a stroke in my life, but I got my feet in the saddle, said, "Lord, I'm in Your hands," and jumped as far away from the horse as I could. I may have gone to the bottom (I later discovered my black hat had quicksand in it so deep I couldn't brush it out), but I came up close to green leaves on a limb sticking up out of the water some fifty feet from the bank. I grabbed it and clamped my feet on the large part of the limb. I was sure this was a tree, but I couldn't let myself down far enough to touch the trunk, and the swift water was swirling around me. I reasoned: "I'll just stay here." Then the swimming cattle saw me and apparently thought I was on a landing; so they headed my way. I held on to that limb tight and tried to push the cattle back with my feet, but so many kept coming that I was afraid they'd surround me. I knew I had to get away.

I plunged toward the bank and came up at a cut bank many feet downstream. I grabbed for roots, but none of them looked strong enough to hold. I carefully worked along the cut bank until I found a place to get out. Then I sat down, thought of all the wicked things I'd ever done, and said, "Thank You, Lord. You saved me anyhow."

I wondered if the rest of the boys were safe. I looked up the bank but couldn't see much. Lots of those little wet Texas steers were crawling out on the bank; just as many hadn't got their feet wet. My horse—with saddle and all my clothing except my hat and underwear—had crossed the river to Frank Partridge— and his horse had come to my side. I made my way through thickets and briars to what was left of the herd, about three-quarters of a mile up the river. I'd gone about half a mile when I met Bill Evans picking his way down the river. He had a catch rope in his hand.

I greeted him, "Where're you going, Bill?"

"To throw you a rope and pull you out," he replied.

"If I stayed in that water for you to get me," I said, "I'd be half way to New Orleans by now. But I thought you'd got in the river and drowned long before now."

"No," said Bill; "the Long X doesn't pay the kind of wages that would get me into that river. I'm a land cowboy, not a duck."

A checkup showed about half the herd had gone across the river, and we had to take the remainder back out of the rough badlands to where there was room to hold them until the next day. After that experience I could say to a prospective cowboy, "Now, young fellow, if you want to have fun, don't go cow punching, for that's not the way it's done."

Next day the river was down. We crossed with little trouble and turned the herd loose. Wilse Norrad and I rode back to Dickinson, and I found Billy Herring getting along fine with the cafe business. In a few days Wilse was ready to go out again. He said to me, "Billy Herring can get along without you. Go back with me. We have a hay meadow on Cherry Creek, fenced in. I've had some of my boys putting up hay for saddle horses this winter. You and I'll ride around and keep the cattle away from the fence till they finish haying. Then we'll go on the beef work and be back shipping in September."

That sounded good to me, and I went with him. Cowboy work is like any other work. If you like it, the hardships don't seem so bad. You get stimulation out of it all. At least I did.

While the haying crew was rigging up to start, Wilse told me to ride over to the Long X headquarters, where there were a bunch of hogs and about thirty old worn-out saddle horses in a pasture. "Kill three or four of those old horses for the hogs to eat," he told me.

This order sent a chill down my spine, but he was boss and I intended to carry out orders. As I rode over, I kept asking myself, "How am I going to do it?" I'd never killed a horse, nor had I ever seen a horse I wanted to kill. Well, I'd never seen one of those old horses—and certainly never ridden one of them. I tried to convince myself I could get the job done.

Nobody was at the ranch in the summer; all the men were out

with chuck wagons till winter. I saw fifty or sixty hogs running around free, rustling a living off grass and weeds. I never had been fond of the swine tribe.

I went to bring in the horses. When I got them in and looked them over I saw that they were old and gentle. They looked so downcast; their life's work was done. Wilse had said to kill three or four, and my problem was to decide which ones to kill.

I talked to myself. "Three are enough. Well, they're all old. It doesn't make much difference. I'll take the bald-faced, lop-eared brown. He looks like he'll die pretty soon anyway. He could never make it through the winter. I'll walk over close and get him right between the eyes."

When I walked closer he made no movement. I stopped. As I drew my .45, old Brownie shook his head and nickered.

"I can't do it," I decided. "That's just like Buck used to act when he expected me to give him sugar or biscuit. I'll bet Brownie here has been some old boy's pet—that he's carried that fellow through swims and taken him to camp when he was lost. I'm not going to kill a one of them. Wilse can do it himself or send somebody else and let me go back to town!"

When I got back to camp Wilse asked, "How many of those old horses did you kill, Billie?"

I answered, "A little thing happened and I didn't get to kill a one." Then I confessed how old Brownie affected me. Wilse hooted, "Old chicken-hearted!"

"Yes," I said, "but you're a big brave man. I'll go with you and see how you shoot them down."

"I can't do it, either; I'm acquainted with them, that's the reason I sent you."

"Well, I became acquainted with them before I got them to the corral."

"I'll send Bill Evans," Wilse said finally. "It won't hurt his nerve to shoot them."

I returned to happier work. Cherry Flat Valley was full of cattle, and they crowded the meadow fence to see what the hay-ers were doing. Every day we rode the fence line and drove cattle away.

One old Longhorn cow let curiosity get the best of her. She

134

went through the fence to see what it was all about. The third time we found her inside the fence Wilse said, "Let's get her out, forefoot her, and throw her so many times she'll want to stay out of there." That we did. I had a good horse, and it was easy to throw a loop over her shoulders and pick up her forefeet. Wilse's horse was no good for roping, and I'd thrown the old cow several times without Wilse making a catch. I got to joshing him about being a poor roper. This made him a little mad, so he spurred his horse and rushed up against her. But now she was mad. She caught his horse in the flank, and, without breaking his hide, broke the stripping inside and ruptured him. We made camp, but the horse died the next day.

I boasted before the other boys that Wilse wasn't as good a roper as I was, or his horse would never have been hurt. He fumed, "I'll bet you a Stetson hat I can tie down a two-year-old steer quicker than you can." The bet was on. All the others saddled up their horses and rode out to see the contest.

I rode the little dun horse named Dude, light for a rope horse but the one I was riding when I had roped and thrown the cow. I knew I could catch on him—and did. I caught, forefooted, and tied a steer in two and half minutes, then made him struggle to show that he was well tied. He squirmed, got up, and kicked off my tie cord. The boys roared.

Wilse then roped him and tied him down so tight he stayed tied. Wilse won, and I knew all along he was a much better roper than I was anyway.

But that didn't end our rivalry. Another incident happened one cool night, the way all summer nights are in North Dakota. We had a cold rain the last days of August, with wind from the north. Wilse and I were sleeping together in a tepee, but when we went to bed, he rolled up in the cover and refused to share it unless I'd go out to the wagon and get him a drink. I lay there a while figuring how to get even with him, getting colder and colder, till I had it planned.

I had on only my underwear, but I put on my hat and boots, rolled up the rest of my clothes, and put them outside the tepee. Then I got the bucket of water and a cup. I put the bucket down, filled the cup, and gave it to Wilse. He drank the water slowly. I asked him if he wanted some more. He answered, "No, that's plenty."

I said, "Oh, yes, have some more." I jerked up the bucket of cold water, threw it on him, picked up my clothes, and ran through a cactus bed. Wilse chased after me, barefooted, until the cactus stopped him.

"Come get me out of here!" he shouted.

"No," I shouted back. "See if you can't find a drink of water in there!"

Wilse spent the rest of the night alone in his tepee, picking out stickers by the light of a lantern.

Soon we went to beef work, to make a shipment of cattle to the Chicago market. Dock Blaylock worked the country west of the Long X Ranch, Wilse Norrad the country east.

We worked north to the rough land of the Big Missouri and to the Fort Berthold Indian Reservation. Since we couldn't take the chuck wagon on the reservation without a permit, we went in and worked through Indian cattle to Independence, thirty-five miles away.

We got tired and hungry. Old Wolf Chief had a store, but not much in it to lunch on. We bought all the cheese, crackers, and canned tomatoes he had, and some sardines. We ate most of it and took the rest with us for breakfast; we were due to have another hard day's ride and work scouting Indian cattle and gathering Long X steers before we could go back to our chuck wagon. We spent the night in the open.

We saw no house or ranch east of the Long X Ranch, except those of Charley Shafer and Chase and Frye, till we got to Independence—though I believe that was the year Frank and Jack Keogh, Leslie and Earl Henderson, John and Charley Foreman, and perhaps H. C. Christensen established their ranches for twenty-five miles along the Indian reservation line. As they hadn't made much progress, I never saw or heard of them. Their ranches are still there, but all have passed to other ownership except for Keogh and Henderson, still operated by descendants.

On this work, I came down with la grippe. My fever ran high. The only medicine we had was a bottle of niter brought along for one of the chuck-wagon horses that had weak kidneys, but

136

that horse medicine kept me going till I came around all right. On the cattle ranges in those days you used what was at hand.

When we'd worked back to Cherry Creek we saw smoke fifteen or twenty miles east, between Elkhorn and Rough Creek. This was about two o'clock one afternoon. When we got to the scene we found that probably everybody in the country who saw the blaze had responded. By one o'clock next morning it was out, and all the fire-fighters gathered on Cherry Creek, two miles above the spot where it runs into the Little Missouri. There I met Charley Shafer, who with his family had been the first settlers in McKenzie County. He also had the first vegetable garden there. Shafer invited us to his ranch to eat, and when we arrived we saw a light shining.

Mrs. Shafer had watched the smoke and glare from that prairie fire. When it began to disappear she had prepared enough food to feed twenty-five men. It was on the table, steaming hot. It included everything that grew in the garden. Those pioneer women! They did more than their part. The frontier was fine for men and dogs, but hell on horses and women.

At the Shafer home I met their eight-year-old son, George, who later became the first native-son governor of North Dakota, elected by the largest majority any governor had ever received.

On September 15 we made our shipment, and I went back to the cafe, thinking I'd spend the winter changing shifts with Billy Herring—two weeks on days, two weeks on nights.

But I was destined for things that I'd never given so much as a thought to.

XV. UPS AND DOWNS—MOSTLY DOWNS

WHEN MY OLD FRIEND Jim Henderson came to Dickinson in October, 1900, he set off a chain of events that would bring variety into my life for the next couple of years.

Jim, as I've already related, I think, had bought the Bellows Ranch from Mr. Ray. He had decided that since there was a lot of open range around him he ought to have more cattle. He told me he could get money from his moderately well-to-do father to buy a thousand two-year-olds.

"I thought if you'd go to Texas, see your old friend Mr. Goodnight, and buy the cattle I want, we might work out a good deal for all of us," Jim told me. "In addition to what we might buy, I want you to propose to Mr. Goodnight that he put in from a thousand to fifteen hundred head more, to share profits with us when they're ready for market in two years. I'll give you a fourth, take a fourth myself, and give Mr. Goodnight half. And I'll pay you a salary to be my foreman and run my layout."

It didn't take me long to decide.

"That all sounds real good, Jim," I told him. "I'm ready to go. When do you want me to start?"

I could start, he said, just as soon as I made arrangements. I knew all I had to do was to tell Billy Herring I'd be gone and that it was up to him to run our business till I got back.

"All right," Jim said. "Your salary starts tomorrow. We'll go to Lawyer Fields in the morning and draw up a contract. I'll pay your salary and expenses till April 1, when you start on salary as ranch foreman."

The next day we went to the lawyer and drew up a contract. Jim gave me my winter expenses. I made them light, as I expected to be home with my people or on the ranch most of the time. Jim also gave me one month's salary and said he'd send the rest each month. I was soon bound for Goodnight, Texas, having been gone four years and four months.

While I was in the cafe waiting for traintime Bob Miller, from Muskogee, Oklahoma, came in. I told him I was headed for Texas, and he said, "Come go with me. I've bought three carloads of horses from the Long X outfit. We've just loaded them. I'll bill one car for you to Muskogee. That'll give you a pass on the railroad. After the horses rest up a few days from this long train trip I'll load them again for Sulphur Springs, Texas, to sell them there."

I took him up on his offer at once, and we had a pleasant trip. Bob was one-quarter Choctaw, and that gave him a landright on the reservation. He was well-educated, a high-degree Mason, and a good businessman. He owned a nice home in Muskogee and had an attractive wife, a three-year-old daughter and a five-year-old son. I spent a day with them, enjoying every bit of it. Then I said good-by to Bob and his family. Years later I was to meet him under entirely different circumstances.

I was now on the last lap of my journey. I'd done very well in the more than four years I'd been away, suffering only brief spells of homesickness. With everything else behind and home just ahead, the miles seemed long. The train crept along. Then the conductor called Goodnight.

All my younger brothers were at the depot—Herbert, Lon, Wesley, Nolle, and Jerome—with my only sister, Maye, now in her early teens. She looked so beautiful! How wonderful it was to see her, and she showed me all the affection she held for her other brothers. My father and mother greeted me at home—the most joyous place on earth. My mother laughed and cried at the same time. My father mostly looked on and listened; he didn't have much opportunity to talk.

Those brothers had grown so much! My sister, fourteen, looked like a young lady dressed up for some special occasion. I felt so proud of her as she hovered close and gave me a feeling that she was my own.

I was the first of our family to go that far away and to be gone

139

so long. We talked until the wee hours of the morning, and I got all the news. Two older boys, Ben and Cy, were married. Clabe, the brother just older than I, had gone away on a trip but would be home the next day.

Originally I'd started home with the intention of surprising the family, but when I left Muskogee I could no longer keep quiet and had wired: "Am on my way home." Many changes had taken place; lots of new people had come into the country. Everybody had a telephone—using barbed wire fences for transmission. You could ring a friend miles away and talk—if you could get the line.

Goodnight Academy was going full blast. Sons and daughters of ranchers from a hundred miles around had brought their wardrobes and bedding in wagons and buggies and on pack horses, ready for nine months in college.

When I met Mr. Goodnight I asked how his calf-branding was going that year. He said, "A good per cent of the cows calved, but I've reduced my herd a lot since you were here and have sold some of the level land near the railroad to men who want to farm. I'm more interested in this school I've started here than anything else. It was badly needed by these young folks.

"I expect some of the smartest people of this nation to come from these plain lands, where it's so level the eye can see for miles around. Broad spaces give a broad vision. I know cattle and horses are smarter and easier to handle in an open country, and I think a man is the same—the farther he sees, the broader his mind becomes.

"I want to see how many minds I can help develop. We have ninety students here now and are just getting started. I'm prouder of them than the calves I branded this year. Your brothers and sister will have a chance to get a college education here, and I'm proud of that. They'll take advantage of their opportunity."

Then I told him what I was doing. I showed him my contract with Jim Henderson to buy a thousand two-year-old steers and explained that if I could get fifteen hundred at market price on shares we'd get the gain in weight from two years on our range in North Dakota and ship them out as four-year-olds to the Chi-

140

cago market. When I started to tell him about the wonderful range around the old Bellows Ranch he said, "Yes, I remember you wrote me all about that good free grass—plenty water, with good protection in winter." Mr. Goodnight never forgot anything anybody wrote to him.

"I have no doubt that it's wonderful range country," he continued, "but I'm getting old. My health isn't good. I'm cutting down instead of spreading out. If I were younger—or if my health was better—I might be interested, but I'm not. The most likely man I know of who might be interested in your deal is Lee Bivins. You know him."

"Yes, sir, I know him," I replied. "I helped Lee take about three hundred two-year-old steers to his ranch near Claude in 1895. He was just getting started in the cattle business then. I spent the night with him. They lived in a two-room frame house with an attic, where I slept. Mrs. Bivins cooked supper, I remember, and Lee milked the cows. Their boys were too small to help."

"He's climbed the ladder fast since then," Mr. Goodnight said. "He's one of the biggest operators in the Panhandle. He's a shrewd trader and has cattle scattered all over the country. Go talk with Lee, and if I can do anything to help you, let me know. Lee lives in Amarillo."

I went to Amarillo and found Lee batching in a small house. Nearby were stables, sheds, and corrals where his freighters stopped when getting ranch supplies. I spent a few days with him and showed him my contract with Jim Henderson. Lee drove to several places close to Amarillo where he had steers, gave me the price for spring delivery, and said, "I'll look your range over in the spring. Then I can see how stock wintered. I might be interested in putting in fifteen hundred two-year-old steers at the same price per head of the thousand I sell you. You run them two years, pay all expenses plus half the shipping expenses, and I'll expect one-half their weight gain, in addition to their original price."

It was now December and I hadn't heard a word from Jim Henderson since I left him in October, though I'd written to him several times. Now I sent him the terms of the deal Lee Bivins had offered. In January, 1901, I went to Amarillo and talked with Lee again, but said nothing about not having heard from Jim.

I couldn't understand it. If our contract was still good, Jim was behind on my salary. If he wasn't able to live up to it, why didn't he write and tell me? We had at all times been good friends. I wrote Jim again, urging him to let me know what to do.

Lee wanted me to go to Motley County, Texas, to look at a herd of steers that he'd either put in our deal on shares or sell outright. My brother Clabe took his buggy and team and drove me to Estelline, where we spent the night with J. C. Thomas, who was running a boardinghouse and wagon yard. Mr. Thomas asked me to go into the livery stable and feed business with him, and I told him that I might do it but that I was on a deal and would have to wait to see how it turned out.

Then we drove to the F Ranch. They told me Estelline was a good place for a livery barn.

We drove on to Motley County, looked at Lee's steers, and returned home. No word from Jim. I wrote to the Dickinson lawyer who'd drawn up the contract to see if he could reach Jim. The lawyer, H. H. Fields, replied that he hadn't seen Jim Henderson since I left, but that he'd heard Jim was staying in Medora at the Rough Rider Hotel and that he'd been there all winter, drinking and gambling. That was hard to believe, for all the time I'd known Jim I'd never seen him take a drink. Jim himself once told me he'd never taken a drink and didn't know one card from another. He had so fine a character that I was proud to associate with him, hoping that perhaps some of his goodness might rub off on me. Could it be true that my bright guiding star had fallen? If so, my castles in the air would soon follow.

Lawyer Fields advised me to stay in Texas till April 1, then to come back. At that time I'd have my first installment of the contract fulfilled, and I could collect my salary and any expenses beyond the cash Jim had given me.

I went to Estelline. We built the livery barn, bought horses, harness, and buggies, and got the business started. I hired a fellow to take my place, and on April 1 started back to North Dakota.

When I got to Dickinson I went to see Wilse Richards, my banker. He had the Dakota State Bank and was a good friend. I needed his advice on what to do. He gave me all his information about Jim and it bore out what Fields had written. Nothing could be done about my contract because Jim was broke. His father had sent him money to buy cattle; he had gambled it away, then had mortgaged his stock and ranch—everything. By false statements he had even borrowed more than his outfit was worth.

"It's all gone, and Jim's in an awful mess," Richards said. "His father's here now trying to get things straightened out to keep Jim out of prison."

After Wilse Richards had told me all this, I said, "I don't want to collect a thing from Jim. I only wish I could help him. Six months ago he was clean and honest, and had never lived any other way. Just twenty-six, with all the good things of this earth in his hand. He's a close friend. I just want to talk to him. Do you know where he is now?"

"He's in town, but they're keeping him hidden until his father gets his business straightened out. Then I suppose he'll take Jim home with him."

"I have to find him and talk to him—let him know I'm still his friend," I said. "Jim needs friends like he's never needed them before. He's no criminal. He's just got off wrong—a weakness I never thought he had."

"I believe you're right, Billie. I can tell you where he most likely is right now, but I don't think you'll get to see him. Go down to Alf White's drugstore. They have living quarters in the back. Jim and his father are staying there. Tell Alf what you want. If he understands you as I do he'll let you see Jim. But don't tell anybody about our talk."

Alf said he didn't know just where Jim was, only that he and his father had been there to visit. Alf and Jim had ranched on the Cannon Ball River and had been neighbors before Jim bought the Bellows Ranch from Mr. Ray; so Alf was just doing what he could to help.

I went back to Richards and told him I didn't have a chance to see Jim. Wilse said, "I'll go talk with Alf."

He did, and arranged for our meeting. Jim was very shy until I told him how I felt about him. Then he put his hand on my shoulder and said, "Billie, I didn't think I had a friend left in the world. I've made such a mess of everything, especially with you. I did you so wrong—sent you back to your people, your friends, to do business for me because I felt your influence and judgment of cattle would be better than mine. You did your part. I failed you."

"We all make mistakes," I answered. "I'm younger than you, and I've made plenty. I don't doubt I'll make more. People must forgive me because they're still friends. I forgive any you've made, and I think others will. Let's forget it. But I would like to know how this happened. Six months ago you told me you'd never taken a drink and didn't know one card from another."

"Well," he said, "as you well know, Medora is just fifteen miles up the Little Missouri from the ranch. I hadn't been up there enough to get acquainted, so I thought it'd be a good idea to go up there, hang around the hotel a few days, and meet more of the cowmen, since we were planning to have more cattle, a wider spread. I thought I at least ought to be acquainted with all the cowmen in the country.

"The Rough Rider Hotel is a good place to meet them, so I wrote my father about our plans—all the details—and told him how much money it would take to buy the cattle. I went to Medora to mail it, and met a jolly, friendly bunch of fellows. They were all drinking beer and whiskey. They invited me to take a drink but I said No. They kept saying, 'Oh, come on, be sociable. Bartender'll fix you up a sociable drink.' He did. I don't know what he put in it, but it tasted good and made me feel good. Then some of them got to playing cards—draw poker—and wanted me to play. I told them I didn't know one card from the other. They said, 'That's easy to learn. We'll teach you. We just play for fun—to pass the time. Sometimes we put in a little money to make it interesting. After you learn the cards and the best winning hands, you'll know as much about the game as any of us. None of us are gamblers. One time you'll be winner, then somebody else will be winner. It's passed around, and we all break even.'

144

"So they taught me which card was high—Ace, King, Queen, Jack, on down the line. Then suits—spades, hearts, diamonds, clubs. Then the winning hands—that was the hardest, but they all knew. They'd tell me as we played.

"For two or three days we just played for fun. White chips were twenty-five cents, reds fifty cents, blues one dollar. I won for fun most of the time, and when we started playing for money I won, quitting a little the winner every game. They told me that was beginner's luck—beginners always won.

"I was drinking what the bartender always fixed up for me. One night I got sick. They said my drink was too sweet, to put a little whiskey in it, just a little wouldn't hurt anybody and would just cut the sweet. I did that, then I started losing. The first night when the game broke up I was four hundred dollars in the hole. They said, 'Well, you'll win it back and more next game.' The next day the game started with white chips fifty cents, reds one dollar, blues five dollars. We played till twelve o'clock that night, and I was more than a thousand dollars loser. I was nervous and asked for more whiskey in my drink. When that game ended, I couldn't have hit the ground with my hat.

"By the time I got your first letter, all the money I'd got out of my beef shipment was gone and I was borrowing. Then my father sent me the money to buy the cattle. I felt sure that with it I could win back my loss, but I lost it all.

"My father's here now straightening things up. I don't have anything. Father's disheartened but he hasn't said an angry word to me. I don't know what he'll do with me. He just asked me to go home with him when he's got everything fixed up, and I said I would."

"You don't owe me anything," I said. "I'll settle for the lesson you've learned. You've paid an awful high price for it. A few months ago your record was clear, and it will be again. Just keep your head up and don't lose confidence in yourself. It's hard to fight uphill, but you've got the spunk to do it."

Sometime later I heard that Jim was in Montana herding sheep, but couldn't find out his address. After that I never heard of Jim again.

Gone were my dreams of a higher financial status. I went

back to the cafe and took over the night shift that Billy Herring had been on during the month I was away. Sybil Anderson, the head waitress, had been in charge of the day shift.

As I waited on the counter serving up ham sandwiches, doughnuts, and pie and ringing up the nickels and dimes in the cash register, it came to me what Mr. Ray had said: "It's too confining for a boy like you who was raised in the open. . . . You won't like it."

When Billy came to work on May 15, 1901, I told him, "I'm ready to sell you my interest in this business."

"I don't want to see you go," he said, "but if you want to get out of this I'll try to raise the money to buy you out."

We figured out a sale price. Billy went to his father and got the money he needed to pay me. But I didn't want to go back to Texas. I was in love with the people and the hills, prairies, rivers, and creeks of North Dakota.

Wilse Norrad offered me an out. "Billie," he said, "I've got about two thousand steers I'm holding here for Uncle Webb Arnett. I'd like to get you to go out, to take my place for four or five days. Just see that everything goes along all right. I have a little business trip I want to make."

I took his place gladly. Then I got a message from home. My younger brother, Wesley, had died. The family wanted me to come home as soon as possible. That was the first death in our immediate family. As soon as Wilse got back, I left for home.

Charles Goodnight and Mrs. Goodnight.

Charles Goodnight's large home was the show place of the Texas Panhandle at the turn of the century. Bottom part of this composite photograph shows part of his famous buffalo herd.

I found in North Dakota wide-open spaces and the best large herd ranges in the United States. The man on the horse in this photograph, taken about 1895, is Wilse Richards.

My first step upon my arrival in Dickinson, North Dakota, in 1896 was the Villard

In the badlands along the Little Missouri River grew some of the best grass in the West.

William C. Ray and Mrs. Ray.

Our appetites were almost as big as the range. We filled our plates and started eating, cowboy style—with legs crossed, plates on legs.

The first picture I ever had taken—of Buck and me—has never been far from me for very long. When I look at it now a spool of happy recollections unwinds for me.

From cook to foreman, we loved our work—or we didn't stay long on the range. This is the 75 Ranch chuck wagon.

During one of the few idle moments at the 75 Ranch headquarters this picture was snapped. Frank Keogh is at the far right, seated.

Across the Fort Berthold Indian Reservation lumbers the 75 chuck wagon.

Near the chuck wagon, 75 Ranch horses wait for riders. Notice the 75 brand on the white horse in the foreground.

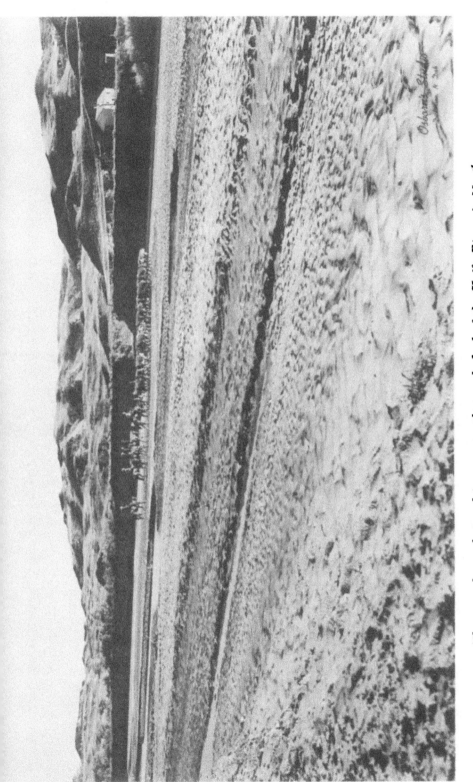

These cattle are being driven across the sandy bed of the Knife River, in North Dakota.

Frank Keogh.

By 1907 the handwriting was on the wall in North Dakota. Most big ranch outfits were out of business; the 75 was the largest one left. It was truly twilight on the range.

October 25, 1910, was a memorable day for me; it was my last day's work as a cowboy. This picture shows part of the last big herd headed for the railroad.

XVI. IN TEXAS AGAIN

AFTER A FEW DAYS in our usually happy home—now so sad-
dened—I went to Estelline to see about the livery barn. That
little Hall County town, on the Fort Worth and Denver City
Railroad, enjoyed an importance in those early days of the
century, in what was a cattle economy.

It was the big railroad shipping point for all cattle in an area
extending 150 miles south. However, spring shipping was over
when I got there and for three months things were very quiet.

My personal situation struck me as peculiar. In North Dakota
I was afflicted with spells of homesickness for Texas. Now, in
Texas, I longed for North Dakota.

I cheered up when Hans Cresswell from North Dakota came
to Estelline and asked me to take him to the F Ranch. It was a
long, rainy-day drive—but a pleasant one, for he talked all day
about cattle and horses and about people I knew on the northern
ranges.

When we got to the Pease River, a quarter of a mile from the
ranch headquarters, we found the river up.

"That looks dangerous," I said.

"Drive on in," he said. "We'll make it."

The current was so swift it turned the buggy on its side and
ripped off the top. We managed to get out, caught the wheels,
and landed on a sand bar. Some cowboys who saw us go in
threw us ropes and pulled us out. We'd had a close call.

When I got back to Estelline I found a shoe drummer from
Boston waiting. He wanted to go into Oklahoma Indian Territory and make all the towns and crossroads stores in the western half of that sparsely settled area. We planned on a thirty-day

147

trip. It took forty—and even then we didn't get into the north-west corner.

This salesman's name was Alfred Baggett, a fine fellow to travel with. At the time there was a smallpox scare and every-body had to be vaccinated. He had already been vaccinated some years before, so this one didn't take on him. Mine took —good. My arm swelled up from shoulder to finger tips, and my fever ran high.

With everybody scared of smallpox it was hard to find a place to spend the night. Most of the time we were in the open country where there were small stores but no hotels. The people didn't want any strangers in their houses.

Once we started looking for a place early in the afternoon. Baggett got out at every farmhouse we passed, but nobody would take us in. My fever was getting higher all the time. After dark we could see farmhouse lights everywhere. I said, "Alfred, I'm feeling tough. I want to stop somewhere. Let me try the next place."

"All right," he said, "you try the next one."

I knocked at the door. An old fellow cracked it just a little, and I said, "Mister, we're trying to find a place to spend the night."

"We can't keep you," he replied.

I suppose the light and the warmth must have made me des-perate; it certainly didn't make me smart. I said, "But I'm sick and I've got a high fever and might be taking the smallpox."

He yelled, "Get out of my yard!" and slammed the door.

"I ought to drive on and let you walk," Baggett said.

About half a mile farther, Bagget knocked on the door of a house and explained that he and I were traveling through, that he was a shoe salesman and we had a spring wagon and four big trunks, that I had been vaccinated—my arm was swollen and my fever high—and that we needed some place to get supper and rest. He added that he'd pay well for the accommodation. They took us in for the night.

The next morning we went back to Quanah, Texas, and Bag-gett got on a train. I drove on to Estelline, where I found a stack of mail, including a letter from Ben Lawless, manager of the

148

W Bar Ranch in North Dakota. He told me they were closing out their cattle and were offering their camps and headquarters. All their holdings, with free range for from ten to twelve thousand cattle, were up for sale. He sent a list, with price for it all.

If I could find a buyer, there'd be a nice little stake for me in commission. Another inducement was that if I could sell it I might get a good cowboy's job, for I'd ridden all over this range.

On October 20, 1901, I sold my interest in the livery barn at Estelline and went to Amarillo, hoping to persuade Lee Bivins to take a look at the W Bar property. Lee gave me some encouragement by saying he thought it was a good buy, with some money to be made. But he'd bought the LX Ranch, just west of Amarillo, and had some work to do there before he could leave.

I went out with Lee until he finished his work. Then I spent a few days batching with him in his Amarillo quarters. His wife was in Sherman, Texas—their old home—and their sons, Miles and Jude, were in school there. I spent some time around Amarillo, hoping Lee would decide to take the W Bar deal, but in January, 1902, he told me he was so tied up he'd decided not to spread out any further. I then decided to go to Mangum, Oklahoma, to visit my old friend, Joe Miller, and find out if he might know of some Oklahoma stockman who'd be interested in the W Bar deal.

I visited with Joe for a few days. He didn't know of anybody who might be a prospect but advised me to go to Oklahoma City and stop at the Hutchins Hotel, a hangout for Oklahoma stockmen, where I might run into someone who would be.

I went there and butted into everybody who looked like a stockman. I talked to a Fort Worth Horse Company man, but he didn't know of anybody looking for a ranch deal.

Then I told him about the fine Percheron horses in North Dakota. He came to life when I mentioned the horses and asked me what they could be bought for.

"I'm not sure right now," I told him, "but October a year ago I came down with three cars of horses to be sold at Sulphur Springs. They'd weigh from nine hundred pounds for three-year-olds to twelve hundred pounds for matured grown horses. They could be bought then for forty-five dollars a head."

"Can you buy me a few carloads?" he asked.

"I don't know, but I can tell you by the last of March or the first part of April. It'll be that long before enough snow melts for range horses to be rounded up and looked over. Horses hold their flesh real good there through the winter—that grass is rich and matures like hay—but until the spring grass is good, they're soft and ought to be held on hay for a week or ten days to stand shipping."

"You're right there. I'd pay that extra expense."

"Give me a list of just what class of horses you want—ages, weight, price, and how many."

He wrote: "Ages 3 to 8 years old; from 900 pounds for 3-year-olds; for matured horses, nothing less than 1,000 pounds; all must be sound; two hundred fifty head, one hundred head in April, the balance as soon as ready, all by July 1st. You load them on cars, we will have a man there to receive them at $47.50 per head. We pay for 10 days haying of 100 head, others if needed. Will accept mares with colt by side at same price."

Still looking for a taker for the W Bar deal, I talked to an El Paso Commission Company man who had a large list of one- and two-year-old steers that he wanted buyers for. He didn't know of anybody I might interest in the ranch, but he said, "You might run into somebody who'd buy some of these yearlings and two-year-old steers when you get back to Dakota. If you do, we'll allow you fifty cents a head on anything you can sell."

"I'll sure see what I can do, if you'll give me a listing—price, grade, and location."

"I'll do that. We have them listed from the Rio Grande to the Panhandle of Texas—the cheapest and poorest, south. Farther north—better cattle and higher prices, though we do have some good cattle on the Rio Grande." He gave me a listing of price and location that also stated my commission, with permission to wire collect to El Paso Commission Company about any likely buyer.

Then I met Louis Chisum. He and his brother, William, were partners, looking for cheaper grass than they could find in Oklahoma. They were feeding about twelve hundred steers near Lawton, and had smaller bunches at other places. I went with them

150

to Lawton to see if we could work out anything from what I had.

Chisum wanted to hear more about the W Bar range. "I'll talk it over with Bill and meet you at Flato Commission Company in Kansas City in just one week," he said. "We do business with Flato, and I'd like for them to look at that listing of property and the amount of cattle the range'll carry. One week from today is the eighteenth. I'll be there."

This meant another week's delay, with expenses eating me up. I needed to find work. I got back to Oklahoma City and found cheap room and board by the week. I looked in the want ads, and I found just the thing. The Van Nuys News Company wanted a news butcher on the Frisco railroad's Kansas City run. I went at once and applied for the job, and the manager wanted to know if I could be ready to go out at 3:30 that afternoon. It was then 11 A.M.

"Yes, sir," I told him.

"Have you got a blue suit?" he asked.

"No, sir, I haven't."

"Do you want to wear that suit?"

It was a light-brown with a little lighter stripe in it. I said I did.

"Then cut the buttons off it," he said. "We furnish brass buttons. Just punch them in where your buttons are now and fasten them on with the cap so they can be taken off when the suit goes to the cleaner. We'll let you run that way for a month. After that you'll have to get a blue suit."

"You understand the orders of the train conductor? When he says, 'Pack your trunks,' do so—about twelve o'clock tonight. He puts you and the trunks off the train, and on his return he picks you up. You lay over here a day and go back with him on his run. We check out your supplies to you; we check them back on your return, and you settle for all goods sold."

"Remember, the conductor is your boss all the time on the train. If you're not courteous and right with passengers, he can put you off his train anywhere and he'll return our goods to us."

I went out with conductor Jack McGinnis, a good, jolly fellow, though on that first run he was very gruff. I thought he was a bear cat. The first thing he said was, "I'm your boss. I have to

151

keep a check on you, and your news company doesn't give me a damned cent for it. So I'll smoke your cigars, read your papers, eat your oranges, apples, and candy, and you won't get a red cent for them!"

"All right, Mr. Conductor," I said. "You're my boss. What you say goes. Help yourself to anything I have, and I'll thank you for telling me if I do anything wrong."

On the next trip I found he was a prince of a fellow. Everybody called him Jack. I used "Mr. Conductor" till he said, "Just call me Jack like everybody else does, and nobody'll know but what we're friends."

It was getting close to the time I had to be in Kansas City to meet Lou, so I told Jack about my deal. He said, "Well, pack your trunks, lie down, and go to sleep; I'll forget to wake you up. Kansas City is headquarters for Van Nuys News Company. I'll cushion for you. But before I do, there's one little business of mine that I want to explain. I have a peach orchard started over in Arkansas. I need some more peach trees in it. They cost a dollar and a half. I just want the price of a tree."

"All right, Jack," I answered. "Here's the price of a tree. I hope we both eat fruit from this deal."

At Kansas City I got a cab to take me near the stockyards where there was a tailor. I got my suit brushed and pressed and the buttons sewed on. Then I shaved and bathed and ate a snack, and at nine o'clock I was at the Stock Exchange with no signs that I'd ever sold peanuts, popcorn, oranges, apples, and candy.

Lou Chisum was there. Soon Mr. Flato showed up. They had some business to talk over first, then I was invited in with the listing of what Mr. Ben Lawless was offering, and the amount of cattle the range would carry. I told them I'd been over every foot of that range. There was water in springs and creeks, and excellent grass. Mr. Flato said, "Lou, that sounds just like what you've been wanting. You'd better go look it over."

"Before you do," I said, "I'd like for you to get the opinion of some old cowman up there about the condition of the range."

"That's a good idea," said Mr. Flato. "Who do you suggest?"

"Either Mr. W. L. Richards or Mr. A. N. Jefferies. They're

both Texas cowmen and have been in that country more than fifteen years. Jefferies was manager of the Long X for Reynolds Brothers. Their ranges joined."

"We'll take Mr. Jefferies' word," Mr. Chisum said. "If he says it's good, we'll go up and see what we can do about it. Write to Mr. Jefferies."

I did so right there and read them what I'd said. As soon as Mr. Jefferies' reply came I was to let Mr. Chisum know. I had a feeling we'd make a sale, for I'd written Mr. Lawless that I had a prospect and asked him to let me know in the meantime if it was sold.

I left them there, rushed back to the depot, cut my buttons off, put on the brass ones, donned my cap, and was ready once again to sell peanuts, popcorn, apples, and candy.

Two weeks later I got a letter from Mr. Jefferies saying that the W Bar range was being overrun by Montana sheepmen and that small ranchers were taking up the best water and hay land, that the range even now wasn't practical for large herds and would soon be worse. I mailed the letter to Mr. Lou Chisum in Lawton, Oklahoma, with a note saying that I could be reached at Dickinson, North Dakota, once more.

Then I unscrewed the brass buttons off my coat, went to the railroad depot and turned in my supplies, never again to be a news butcher.

I saw Jack the train conductor and told him my deal fell through but that I had the price of a peach tree. "I'm heading for North Dakota," I said.

Jack replied, "You're a good sport. I'll see the Pullman conductor. I think you can ride to Kansas City with us."

I did.

XVII. BROKER AND FOREMAN

I ARRIVED IN DICKINSON on March 30, 1902, anxious to try my hand as a broker. After visiting Mrs. Ray and her family I called on Wilse Richards at the Dakota State Bank, showed him my propositions with the Fort Worth Horse Company and the El Paso Commission Company, and asked him what he thought I could do with them. Wilse said to let him think it over and come in the next day.

On the street I met Louis Randall. After we had talked awhile he asked me if I'd found a room yet. When I told him I hadn't he said, "Three other boys and I have one at the Gem Hotel. We keep it all the time so we'll have a place to keep our clothes. It's never locked. Nobody's using it now—the other fellows are out of town and I'm leaving now." I thanked him and told him I'd like very much to use the room.

Lou left for the DZ Ranch sixty miles south of town and I hadn't thought to ask him who was renting the room with him.

After he left I met Mary Riley, an old friend who was staying at the St. Charles Hotel. Mary's family were among the first settlers in western North Dakota, so she had the friendly, Western way. She said, "Billie, come up to the hotel and let's get this visit out."

I told her I'd be there at eight o'clock that night. But my suits needed cleaning and pressing, and I was afraid there might not be time to have this done. The one cleaner in town was also a tailor, and if he had an order to make a suit he wouldn't get mine cleaned for a week. I took my best suit out of the valise, brushed it, and tried to stretch some of the wrinkles out of it.

As I hung it in the closet my eye caught sight of a beautiful new gray suit hanging there. I looked at it alongside that dirty, crumpled one of mine, wondered who it belonged to, and wished I'd asked Lou who his roommates were. I knew it couldn't be Lou's, for he was taller than I. Examination had showed the trousers were just the right length for me. I hung it back.

After supper I went back to the room. It was past seven o'clock and that new suit was still hanging there. I reasoned that if its owner didn't have it on by then he wouldn't be using it that night.

At eight o'clock I had on the gray suit and was at the St. Charles Hotel visiting with Mary. We talked for about an hour, and just as I was thinking of leaving, Clint Randall, who worked on the Long X Ranch a hundred miles north, came in. Clint was an old friend I hadn't seen for a year.

I soon realized that he and Mary were sweethearts, for he'd come up at a late hour dressed just like he would have been on the ranch. As soon as I could, I excused myself and went to the lobby and began chatting with friends.

When Clint came down I was standing with my back to the stairway. He whacked me a real wallop between the shoulders and said, "Listen, boy, if you want to go see my girl, get yourself a suit of your own."

That cost me the treats. Mary knew all the time whose suit I was wearing. (She told me fifty years after she'd married Clint that she never was at any gathering of old-timers that somebody didn't say something about my coming to see her wearing Clint's new suit.)

I spent the next couple of months acting as "broker" in the horse and cattle deals. With Wilse Richards' help I lined up what looked like a sure-fire arrangement for getting some horses that could be sold to the Fort Worth Horse Company. Bill Lang had four hundred head at his ranch on the Little Missouri that he was willing to sell at twenty dollars each—eight thousand dollars. Wilse didn't want to go into partnership with me on the deal because he already had too many irons in the fire but he was willing to lend me the money to take care of it myself.

But when I telegraphed Fort Worth they wired back that there'd been so much death loss during the past winter on horses that had come in from Montana and the Dakotas that they didn't intend to handle northern horses again unless they were first shipped to West Texas or Oklahoma for a year to get used to the climate. That ended the horse deal for me.

I then got busy trying to sell the steers for the El Paso Commission Company. I was looking for any cowman who might buy 1,000 or 1,500. One of the men I met was Mr. Webb Arnett, who would often buy from 1,000 to 2,000 head and sell them to smaller stockmen who could handle only 250 or 300 at a time. He told me, "Billie, I've got 1,212 steers out here that I've just shipped in from Oregon. If you find anybody who'll buy them I'll give you fifty cents a head for all you sell—and when they're cleared out I'll buy 1,500 of your Texas steers."

Three days after my talk with Mr. Arnett, Mr. George Woodman came to town. His ranch was fifty or sixty miles southwest of Dickinson. He'd been manager of the HT Company when I was in the livery and feed-stable business and he'd given me all the HT business. We were very good friends.

Woodman had invented the chain fire drag which all Western stockmen used to fight fires. It had rings linked together 8 by 10 feet with an asbestos blanket on top. It dropped into low places and cut or smothered out all fire. On the right and left end of the drag were chains that were 6 feet long. Ropes would be attached to the chains and then secured to the saddle horns of two riders, one on each side of the fire. This would keep the two riders out of reach of the flames. Before Woodman invented this device, which missed nothing, stockmen had used sheetiron drags, which sometimes slid over low places and left the fire burning.

Mr. Woodman asked me what I was doing. I said I was trying to sell some two-year-old steers for the El Paso Commission Company.

"I might talk to you about some of them in September," he said. "I'll be wanting from 1,000 to 1,500."

I tried to sell him on buying now, as he had so much free range. I stressed the growth to be expected and the better condition they'd be in for winter. But he said he didn't want to borrow money. I saw I was getting nowhere.

156

Then I said, "Mr. Woodman, I've got a deal for you right here. You'll have to pay just a small rate of interest. Mr. Webb Arnett has 1,212 two-year-old Oregon steers that I'm selling for him. They're good Herefords and Durhams crossbred, worth the money he's asking. He told me I could sell them without a dollar down to any good man, and I couldn't hope to find a better one than you. I wish you'd go out with me in the morning and look at them."

He agreed to do that, and I suggested that we meet at the cafe at five o'clock.

We drove out in a buggy. By seven o'clock Mr. Woodman said, "I'll take them if Mr. Arnett will accept my paper."

Mr. Arnett was glad to take the note. I helped run the U Bar U brand on them, then helped drive them toward Mr. Woodman's ranch. Mr. Arnett was anxious to cut expenses and had paid off his men. But Wilse Norrad, Arnett's nephew, went along to help me.

Later I met Mr. Arnett at the bank. He handed me a check for $35.

"What's this for?" I asked.

"For helping with those cattle," he said.

"You don't owe a dime for that," I answered. "I did it for Mr. Woodman. He asked me to. What you owe me is $606 for selling them."

"I wouldn't pay anybody anything to help me sell cattle to George Woodman. I could've sold them to him without your help."

"Mr. Arnett, I don't doubt that you could sell to any man in the Northwest without my help. But you didn't sell that bunch to George Woodman. I did. And you can't deny that you told me to sell them just as I did. According to your own agreement you owe me $606. And what about the 1,500 Texas steers you were going to buy from me?"

"I'm not buying any Texas steers," Mr. Arnett said. Then he walked away.

Wilse Richards knew about my deal with Arnett to sell his steers. I went to Wilse and told him what Webb Arnett said about my commission. "All right," Wilse said, "Webb owes you and ought to pay you. But if he says he isn't going to, what can you do about it? Did anybody hear Webb say he'd give you fifty cents a head to sell them?"

"No," I answered. "We were standing out there on the street in front of this bank. I came right in and told you. I also told Wilse Norrad, and he knows very well I sold them to Mr. Woodman—Wilse Norrad is a good friend of mine."

"I know what you told me," Richards said, "and I know it's true. But that's only what you told me and what you told Norrad. Remember, Norrad's a nephew of Webb's and works for him —and friendship sometimes doesn't stand a very rugged test when there're dollars involved.

"Webb is a long-time friend of mine. I'll talk to him, and we'll get his side of your deal."

Shortly afterward Wilse told me he'd talked to Webb, who told him what he'd told me—that he didn't need any help to sell cattle to George Woodman. But he didn't tell Wilse whether or not he'd ever had an agreement with me, and Wilse asked him the direct question—"Didn't you tell Billie you'd give him fifty cents a head to sell them?" Arnett repeated, "I didn't need any help to sell to Woodman," and walked away.

That settled, Mr. Arnett and I had friendly relations thereafter.

A short time after my activities as a "broker" came to an end, I went to work as foreman for the Dakota Land and Cattle Company at the age of twenty-three. Wilse Richards, A. N. Jefferies, and George Frye were the owners. They were all real cowmen, having begun as cowboys, and they knew all the problems.

Mr. Frye was occupied principally with looking after their land. Therefore, I got my orders from Mr. Richards and Mr. Jefferies, and in time I came to deal almost exclusively with Mr. Richards, who was a remarkable man. The present generation of Americans has heard too much about the bad man's West. I saw the ranches disappear and the settlers come. The West I knew was the good man's West, and it always was. The bad were a minority, and most of them got their just deserts, though at times it seemed long overdue.

It took real men to follow the wagon trail all summer and to be ready for the next spring's work; then to take the hardships all over again, to face storm, hail, rain-swollen creeks, foreboding nights, stampeding cattle, and especially loneliness. A flickering lantern on the side of a chuck wagon on a stormy night can mean a lot to a cowboy.

Wilse Richards was of the breed who had more than the endurance necessary to spend from dawn to dusk in the saddle, and he had the sort of self-sufficiency needed to live for weeks away from human companionship. He also had more than the usual qualities of a cowboy. He was, to start with, a good businessman. He was courageous and always acted on the square. The only reason ever to have any agreement in writing with Wilse Richards was the chance of his death—and he lived to be ninety-one. You couldn't have wrung a lie out of him.

He wasn't the "type" cowboy the present generation hears about. There weren't any such cowboys in my experience; each one was different.

Wilse was older than I, as most of my early acquaintances were, for I'd started on the Goodnight ranch when I was fourteen. He was born in Alabama during the Civil War, but grew up at Mineral Wells, Texas. He'd been a cowhand and freighter, and had trailed a herd to North Dakota for Reynolds Brothers. Later he trailed another herd and decided to stay in North Dakota.

He began his own spread while managing the big Crosby Ranch near Dickinson, and in 1897 he bought it. At one time he leased more than 100,000 acres of Indian land, and he owned thousands of other acres. He developed herds of both purebred Hereford and Angus cattle.

Not only was Richards a leader in developing the livestock industry, but he was interested in the welfare of Dickinson and other towns. A well-built, stocky man, he had a solid, stable look which inspired confidence. If at the turn of the century there had been a Cowboy Hall of Fame almost everybody in western North Dakota would have picked Wilse Richards to be enshrined there (as he was in 1958).

In employing me as foreman, Richards and Jefferies, who talked to me together, told me what they wanted done. I was

159

to find the help I needed, keep it only as long as necessary, buy anything I needed but watch expenses. These things I did. There was some paperwork, but not much.

They also impressed on me that I must cooperate with neighboring cowmen and help them when they needed an extra hand with their cattle. These neighbors would in turn help me, a custom of the country. They were all substantial people; most of them were just starting off in the cattle business. Some of them I'd known as cowboys.

One cowman in the area was John Goodall, who had a record worth mentioning. At one time he'd been foreman on the Marquis de Mores' ranch near Medora. One of his spring roundup pupils there had been Theodore Roosevelt, and he'd made a competent ranch hand out of the future President of the United States, cracking the whip over him and making him work from fourteen to eighteen hours a day. (Goodall is another Cowboy-Hall-of-Famer; he was elected along with Wilse Richards.)

My first assignment with the Dakota Land and Cattle Company was to go to the Fort Berthold Indian Reservation and round up 1,500 steers turned loose there in charge of two men, who were to hold them on 200,000 acres of land. There was no Indian stock on this part of the reservation, and the Indian Agency had given orders that ours had to be moved off.

One of the line riders, Jim Stedman, was an Oklahoman who'd come up the trail a few years before from the XIT Ranch in Texas. The other line rider was John Blocker.* But Blocker had never ridden any, and Jim didn't like to ride. He preferred to cook. The result was that the steers had drifted as they liked, and they were widely scattered.

I hired Jim Wilson, a good Texas cowboy who knew every foot of the reservation and was acquainted with most of the Indians, and three Indian cowboys—Edgar Crowhart, Louie Baker, and Charley Burr. Jim Stedman cooked, and John Blocker became horse wrangler.

In hunting our steers, we worked through our neighbors' cattle. But we hoped to disturb their herds as little as possible, so we didn't round them up. We merely drifted or rode through

* Not the John Blocker of Southwest Texas.

160

them to get any of our own VVV (Three Vees) steers we could locate.

After riding down into the Indian country we crossed creeks and watering places on about 300,000 acres of range land and got 1,365 of our steers. We pushed them on to their summer range on Spring Creek, leaving the missing 135 head for a later search. Then we brought together there stock cattle from Crooked Creek and other steers that had been bought, giving us around 3,000 head of cattle and 40 saddle horses on the summer range. We built our summer camp on land that belonged to Jim Stedman and John Blocker.

That year, 1902, I worked Newton McCollum, a roper. I'd met Newt in 1896 with the Three Sevens outfit and knew what he could do. But when he got to town, he'd get drunk and stay drunk till his last dollar was gone. After that he hung around saloons. He was a real bum. Everybody was always looking for ways to get him out of town. When I became foreman, they asked me if I could take him out and use him for a while. I told them I could, if I could get him sobered up.

We didn't have any corrals to brand in, and our calves were big. Newt was just the man we needed to brand these husky calves. I took him down to the feed stable in Dickinson where he had an old pony and saddle, paid his feed bill there, and took him out to our camp.

Newt couldn't have been made up to look any more like a tramp. He was wearing dirty worn-out boots and a little old hat that looked like anything else but what it was. Still, I knew he was a top roper. I got some discarded sugans—blankets—and made a bed for him. Cowboys don't spend much time investigating the pedigrees of their companions, but the boys wanted to know what I was going to do with that dirty bum. I passed it off by saying that I'd brought him out to sober him up.

Then I announced that we'd get ready to brand the following day. We would, I told them, bring in just a small number, rope the calves, and brand them—as they were too large and nimble for our small crew to bulldog. That was good news for our cowboys; they all wanted to try their luck at roping.

I assigned Newt three old, gentle horses, told him to stay with

161

the wagon, and to start a fire to heat the branding irons. Jim Stedman was to take the chuck wagon, wood, water, and branding irons to where we'd begin rounding up and branding. By the time we got the first roundup completed, Jim and Newt had arrived. I left two boys to hold the herd and the rest of us went to the branding fire.

I told Newt we were ready to bring the calves in. Newt started his horse in a little trot and never slackened. At every throw his rope caught a calf by the heels and his trained eye read the brand of the mother cow. If it wasn't our calf, we put her brand on it.

When branding was over, nobody except Newt had had a chance to get a rope on a calf. He didn't miss a throw. Every loop caught a calf and Newt brought the struggling animal to the fire in a trot. There was no wrestling with the calves—they were down. One man simply held a front foot and another man held the heels till they were marked. Newt kept us all busy in the easiest branding we ever had. When the work was over he left us, and we never saw him again.

We shipped our beef and shaped up our cattle for winter. All stock cattle, cows, calves, and yearlings went to the Crooked Creek Ranch, where Scotty Campbell would feed hay as needed during the winter. I took all steers and saddle horses to the badlands on the north side of the Little Missouri, at the mouth of Cherry Creek in McKenzie County.

This was the home range of the W Bar and Long X cattle companies. I'd ridden this range with those outfits when they controlled all this vast area except about 200,000 acres of Indian land on the Fort Berthold Reservation.

There'd been only a few small ranches on the Big and Little Missouri up to 1900; then the number began to increase. Ranches of smaller cattlemen sprang up on the tributary creeks of the Big and Little Missouri Rivers.

I met many of the new ranchers in this summer of 1902, and I needed to be able to identify many new brands, and the only way I could do it was to get Montana and North Dakota brand books. Since it was open range, cattle wandered a long way from home.

162

A number of the small ranchers didn't have their brands listed in the brand books, so, wanting to have a complete record, I started a brand book of my own. I got the name and monogram of every rancher I heard of and put them in my brand book. I carried these books in my saddle pockets, and could quickly locate the owner of any stray cattle we got in our roundups.

At shipping time the strays were sent to market, and the money they brought was mailed to the owners, if known. If the brand was correct on the shipping list and the owner's name and address were known, there wasn't any charge for inspection at the market. But if there was any doubt and the inspectors had to clip the hair off a cow in order to read the brand, they charged a five-dollar fee. If the owner still wasn't known, the money was sent to the Montana Stockmen's Association. There an inspection of the brand records was made. If they found the owner, they sent the money to him. If the owner wasn't found, the Association kept it.

Frank Brennan, from Wyoming, was head inspector for our states at the Chicago market. I didn't want Frank to get a five-dollar charge against anything that I shipped—and he never did. I was careful about listing all brands correctly, including also the names and addresses of the owners.

In January, 1903, I filed on a homestead on Cherry Creek, a mile from its mouth. There was a state school-land section between me and the creek, and I was six miles down the stream from Robert Monroe.

I conceived the idea of leasing Section 36, which lay between me and the creek, and also leasing Section 16, another school-land section up Cherry Creek. Lying along the stream between Sections 16 and 36 was homestead land which hadn't been claimed by anybody. Four tracts of 40 acres each made up a 160-acre homestead. If I could find four agreeable homesteaders they could align their sixteen 40-acre tracts to take in all the land between Sections 16 and 36, on both sides of the creek. If I could work out an agreement with them, I'd have a good right to the water. I could, in short, be a rancher.

With the idea of leasing this land from them later, I decided to ask four girls to homestead it. They'd be required to retain it

163

for fourteen months and then pay the government $1.25 per acre and prove up on it. I expected to build a log hut on each claim. Under the homestead law, the girls would have to live on the claim for a short period once every six months, two or three nights in the spring and again in the autumn, and the next summer they could prove-up—that is, acquire title.

I went to Dickinson and told Agnes and Eleanor Ray of my plan. They liked the idea. It would be merely a little lark—three trips to the country, horseback riding, and a chance to continue some of the explorations of the Little Missouri badlands they had started when their father owned the Bellows Ranch.

I also went to see Katy Coleman. She like the idea too. Agnes had a friend, Katy Burk, in Valley City, who often visited her. Agnes declared Katy in, and I went back to my claim. It had a good house of hewn logs on it, put there by George Frye for a hunting camp in 1883. I hired Frank McCluskey and put him to cutting logs to build the four claim-houses and posts to fence them with.

When Mr. Frye heard of my plan he agreed it was a good idea to own the water land on Cherry Creek, but he advised me to discard the plan I had for the girls. He said he had a better idea. The United States government issued land scrip to former Union soldiers. It entitled them to 160 acres of public domain, and they could place it on any government land that was open for homesteading. They weren't required to live on it.

Mr. Frye bought old soldiers' scrip and placed it on the four homesteads I had selected for the girls. That ended my plans in that direction.

XVIII. OF PEOPLE AND HORSES

MOST CHAPTERS IN THIS BOOK tell about some event or experience that either changed the course of my life or influenced it in some way. These were the landmarks on my ride through new territory, for they always pointed the way to something else. But to a man in the autumn of life, other, gentler, memories of day-to-day living come crowding back, too. They may seem dull and humdrum to a person who hasn't experienced them, but they—not the lush patches—were the broad prairies of my life. I find these memories boil down to just about two things —the goodness of the people I have known and the appeal horses had for me. Maybe I ought to put the horses first, for I wouldn't be quite honest if I didn't admit that when I think of the Texas Panhandle or the green hills of North Dakota, I am apt to think first of a particular horse, now long since departed. Other horses, too, were my companions in times of hardship and danger, and under the twinkling quiet of summer stars and the warming rays of the sun.

Sometimes you can get a great affection for a contrary horse. We had good saddle horses on the Dakota Land and Cattle Company Ranch. All were gentle, though high-spirited, cow-horses except three which the West called "outlaws." I have a warmer spot in my heart for at least one of those rebels than for the good horses there.

One of the outlaws we called Sunbeam, because when any-body got on him he went through such gyrations that the sun saw more of his belly than his back. Nobody in our outfit was good enough to ride him. We gave him to Ed Partridge, one of the best riders in the country. Ed could ride him but didn't have much heart for it.

"He's too hard a bucker," Ed said. "No horse that hard to ride is worth it."

Ed turned Sunbeam over to Scott Gore, another top rider. Scott could stay aboard, but he wasn't any more enthusiastic about taking the punishment than Ed had been.

Number two of the trio was a lean, limber boy named Bicycle, whose hangout was on Bicycle Creek. Everybody who knew anything about Bicycle called him a mean horse. He didn't like any man, and I was always sure that this was because some man had been cruel to him. Bicycle not only didn't want anybody on his back, he didn't want anybody in his immediate vicinity. He had a bag of tricks to prevent it, too; he'd paw, kick, or bite you if he thought you were poaching. If you got on him he'd buck you off or fall with you, and he had figured out a way of falling that was sure to hurt the rider. I took him into my mount one day and told the other boys, "I'm going to see if I can't make him like me." It was a tough job.

We ran him into a corral, forefooted him, and tied him down. We put a hackamore on him and wired a dried cowhide to his tail so he wouldn't be able to kick it off. We freed him in the round corral for the rest of the day and one night. Then we tied him to a log so big that he could hardly move at all.

I left Bicycle for three more days, without water. Then I went to see if he'd let me rub his nose without biting or pawing me. I found that still got his dander up. I'd been told that a horse could go nine days without water and it wouldn't do him any great harm. That left five more days to go. I knew they'd be hard days on me and I supposed they would be on him. But I steeled myself and said, "Old boy, I'll try you every day, and when you like me enough to let me pet you, I'll lead you to water."

The fifth day I tried him, he was looking bad—drawn and thin—but was still of a disposition to fight. Mr. Jefferies drove by, caught sight of him, and wanted to know what I intended to do with him.

"Mr. Jefferies," I replied, "that's Bicycle. You know, he's an outlaw. I'm going to conquer that fighting spirit and get him so he'll like me. Then he'll get water and I'll be good to him. After that, if he gets bad again, back on that log he goes without water until he learns to behave."

The seventh day I could rub Bicycle's nose, head, and ears. In

166

fact, I could rub him all over. I led him to water, let him drink a little, then tied him back to the log and moved him to fresh grass. After he had grazed for six hours I let him have all the water he wanted.

After I'd petted him some more and let him graze some more, I led him to water again and got the old cowhide loose from his tail while he drank his fill. The third day after the first watering I rode Bicycle. Never again did my convert bite, paw, kick, or buck. Anybody could ride him. He made a good cowhorse, and I had great affection for him.

The third rebel, Cyclone, was a tall gray horse, so named because he bucked in circles. He wasn't too hard to ride, but he'd taken out a patent on the trick of scraping you with his hind foot when you tried to get on him.

I took him in my mount and after so long a time used him for long, hard rides. I tried to tame Cyclone by tying up his right hind foot—his business foot—and mounting him from the left side. After wearing him down by getting off and on while he was trying to kick, I'd rub that left hind leg and let down his foot, which was held by a rope tied to the saddle horn and secured to his foot by a half-hitch.

Cyclone's deportment improved, but he didn't earn any gold stars. He never was safe, and you never could let yourself be caught off guard with him. As long as he was in my mount I always got on him by holding the cheek of the bridle, turning my back to his head, and twisting the stirrup to get my foot into it. As I turned the stirrup loose I grabbed the saddle horn, vaulted into the saddle, and was ready for a hard ride if Cyclone didn't throw me—and he sometimes did. Like a lot of other Rebels in those days, he just didn't take to Reconstruction. He never hurt me much, though. Cowboys get many a bruise, but they heal fast.

In June, 1903, we rounded up to brand. Dick Blackburn, who ran a cafe in Dickinson and also had a ranch west of Killdeer Mountain, came over to work with us. He was an old hand as a roundup cook, and a good one. He said he'd rather cook if Scotty Campbell, our regular cook, would ride, and we could look after any of his cattle when we brought all the herds together. This was agreeable to Scotty, so I gave him six horses in his mount—and included one that I generally rode, a good-looking buckskin that was gentle enough. When we caught our horses that morning Scotty chose this buckskin, whose name was Rondo.

As Scotty mounted, Rondo got scared and took off running. Scotty couldn't hold him. He'd circle and come back to us but wouldn't stop and we couldn't head him off. When Rondo came racing by, I could see Scotty was mad, for some of the boys thought it was funny. I knew it was the wrong time to laugh, for Scotty—a man with a temper—thought he'd been the butt of a joke. I told the boys that Scotty wasn't taking that ride any too well—he obviously thought it was an old trick of Rondo's—and that it wasn't any laughing matter. I was scared as bad as Rondo and worse for Scotty, but I couldn't run and was wondering how I was going to square myself with Scotty.

It was the first time Rondo had ever behaved that way, but how was I going to make Scotty believe it? I had to, somehow, because I'd seen Scotty in action, and I didn't want him mad at me.

Then I saw that Rondo had stopped his running about half a mile from us, and I said, "Now you fellows meet Scotty one at a time and try to convince him Rondo never did that before, and I'll ride out last."

When I reached Scotty, I said, "Let's take a look and see if we can find out what caused that fool to take a notion to run. He's never done that before." I found there wasn't any curb strap on his bridle bit. Curb straps go under a horse's jaw to the bit, so when you pull on the reins you're giving your horse the message that you want to stop. All that time Rondo thought Scotty wanted a wild ride and he was cooperating.

When branding was completed on the twenty-fifth of June Mr. Richards sent Frank Ray, son of my late friend and backer William Ray, to the ranch with a letter telling me that as soon as I could find time he wanted me to take as many men as I needed and scout over the Indian reservation and see if we couldn't get the 135 steers we hadn't found the year before.

Again there wasn't any roundup. We followed the same method we'd used to locate the bulk of the herd. We just scouted—

meaning that we rode through. Each man knew exactly what he was looking for and the place where he was to meet the others so we threw all the cattle together.

After we finished on the reservation, we were to scout all of the range from the reservation west, an area lying between the Big Missouri and the Little Missouri to the town of Schafer and the Birdhead Ranch.

On June 30 Bill Taylor, Frank McCluskey, Frank Ray, and I, with twenty saddle horses—two of them packed—crossed the Little Missouri to Mr. Hans C. Christensen's ranch on the west side of the reservation. Nobody was allowed on the reservation without a permit, and I didn't have one. I decided just to scout it as we had the Long X in 1900. We'd had no trouble on that earlier scouting, but for this trip I decided we ought to take just as few horses and as little equipment on to the reservation as we could get by with.

We left our surplus riding horses, as well as the pack horses, at Mr. Christensen's. Each of us led one extra horse. We planned to eat with the Indians. I knew that Pete Frederick—his wife was an Indian—lived on the Little River, Tom Smith on Hanes Creek, Dick Burr on Shell Creek, and Charley Burr on the Little Missouri. The two Burrs and Smith were Indians. The Reverend Hall lived at Shell Creek Mission, near the Big Missouri. The parson wasn't an Indian, but he'd been a missionary with these Indians for thirty years.

I'd met all these reservation residents before—as well as Wolf Chief, who had a store at Independence, an Indian post on the Big Missouri. I liked every one of those Indians, and I knew that they were clean enough for us to eat with. Their tepees were convenient, too; we could do our work between them and get one or two meals a day. We scouted down the Little Missouri from Tom Smith's to Pete Frederick's, then over to Dick Burr's on Shell Creek.

We were at Shell Creek Mission on July 4, and we watched the Indians celebrate Independence Day. Frank Ray was very much taken with a good-looking Indian girl wearing a white dress, and he made signs to her that he wanted a drink of water. She smiled and said in as good or better English than any of us

169

used, "We haul our water from the river. It's behind that tepee in a barrel. Help yourself."

The corn dance intrigued us. Watching it, Frank located his beautiful Indian maid. The white dress was gone; wearing a shawl and moccasins she was at home with her people, reveling in the dance. Doubtless she was home from college, but she hadn't lost her love for her people and the free life around the campfire. All of them joined in singing ancient tribal songs or beating drums. The old men chanted.

Bill Taylor was extra good at the sign language. He would have liked to linger there, even though we were missing too many meals. But everything we ate with them tasted so good that Frank McCluskey said he'd be content to live with the Indians. However, I was sure we'd all enjoy life more with our own tribe and was hankering to get off that reservation. We were spending the nights as usual—saddles for pillows and blankets for beds.

We hobbled our horses with catch ropes on four, so we could get them at daylight. Then we ate an early breakfast at Charley Burr's and pushed on with our cattle and horses toward Saddle Butte, where we left the cattle and horses and went back to Independence. We were real hungry and all we could think of was filling up on cheese, crackers, sardines, and salmon at Wolf Chief's store. When we got there at four o'clock we found that old Wolf Chief didn't have one thing that we could eat.

We decided to see what the missionary lady had. I introduced myself to Miss McKenzie and told her my errand was to see if she could feed four hungry cowboys. She asked if we'd rather wait till she cooked something or have just a lunch. When she called off what she had for "lunch" it made our mouths water. We didn't see any reason to wait for cooking.

She put the meal on the table while we washed and cleaned up. As spokesman for the group, I thought I'd show my good manners by washing last and I tried to wet and comb my hair so it would stay down. I also did my best to tell Miss McKenzie how grateful we were. She said, "Will you ask the blessing and help the plates for these boys?"

All the boys dropped their heads quick and cut their eyes at me. "Thank you, Lord, for all this good food," I managed to say.

She was so nice and so kind to us that I didn't like the idea of leaving her there all alone, with nobody around but Indians. As we rode away I said to Frank McCluskey, "I, too, know a place on this reservation where I wouldn't mind living."

We each went away carrying a package of food for breakfast. When we got near Saddle Butte it was getting dark, and we camped for the night. On July 6 we got back to the Figure 4 Ranch and had a good supper—and beds. Off came our boots and clothing, for the first time in a long time. We had 95 of our steers in tow.

From Mr. Christensen's ranch we rode back into the reservation and worked his cattle, then went to Henderson Brothers Ranch and continued the sweep along the border of the reservation till we had 125 of those 135 steers.

There were mighty few Indians in North Dakota who'd steal cattle. Most Fort Berthold Reservation Indians lived like honorable men live anywhere. I liked them. I never met one I didn't think was on the square.

From the Hendersons' we worked Jack Williams' cattle and went on to the Bert Dimmick camp and then spent some time seeing if we could locate anything on North Fork Creek. Mr. and Mrs. Jeff Handley and Mack and Thad Uhlman were the only ranchers on North Fork Creek range. We ate with them and made it a point to miss no meals, for those pioneer ladies knew how to touch a cowboy's heart through his stomach. They set the pace that all later settlers followed; hospitality was the order of things. No matter where they came from—Minnesota, Wisconsin, Norway, Germany, Sweden—North Dakota was settled by good people. Up there it was the easiest thing in the world to "love thy neighbor as thyself."

One morning while we were scouting the country around Dimmick Lake a coyote came out of the tall grass. She had six puppies and they were getting large. We'd been losing a lot of calves to coyotes, and that many could lose us a lot more.

I was riding a very useful horse, Good Eye, who got his name because he could keep his eye on anything. If it was a jack rabbit he'd chase it, stop, and turn with it. Good Eye ran down all those

171

puppies, and I knocked each one with the end of my quirt so the boys could put them to a painless end. Good Eye took me so close to the mother coyote that I shot her with my .45.

We drifted through Cal Dodge's cattle that day, and while Bill Taylor and Frank McCluskey drove cattle to Mendenhall Brothers Ranch, Frank Ray and I said we'd go to the Keogh Ranch to look through their cattle—but it was principally to see Frank and Jack's sisters, Sadie and Margaret, who we'd heard were living at the ranch.

Girls were a lot scarcer than steers in that country, and we didn't want to overlook any of them. We also wanted to sample their cooking. But after a long, hard ride we met with disappointment. Nobody was home. Cattle and horses were all we saw.

Then we went up the river to the Birdhead Ranch, where Tom Moat was foreman. Wilse had told me to leave our steers with Tom to ship out. Frank Ray, Frank McCluskey, and I went south seventy-five miles to our camp on Spring Creek, arriving there August 8. Bill Taylor went up the river to Frank Poe's ranch. Mr. and Mrs. Poe were from Texas. Frank was an old Texas cowboy who had worked on the T Anchor near Amarillo in 1882. They had a little girl, Irene, about ten years old, that Bill had been going to see for five or six years. Being that close, he had to see Irene.

Four days later Bill started back to our camp and found the Little Missouri up bank-full. He had a good swimming horse and he made it across all right. On the other side of the river he found a man, his wife, and five children stranded, about out of food, and with no money. They were heading for Regina, Canada, where the man had a job as bricklayer waiting for him. They'd set out from their home in Nebraska, thinking that they had plenty of money to see them through. But there'd been so much rain, mud, and water that their progress had been slower than expected.

When they got to the Little Missouri they felt they had to go on. Their nineteen-year-old boy rode his saddle horse into the high water to see whether or not the team could make it. The swift current swept him under, and they never saw him or the horse again.

172

Free-hearted Bill told me that if he'd had any money with him he'd have given it to them. It was Sunday morning, and we'd heard there were going to be two young preachers at Oakdale, where Mike Cuskelley had put in a post office, a store, and a community center. These were to be the first church services ever held there in the open.

It seemed to me the only thing to do was to go to the church and have the preacher tell his congregation about the family's plight and get him to take up a collection for them. Scotty Campbell advised, "Don't have the preacher do it. Do it your-self and you'll get somewhere."

But I decided I'd better talk to the preacher first and see what he thought. I did, telling him what Bill had told me. He said, "I wouldn't have any part in such a collection. I don't know one thing about those people—whether it's a worthy cause or not. I do have a worthy cause that we're going to ask a donation for."

"I don't know what your worthy cause is," I answered, "but I have a knowledge of ours. A man, his wife, and five children need food. That's as much of a worthy cause as you're likely to meet up with."

After the service was over I got up and asked the people in the congregation to come over to Mike's store. There we told them about our worthy cause. The little handful of men who came got up enough money to buy groceries to last seven people thirty days, and we had twenty-eight dollars in cash left over.

Bill took Mike's team and spring wagon and delivered the things to the family that afternoon.

I guess living helps you recognize a worthy cause when you see it. Those young preachers hadn't done much living.

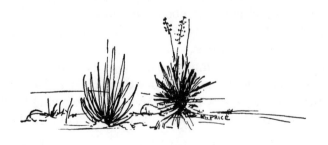

XIX. SOCIAL ITEMS ON THE RANGE

A COWBOY LOVED HIS JOB, as I've been trying to make plain on these pages. If he didn't, he soon left it for an easier life. But a lot of us stayed. I've seen it estimated that during my early years as a cowboy there were thirty-five thousand boys and men in this work.

Still, the old saying about "all work and no play" was as true for us as for anybody else, and we had to have diversions. I'll tell you shortly about three of them—a penny-ante game, another dance, and about entertaining a bunch of deer hunters. The last diversion, as you'll see, was a little different from the first two.

But work always came first, and we didn't think about anything else until we had some time to spare. And July and August were always very busy for us. When North Dakota grass got ripe in those two months it put beef on cattle and weight on horses. This was hard on the horses' hoofs, especially if you were doing a lot of autumn riding shaping up the herd for winter.

A cutting horse has to do a lot of hairpin turns, so it was customary to shoe him before the fall roundup started. Every cowboy did most of his own shoeing, but they helped one another, if help was needed, on what was usually a one-man job. Most horses needed only their hind feet shod, as those were the ones they turned on. This was true almost without exception in the case of dark-hoofed horses, usually tough ones. In the case of white-stockinged legs, the hoofs were always soft and wore off easily. When their hoofs got smooth they were apt to fall. So in August we shod our horses.

Then I began rounding up early and by September 13 had gathered 550 head of cattle. About three o'clock that afternoon it began to snow, and within an hour it was blowing hard. This was a biting snow, and I knew we couldn't hold the herd that night, so we turned them loose and went into camp on Spring Creek, where we had two good log shacks and a horse pasture. Now came some spare time—and the penny-ante game.

I had six men with me—cook, horse wrangler, and four other riders. There were also fifteen "reps"—representatives of other cattle outfits who came to the roundup to gather any of their own cattle that might have mingled with ours.

Twenty-two men couldn't all roll out beds to sleep in, so the game—the most usual pastime for cowboys—got started. It was a sort of draw poker in which nobody was likely to get off with much money. In fact, it was my business to see that it stayed in bounds so nobody got fleeced.

All you could ante was a penny, and bets were limited to from five cents to twenty-five cents, whatever the players set. The game and the storm went on all night, and as the first players got tired they lay down and slept. The next morning it was still snowing and blowing into big drifts, and the game was still under way.

Jim Stedman got three fellows who didn't play poker to help him make coffee and sour-dough biscuits and to fry steak and potatoes. Then by two o'clock clouds began to break and it quit snowing. "The storm's over and so is the game," I said. "The ground's warm, the sun's shining. By noon tomorrow there'll be nothing except some drifts, and tomorrow we have to get five hundred of our herd together—more if we can, because we're going to town." Back to work we went.

But a few weeks later came another chance for diversion. We'd worked the country back to Bill Connolly's ranch and decided to stop there and make up for some lost sleep. Bill wasn't around, but I felt free to use anything of his without asking, knowing we were welcome. We put our cattle in his feed corral, turned our horses loose in his pasture, and camped our wagon at the spring near his house. We got all this done before the cook had supper ready. Then Bill drove up in his spring wagon, accompanied by a well-dressed young lady and two city men from Stoughton, Wisconsin. The men were bankers—George and Read Dow. The young lady was their niece, Miss Georgia D. Townsend, whose mother and uncles were interested in three townships of railroad land they'd bought. They were there to look over their holdings.

Bill came down and said, "There's a young lady up here I want you to meet. She'd like to eat with you cowboys." I told him he knew which way the pleasure lay. Then I met Miss Townsend (now more than half a century later still a close friend). We invited her to have supper at the chuck wagon! She thought it quite a treat.

Then Bill said, "I'll bet Miss Townsend would like to dance with some cowboys. My hayloft's empty, and it's a good place to dance."

Georgia said she'd like that, and I told her, "Miss Townsend, if we can locate a fiddle and somebody to play it, you'll certainly have a chance to dance with some long-haired and whiskered cowboys."

Charley Partridge and I hitched up our lead chuck-wagon team to Bill's spring wagon and drove out to see if we could get one girl and a fiddler. As the big percentage of cowboys then were like me and not very graceful at such things, the dances were mostly square ones. To have four women—one more besides Georgia, Mrs. Connolly, and the Connolly hired girl—we had to get another.

We knew where to find her—six miles east. She was Sophia Beaner. But when we got to Mr. Beaner's house, Sophia said she wouldn't go to the dance unless Sam Pelton was going to be there. She was engaged to Sam and wasn't going to a dance unless he was there.

This was a desperate situation. We didn't know where Sam was. Luckily we didn't let on to Sophia that we didn't know, for to get things going something had to be done. It wasn't that making up some sort of ruse would have bothered Charley or me. We were used to that. It was that we knew any scheme we thought up would be found out in a few hours. We didn't wait long to decide, though. We took the chance.

We told Sophia that Sam would be there, that he'd just gone to his brother's ranch, several miles away, to dress up so he could meet her at the dance. He was expecting us to bring her, we said.

176

Sophia came with us. Ten miles farther on we got Paul Palson and his fiddle. By eleven o'clock we were back at Bill's barn.

The dance started with Sophia, Charley, and me expecting Sam at any moment, but he didn't come. Mrs. Connolly wasn't feeling well, so she couldn't take part. But with a boy taking the place of a girl and one or two sets of boys dancing together, the dance was on.

Panch Arnett showed the most signs of trying to spruce up for the occasion. His hair had grown so long that unless he kept his hat on, stray locks would flop down in his eyes. At the barn he'd found some old sheep shears, which Billy Connolly kept to trim fetlocks, and he'd trimmed the front of his hair almost even with his head. It was a sort of a bangs appearance. He looked cute, and seemed to have a wonderful time.

At two o'clock Dick stopped the dance to serve beefsteak, fried potatoes, corn, hot biscuits, and coffee. It was evident that the first gray-pink streaks of dawn would soon be appearing, and we'd have to tangle with Sophia, no matter what.

Her manner left no doubt that by now she knew we'd lied to her and that she looked upon us as contemptible frauds. Earlier in the evening she'd been cheery-voiced, charming, and delightful. Now she wouldn't dance anymore.

A heavy fog hugged the country for miles around, and nobody could leave until daylight. Time dragged. Still I couldn't muster enough courage to face Sophia.

Just as the first rays of the sun were filtering into the barn I went to Charley, dumped the job of handling Sophia on him, and walked out into the crisp morning air. She was very mad at first, but she got over it. (After she and Sam got married I visited them in their home. By that time she thought our trick amusing.)

It developed that that night of fun in Bill Connolly's hayloft had been a pleasant interlude between a rough fall and a very harsh winter. With Frank McCluskey and Joe Woods to help, I went into winter camp. But from the outset we were to have a lot of company.

November was open deer season, and we got a good many hunters from the eastern part of the state. They'd come to Williston by train, then get a livery man to bring them to Schafer. From there Charley Schafer would bring them to our camp. One day Charley brought ten at one time, and they asked me if they could stay for a few days and hunt. I told them they were welcome if they could find room to sleep in our 20' × 22' shack.

All the furniture we had was a chuck box and stove in one corner, two rolled-up beds, a few homemade stools, and a table. A big tin-covered trunk containing some extra summer and winter clothes we put outside the door. Each of us had a warsack that hung on the wall. In it we kept summer clothes and those we used for winter and weren't wearing at the time. But we never had many extra clothes after we'd dressed for a cold day's ride.

The ten deer hunters moved in with their bedding, extra clothing, and grub. When they all got in we had a bulging house. Their stuff was stacked high against the walls, leaving a little path in the center so we could get around the table. It looked like we were going to have a good time, though, anyway, for these men were pretty jolly and had come out expecting to rough it.

Guy Curr and Frank McCluskey were out riding when the ten men descended on us. I knew they hadn't eaten since breakfast, so I felt that I should have supper ready and not keep them waiting.

When I started to move around to get the meal ready, I found out how really crowded we were. Somebody was in the way every time I wanted to turn around. I wondered if Guy and Frank mightn't think we'd taken in too many lodgers. When they got in they were surprised, but they didn't seem to mind. I was sure, though, that that first flush of good fellowship would soon wear off. There wasn't much I could do about it.

When their ten beds were rolled out on that floor there wasn't enough room for a mouse to get to the door. And getting breakfast the next morning was even worse than getting supper. When Guy and Frank left for the barn to saddle, I went with them to talk it over. I said, "It's crowded, but I don't think they'll be here more than three or four days. I won't charge them anything. I'll tell them, though, to give you boys any tips they

178

want to, to make up for your trouble." That suited Guy and Frank.

We had nine very sociable men, and we enjoyed their company. But there was one—from Rugby, North Dakota—who was in a class by himself. He knew the last word on any subject that came up and looked for the best of everything for himself all the time. Soon nobody liked him.

We were pretty unnerved when we found that the hunters had told the Williston livery-barn man not to come after them for ten days. There wasn't any choice but to bear it. All my time was spent cooking and washing dishes. I'd send Guy and Frank out with pack horses to bring in their deer. Two hunters got four deer, five got five, and three hunters got nothing.

When time came to get to Schafer to meet the livery man I told Frank and Guy to take them. As they were loading the hunters' gear on a sleigh, I came out with my saddle horse. Nine of the hunters wanted to pay me something for the accommodation. I wouldn't take anything, telling them, "I won't charge you anything. If you want to, give Guy and Frank some money to buy themselves some good winter clothing."

An old lawyer from Devil's Lake spoke up, "I'll give them ten dollars." The other eight fell in line with ten dollars each. That was scads of money in those days. Right away I regretted I wasn't in on that deal, but it was Frank's and Guy's.

The Rugby man hadn't said a thing. Frank told me, "He's not going to give anything."

I told Frank and Guy, "You boys take them twelve miles to Schafer. I'll be there soon after you are. Don't let our friend from Rugby unload anything till I arrive. If he doesn't give you the ten dollars willingly, I'll charge him fifteen."

When they got there the Rugby man said, "I'm not paying anything. I brought my own chuck."

When I came up, my boys told me what he'd said. I went over to him.

"You owe me fifteen dollars for furnishing you a place to sleep and for doing your cooking and washing your dishes," I said. "Don't take anything off that sleigh until you give Guy and Frank fifteen dollars."

179

"I'll give them ten dollars like the others did."

"Theirs was a free-will offering. This is a charge, and it's fifteen dollars cash."

He paid it.

From Schafer I rode over to Killdeer Mountain, our summer camp, to attend to some business and to pick up any mail we might have at Oakdale.

There I got a Bible my mother had sent to me. (I have it now, fifty-five years later, much worn but all together.) At the same time I got a box of schoolbooks and a few good storybooks from the Ray family. All the books had the children's names in them —William, Agnes, Eleanor, Frank, Walter, and Donald. The Ray family knew I needed books of all grades.

I'd discovered long before then how limited my education was. Sometimes words came so hard that I had trouble expressing a thought. I studied those books for the next ten years and learned more from them than I'd learned in my brief school days.

XX. SPEAKING OF WEATHER

WEATHER IS UNPREDICTABLE almost everywhere. But I doubt that anywhere else on earth do you get more surprises than in North Dakota, especially in late spring or early autumn. Whatever plans you make are likely to get a climatic rebuff. Sometimes I think the most important requirement for a North Dakota cowboy was that he be able to take sudden weather changes.

October, 1903, was a balmy, delightful month. But early November brought sudden cold, with snow that lasted till April. The Birdhead outfit, of which Tom Moat was foreman, had put seven hundred head of their steers in with ours for us to look after.

There weren't any social affairs close to us. The entire feminine population within twenty miles of us consisted of six ranchers' wives. It was men we met—when we met anybody—as the snow got deeper and the weather colder. The January low was 20 degrees below zero, and the thermometer played around 30 and 40 below for a time.

Rheumatism really took charge of me. I wasn't able to even saddle my horse. One of the boys would saddle him for me, and then I could ride all day—with pain that was at least bearable. But at night I couldn't get much sleep.

Tom Moat wrote me to come over and visit him and we'd go to Williston. I did that, thinking I'd see a doctor who would know some way to help that intense pain.

It was forty miles to the Birdhead Ranch. The snow was deep, and the mercury down to 40 below, so the trip was hardly a pleasure jaunt. It was just fifteen miles up the Big Missouri from Birdhead to Williston.

We started out early the next morning, since Tom wanted to make the round trip that day. As we rode up that bottom we could hear cottonwood trees pop from the cold. It was easy to see the thermometer had lost its grip on the 40s and was plummeting. At Williston it registered 53 below.

I said to Tom, "When you get ready to go back to the ranch, don't wait on me. I'm going to get a room at the Great Northern Hotel and stay there till that thermometer shows me it can climb up to the 20's."

When I saw the doctor he asked, "When did you come in?" "Today," I told him. He gave me a long look and commented: "If a man with your kind of rheumatism will go out on a day like this, he's wasting his time going to a doctor."

He rubbed me with some sort of burning liniment, gave me a bottle of it, and told me to stay in a warm place. There was nothing more he could do for me. For six days I stayed in the hotel, rubbed on the liniment, and rested till the thermometer rose to 30 below. Then I rode out to Birdhead and on to our camp on Cherry Creek.

181

The bitter cold was taking its toll. All the cattle looked scrawny. We just had feed for the saddle horses we rode. All we could do was to get around and see where the cattle were. They'd made their way into coulees or brushy places on the river or creeks. There wasn't a chance for them to get any grass. The few points, on hills, where the wind kept the snow whipped off the grass were so cold that nothing but a polar bear would have had enough blubber to stay there long enough to graze.

In the river and creek bottoms the cattle ate the sage brush down to stubs. Any brush as big as your finger was nipped off. We covered some part of the range every day trying to do everything we possibly could, like not letting too many of them bunch up in one brush patch or get blocked by snow drifts, which would bank high around the patches. Cattle won't break trails for themselves through snow, so we'd ride our horses back and forth to make a path for them so they could get out if there were too many in one place.

There was gloom on all nearby ranches, with everybody certain they were taking heavy losses. Feed lots were hit heavy. Nearly everybody ran short of hay, and that was all anybody fed in those days. Feed lots could count their losses every day, for their cattle were huddled. We couldn't, for ours were too scattered. Those we did see all looked like they were going to die.

We heard of some good cowmen who were working their cattle out of the brush patches and driving them up on hills where there was a little grass. But in that cold the cattle would stay only as long as the men kept them company and made them stay.

I was in a situation where I had to use my judgment. I decided I wouldn't follow the example of those who were driving cattle to high places. Going through deep snow took strength, and I thought the cold and cutting wind would probably keep them from grazing. Then more strength was sapped getting back to the brush.

When I saw three dead steers, one of them with an HK brand —the brand on sixty-five head I had bought for myself—I began to mistrust myself. Still my judgment kept telling me not to drive those cattle through the deep snow but to let them keep all the strength they could—if they were going to die anyway

182

there wasn't any reason to take them to the hills. I stood by that judgment till I saw some more dead ones, including four HKs.

On March 15 it was still storming and was a long way to warm weather and green grass. I said to Guy, "You and Frank keep riding. Do just like we've been doing. I'm going to Dickinson and see Wilse Richards; I want him to know how this deal looks and how we've been handling it. He might know somebody he thinks could handle it better. If he does, he can send him out to head up this job."

I rode that seventy-five miles to Dickinson through biting cold and deep snow. On the eighteenth I walked into Wilse's office. He smiled when he caught sight of me and said, "How're you, Billie? What brought you in in this kind of weather? Does it look so bad you figured we were going broke and you'd better come in and collect what pay you have coming?"

"I don't think I'll have anything coming for a long time," I answered sadly; "not till I get those HK steers paid for, and they're all dying. And if those steers of yours were the only prospects you had for keeping you out of bankruptcy you'd be in bad shape, too. But I'm not thinking about myself. I know I'm broke, but I'm used to that. It's the way I'm handling your property that's got me worried."

"The only thing that's worrying me, Billie, is the suffering the cattle are having to go through," Wilse said. "Let's not worry about anything else. We won't go broke even if we lose them all. We'll get some more in the spring and you'll have a job."

He asked how many I thought were dead.

"I've seen only a few dead," I answered. "I saw five HK steers and probably there are at least that many more. All the rest are mighty thin. My guess is that 20 per cent of my HKs are dead now and 10 per cent of your Texas steers. If this keeps up for thirty more days it's doubtful if any will be left, with all of them already looking like they've had about all they can stand."

He commented that I was giving him a pretty gloomy report, and I went on:

"I know it. But I didn't see anything out there to report on that would have sounded any better. I wish I had. I came in to tell you just what we've been doing—and it's not very much."

I told him how I had handled our cattle and how other good cowmen—men he knew—were handling theirs different.

"There're days," I told him, "when storms are raging so we don't go out at all. But as I see it, we couldn't do any good. Other men come to our camp on such days getting their cattle out of the brush and trying to get them to grass, while we don't do anything till the storm's over. News travels even through snow-storms, and I wanted to give you my report firsthand. I have to go on my own judgment, not on what somebody else does. I'm in here to give a full accounting. If you know somebody else who can do a better job, send him out. It won't make me mad."

"I've had no bad report about how you're handling your out-fit," Wilse said, "and I've never had one. But even if I had, it wouldn't make any difference to me, for I know what you're doing and your judgment suits me. No matter how we come out in the spring I'll know you did your best."

I rode back to camp in a different frame of mind. I hardly noticed the snow and cold wind after this expression of confidence. Even the rheumatism wasn't so bad and some of those miserable old steers began to look like they'd make it till grass came. There's nothing like a pat on the back to raise your spirits.

I sent Frank and Guy to Oakdale to Mike Cuskelly's store to get enough groceries to last through spring roundup. We'd thus be stocked up before the snow melted and high water came, and we'd be ready to get right to work.

Wilse and Tod Richards and Frank Banks had bought the Birdhead Ranch. Frank and Wilse were old friends who'd come up the trail together with a Long X herd from Texas in 1885. Banks was foreman and manager of the ranch. He came over to find out when we'd start the roundup and to ask what I thought was left over from the hard winter.

"We won't know till we round up and tally them," I answered. "The first thing I want to do is go through these river-bottom brush patches. There're some old Long X steers in here that were here last year. I don't know how long they've been running wild. We'll have to get them early in the morning. They come out at night to graze. After sunup they go back in the brush and you can't get them out.

184

"My idea is not to wait till spring roundup for them, but to get them just as soon as the Little Missouri goes down to where we can cross it without swimming. They range on both sides of the river, and they don't mind swimming it. We want to get them, because we have steers with them. Their bunch gets bigger every year."

"Let me know when you're ready," Banks said, "and I'll come with two good men."

I told him I had two men, Guy Curr and Frank McCluskey, who didn't know any better than to follow a cow wherever she went. With his men we'd have help enough if we could just catch the Long X animals out of the brush.

When the river got to where we could ford it, I sent for Banks, and he came with his two men. We already had the wild bunch spotted. They were ranging on our side of the river and down it two miles from our camp. We had to ride over slick, muddy hills that still had some snowdrifts on them to get there.

We found the cattle. Sure enough, they were grazing toward the hills at daylight and then at sunup they'd turn back toward the brush. I gave Guy one of my winter-fed horses—a rangy sorrel, easy to manage and fast. He'd go anywhere you wanted him to.

With our six-shooters ready to fire to keep the steers out of the brush, we sallied forth on our best horses. We had to get rid of these wild animals, for they were getting others to join them each year. We slipped around them and made for the brush, keeping out of their sight. We could see them peacefully munching their way toward the hills.

We got down to let our horses rest while we took a smoke and waited for the sun to come over the hills. We knew that was when the herd—unless it had a change of plan—would turn back toward the brush. When it did, it was time to rush them. Everybody was to blaze away with his six-shooter, to make enough noise to turn them toward the hills again.

But those dumb beasts weren't so dumb. When we fired our volley they made for the river alongside the hills. Knowing there was a bank there ten or twelve feet above swimming water, we thought we'd outguessed them. But we hadn't. They went right

185

over the bank and hit the water swimming, with Guy Curr and his speedy horse Slivers right with them. Both man and horse knew exactly what they wanted to do, but just in case the horse might lag Guy was using his quirt and spurs for all he was worth. He was able to get into a spot where he could hold the cattle on a sandbar till the rest of us rode down the river to a place we could ford.

Guy and Slivers had saved the day. We got the wild cattle to our camp and corralled them. Banks took them to Birdhead, thirty-five miles from their range. That ended the wild cattle in our area.

When spring came, our cattle drifted out north and west on Spring Creek to its mouth on Cherry Creek, then up and down Cherry Creek. There we had a big spring roundup. Every cowman in the country had cattle in that lowing mass. There were at least six thousand head brought together.

At this time I had another duty. Wilse had written to me about an old cowboy friend, Milton Brooks, a capable man he wanted me to try to straighten out. Milton's weakness was liquor, and when he got fired-up he didn't cool off easy. Wilse told me that Milton didn't know how to stop by himself, and he thought I could help him.

Wilse had heard that Milton was at Schafer, where there was a "blind pig" that sold a vile sort of drink. He wanted me to go over there and get him. The only time I'd be able to spare would be the night before we started screening out the big herd the next day. Once that job began everybody would be busy till it was finished. After that we'd be shorthanded in getting our cattle to the summer range on Spring Creek and Killdeer Mountain, and everybody else would be busy moving their cattle home at the same time. We could certainly use an extra cowhand.

So, after supper, Banks's man Lin Rivets, Frank McCluskey, and I rode the five or six miles down to Schafer to get Milton. He acted glad to see us and was enthusiastic about going back with us. Getting out on a spring roundup was exactly what he wanted to do, he said. Frank went to the barn, saddled Milton's horse, and brought it over and tied it with ours.

186

Milton had been there two weeks, drinking heavy. It was easy to see he was pretty well shot. I told him we'd take a pint with us, that he might need it in the morning.

"I don't think I'll need it," he said, "but as long as you're going to take a bottle you might as well take a quart."

"All right, Milton," I agreed. "What you say goes. Let's go. We've got a big day's work tomorrow."

Milton stepped back to a chair, sat down, and said, "Billie, I've just been thinking. I'm real happy you boys came to see me. Now, you fellows go work that big herd, drift them to their summer range, and I'll meet you at the home ranch across the big divide." And there wasn't anything we could do or say to budge him.

We divided the big herd into three parts and made three cuts. Experienced men were on the job and at four o'clock in the afternoon everything was cleaned up and the herds—north, east, and west—were on their way home. Next day we crossed the Little Missouri, strung them out, and made a count. We had 95 per cent of our count that had crossed the river in October. I had sixty of my own HK steers. The five dead ones I had seen were all I'd lost. I learned this lesson from that bitter winter of 1903–1904: Be an optimist till there isn't any hope. Then it's too late to be a pessimist.

This summer was a quiet one for the Dakota Land and Cattle Company. No new cattle were put in. Some land was sold and some homesteads were taken on what had been our range. With the range getting crowded, the herd was cut down at beef-shipping time.

Goob Saunders and I faithfully rode the range, not only to see where our cattle were and how they were doing, but with some romantic notions also. There'd been a big influx of settlers, and we wanted to find out whether they had daughters—and if so what the daughters looked like. Some of the new girls were old enough to file on homesteads, and we were on the lookout to see if any of them were on our range.

Georgia Townsend had filed on her land fifteen miles east, near Bill Connolly's ranch, and was closest to us. Her father had told her that he'd give her a section of land if she'd give up the

187

idea of homesteading. But she wanted to do what some other girls she knew had done—earn her own land. It wasn't hard to do. She lived at Bill Connolly's, kept a horse, and inspected her acreage now and then. Goob and I liked that.

Mr. and Mrs. Connolly were fine people. Mrs. Connolly always had a big assortment of good things to eat. On our visits to their home we usually saw Georgia, who was good-looking and friendly. We went there often. We were certain that if we had any cattle mingling with Bill's they were on good grass and we'd see them at the beef roundup anyway. So we looked after other things we were interested in.

Beef roundup came in September. We shipped all Texas steers and all other fat four-year-olds. We also shipped the HK steers I'd bought and they paid out well. The Dakota Land and Cattle Company didn't lose many of the steers that wintered in the badlands, for they were three- and four-year-olds. Their biggest loss was in the stock cattle around feed lots. That was pretty generally true throughout the whole range country.

After shipping, Goob said he'd give a dance before we picked up the cattle we were going to move to winter quarters. He had a big two-room rock house. We took everything out and scrubbed the floors. Word was sent for miles around. There were so few ladies in our range—and even these widely scattered—we had the problem of rounding up enough of them. But we were young, brave, and hopeful. We went ahead with plans.

The day of the dance the floor looked clean, but it was too rough. It was just seven miles to Oakdale. I got on old Cyclone and loped over to see if Mike Cuskelley had any floor wax in stock. He did. I got a box and Mike put it in a big sack so I could carry it easily. But as I mounted Cyclone the sack rattled and scared him. He threw me before I could get settled in the saddle. I landed on rocky ground and it peeled the skin off one side of my face. That ended any chance for me to "cut a shine" at the social event, for there were some handsome boys who'd be there.

With one side of my face peeled, I kept wishing it was going to be a masked ball. Then we found that we had delayed the dance too long anyway. Georgia had gone back to her home in Wisconsin for the winter and some other young ladies had left.

Only Mrs. Austin Pelton and two women I'd never met showed up. Thirty-five boys came. We put handkerchiefs around our arms so you could tell a lady from a gentleman and had a very good time—for a bunch of disappointed cowboys.

Then we started the roundup. Rain and snow started at the same time. For days, when it wasn't snowing it was sleeting or raining. The work was going at a snail's pace. Under these conditions the cattle were naturally hard to handle. It was November before we got the stock cattle to Crooked Creek Ranch and moved the steers and saddle horses to our winter camp on Cherry Creek.

The old rheumatism was giving me fits. Dick Blackburn had been with us all during the work and knew what I was going through.

"Why don't you quit trying to ride in winter?" he said. "Stay in a warm place until spring. I'll give you $100 a month and pay your room rent to go to Dickinson and take charge of my cafe until spring. You can be warm there. I want to stay on the ranch with my cattle this winter, as it looks like it might be another hard one."

"Your offer sounds good, Dick," I replied. "It might be best to do that. I'll get these cattle across the river to their winter range and settled down a little. After that I can leave Adam Blank and Frank McCluskey with them. If I decide to do it I'll come over to your ranch in a few days."

When we got to Cherry Creek I wasn't any better. My arms and shoulders were so bad I couldn't saddle my horse. I decided to go to town. Wilse Richards thought I was doing the right thing to get out of the harsh weather. Wilse's bank was just three doors from Dick's cafe.

I saw Wilse practically every day. I liked that, for I had grown extremely fond of him. If he had a fault I never discovered it. He was always in a good humor, and I never knew a man who had more balance or a deeper sense of fairness. We were closing out the Dakota Land and Cattle Company and I never worked for him again, but we remained close friends until his death.

XXI. BACK TO THE CATTLE

DICK BLACKBURN was an old roundup cook who worked fast when he had a job to do. He believed in doing it as well or better than anybody. I'd been around him a great deal, and liked the way he moved and his jolly manner.

He was what we call "middle-aged" when he married a girl from Ireland. There were several of those good-looking Irish girls in Dickinson, and Dick wanted a family. He soon got one.

First year, a baby girl. Next year, twin boys. The third year, triplets—Faith, Hope, and Charity. In three years Dick had himself a wife, six children, a cafe, and a cattle ranch. He was established as a man who accomplished things.

I was proud to do business with him, for he was honest, respected, and well liked. With a few words he turned the cafe over to me by telling the help that I was in charge and that it was my responsibility to hire or fire as I saw fit. He said to me, "You know how to run this business. It's all up to you. If the weather's not too bad I'll see you Christmas. I have to get out to the ranch." And he was gone.

All the people who worked at the cafe—mostly Irish girls— knew how to handle their jobs, so I didn't have any greenhorn trouble. Maggie and Delia were the cooks.

This was a pleasant, though could, winter. I rented the same room with Mrs. Frank Lish I'd had when I'd been in my own cafe business, and her house became one of my homes. I had great affection for the Lishes and their children—Emma, Beatrice, John, Peter, and Marguerite. Lucille had been their baby girl when I'd been there some years before. But she had died, and Marguerite now was their baby—two or three years old. She soon became my sweetheart.

I'd found out that was about the proper age for a sweetheart. My experience has been that if you want a sweetheart to stay with you, you have to start early. I gave Marguerite a rag doll which she carried around so much she wore it out. Her mother wanted to throw it away, but Marguerite clung to it, saying, "Billie gave it to me." She kept it till she got married, though it wouldn't have cut much ice in a "breach of promise" suit.

Dick Blackburn came in to spend Christmas with us, then went back to his cattle, for it was another hard winter. I was in a warm place, so I seldom had a rheumatic pain. Everything moved on smoothly until the night of March 11, 1905, when a fire broke out in the building next to us. I'd just started for home, about eleven o'clock. It was very cold, and deep snow.

The burning buildings were all made of wood, and I could see that our cafe was soon going. I knew Dick probably didn't have enough insurance to cover everything, so I got everybody around to help carry out the cash register and all the papers, first, then the cigar showcase and the rest of our stock. I stood out in the street and guarded the stock, which had got soaked by the fire hose. I waited in an icy wind till a dray could get there. When it was loaded I sent the stuff to Dick's house to be put in his basement. Then I hurried to the St. Charles Hotel lobby to get warm.

I pulled a chair as close up to a radiator as I could and tried to unthaw. Fred Dickinson and I were talking about the fire when a severe pain struck me in the elbow. I said, "Fred, it's two o'clock and this pain is getting me. I'm going home."

I undressed and went to bed, but not to sleep. It was a long time till six o'clock—when Mr. and Mrs. Lish usually got up. I decided I'd dress and go downstairs. I got up but couldn't dress myself. That left arm felt like it was paralyzed. I couldn't use it, couldn't even move it without lifting it with the right hand. I lay back down, thinking that if they were having pancakes for breakfast Mrs. Lish would send Frank up to wake me—she knew that was my favorite breakfast. If she didn't do this I didn't know how I'd get dressed, without help. Still, I didn't want to tell anybody I was in such bad shape, for I thought I'd get better in a little while.

When I heard Frank coming up the steps I knew I'd have to tell him, for Mrs. Lish was surely inviting me to breakfast and she knew I wouldn't turn down her invitation without some mighty good reason.

Frank helped me dress. Those pancakes looked good, but I could eat only a part of one. I usually made way with from six to twelve, so Mrs. Lish knew I must be in bad shape. She had Frank put me in their bed so she could look after me till she got a doctor.

We sent for Dr. Perkins. He was a young physician who'd come to Dickinson in 1898. Before he married he and I had been pals, and I liked him. He couldn't determine exactly what was wrong, but said it was something so serious that he'd have to take me to the hospital.

There we discovered that I had inflammatory rheumatism. The swelling was so bad from my shoulder to the tips of my fingers that I couldn't move a finger. The pain was centered in my elbow joint; it throbbed steadily for fifteen days and nights. Dr. Perkins couldn't find any way to ease it, and I got no sleep without drugs. He gave me drugs every twenty-four hours—all he thought my heart would stand. It didn't take Dr. Perkins long to become discouraged. I think he must have read up on all the worst that could happen and he told it to me. "If I can't move that pain in ten days it might leave your arm so crippled you'll never be able to use it again."

Ten days passed; the pain hadn't budged and the swelling was just as bad as ever. Then he said, "If I can move it down, good. But if it goes up to your shoulder it might go to your heart, and that would be too bad. Let me write your folks and tell them about your condition."

"No, Doctor," I said. "That would only cause them to worry, and we don't know where this pain is going or if it's going anywhere else. If it does go to my heart, then you write and tell them what happened. That's soon enough."

"I'm going to have Dr. Stickney and Dr. Davis come in tomorrow morning," he said, "and see if they can suggest anything."

They came in, looked me over, and reviewed Dr. Perkins' report of what he was doing. Then they told me cheerfully,

"Your doctor's doing all he can. In a few days you'll know you're on the road to recovery. Nobody could do any more than Dr. Perkins is doing. He just has a stubborn case."

At noon Dr. Victor H. Stickney returned and said, "I came back because I wanted to talk to you alone. Dr. Perkins has your case at heart and he's doing the best anybody can do. But he's made one mistake—he's become discouraged and has let you know it. That's bad for him and worse for you.

"Forget this talk about a crippled arm or the pain going to your heart. [I knew Dr. Perkins had told him this; I hadn't.] You're going to be all right. I'm leaving for St. Paul on the train this afternoon. I know a specialist there and I'm going to see him. If he thinks he can do any good by coming to see you I'll send him up here and pay all the expenses myself. So don't fret about that.

"Suppose that pain did leave you with a bad arm, there'd still be plenty things you can do. Mrs. Jack Linberger has her restaurant and bakery up for sale. I've got $85,000 in the First National Bank, and I'll help you start something you can handle. I also have a good many cattle scattered around the country. We can start a ranch and you can run it. Don't lie here and worry because your left arm might not be as good as the right one."

When Dr. Stickney left, I was in a completely different frame of mind. Three days later the pain did go to my shoulder, but it wasn't so severe. I went to sleep without a drug.

I was soon up and around the hospital but in no hurry to leave, for I liked it there. I had lots of visitors—and I became very fond of the nurses who put in every spare minute they had massaging my arm and trying to relieve the pain. Johnnie Goodall and his wife had a room there for a short stay, being there only because there was a spare room.

As soon as I could get downtown I visited Wilse Richards at the bank. He told me that most of the Dakota Land and Cattle Company saddle horses had been sold to Arnett and Jefferies, who'd put four thousand steers on the Fort Berthold Reservation, and that Dick Arnett was foreman. He said, "When you get so you can ride I'll have something worked out for you."

193

Dr. Stickney had been on my mind ever since he'd given me that boost of morale in the hospital. I knew I didn't want a restaurant or bakery if I could ride a horse, but my arm was still in a sling, and I hadn't been able to straighten it out. But I didn't want a ranch if I couldn't work. Dr. Stickney had good men looking after his cattle, and he certainly wouldn't want to take the cattle away from them. I said to myself, "I'll go over to his office, see if he's in, and have a little visit with him, anyway. That might have just been booster talk, and he might not say anything more about it."

He was in his office. He looked at my arm and said, "It's going to be all right. Rub it often and try to straighten it out every few hours, but watch out that you don't make it sore. What do you want to do—buy out Mrs. Linberger or start a ranch?"

"Doctor," I replied, "I've thought a great deal about that talk you gave me at the hospital. You gave me the lift that got me out so soon and I'll never quit thanking you for it. But I don't want a town business if I can ride a horse. And I don't want a ranch if I can't make a ranch hand. To do any good with a ranch you've got to take the lead and say, '*Let's* do it,' not 'You do it' for everything. I don't see how I can plan my future yet.

"I've been wondering how a doctor in this small town and the thinly settled country could get together so much money."

He laughed and said, "I have a practice ranging from 100 to 150 miles north, south, and west, and some east. Not many people get sick, but sometimes horses fall on them and break their bones. Some get shot. None of my patients ever die. Oh, sometimes they're dead when I get there, and I don't charge them anything. In fact, I've never yet sent out a bill or asked anybody to pay me. I think everybody pays who can, and if they can't, they don't owe me anything. I'm just a doctor, not a collector. Most of my money is in bank stock. That's fared well. Then I have those cattle."

Dr. Stickney was a special breed of man. I never missed a chance to visit with him.

About this time Billy Marsh came to visit me. He was an Indian who'd been left an orphan when quite young and he'd been raised by a white family near Mandan, North Dakota. He'd worked for the William Badger Cattle Company around Mandan, then had started ranching on the Fort Berthold Reservation. I knew Billy well; I'd stopped at his ranch and met his wife and their two children.

He asked me what I was going to do that summer. I told him I wouldn't know till I got the arm out of the sling.

Billy said, "Come stay with me till you can ride a horse. Billy Badger said he'd put in a thousand one- and two-year-old steers for me in May. If you're able I'd like for you to take an outfit down there and get them for me. He's wintering them on Standing Rock [Sioux] Reservation."

I went with him. Every day I got better, and soon I could saddle my own horse.

In May the grass was getting green, and we went after the steers. That kept me busy for a while.

Then in 1905 I went to work managing the HE outfit for Hiram Eliott, who had learned the cattle business while working for Charles Haas Commission Company of St. Paul. He was industrious and alert, but his knowledge of handling cattle on the range was limited.

Mr. Elliott was puzzled about what to do when he saw conditions. Few of his cattle could be located. He and Robert Cochran, who was then in charge of the ranch, talked it over with Frank Banks, an old cowman whose advice they felt they could rely on. Banks told Mr. Elliott that the Dakota Land and Cattle Company had closed out most of their cattle the past fall, that I was no longer with them, and that I was somewhere on the Indian reservation. If I'd take their outfit, Banks said, he was sure I'd find a solution to their problem.

Mr. Elliott sent for me, and we talked for quite awhile about their troubles. My idea was that the best thing to do was to cut their herd as soon as possible, ship all beef, cut them close that fall, and take all the steers to my place in the badlands for the winter. The stock cattle could winter at their ranch. The next summer we'd ship everything that looked good, and the next fall we'd cut their herd till it would be easy to handle.

This plan suited Mr. Elliott. He returned to Duluth and left the HE cattle problems to Robert and me.

I went back to the reservation for my warsack and bed—and to visit with Frank Keogh. I told him what I'd done and the problems I could expect. Frank, in turn, told me what he was planning. He had several thousand cattle; good cowboys were hard to find; the reservation was open country with no fences. He wanted me to stay with him. They were starting to fence the reservation and they'd bought the Dakota Land and Cattle Company's saddle horses—my old horses—and I could pick my mount. I was fond of Frank, and those old horses and I were friends.

"But I promised Mr. Elliott," I told him. "I think he's a top-notch man and he's depending on me to carry out his plans for a year or two. I can't disappoint him."

Mr. Elliott's ranch was in McKenzie County, the largest county in the state. Some boasted that it was larger than some of the New England states. It is bounded on the north and part of the east by the Big Missouri, on the southwest by Dunn County, and on the south by Billings and Golden Valley Counties. It was called the "Inland Empire" because so much of its boundary was water.

This vast range of McKenzie County, when I first rode it in 1899–1900, was primarily controlled by the W Bar and Long X, and a few smaller outfits. It was called the cowman's paradise —it had fine grass and springs and creeks, but no taxes, no county offices to fill, no political strife, no schools, churches, jails, or poorhouses, no roads or bridges. To these pioneer people, the burdens and benefits of organized society were unknown.

The first census taken in McKenzie County, in 1890, showed a population of twenty-seven persons, including three women and one child. George Shafer, whom I first met in 1902, was the child. He was then fourteen years old, a boy with good manners, intelligent and friendly. Later I was happy to see him climb the ladder of fame—first to County Attorney, then Attorney General, and finally the first native-born and youngest Governor of his state.

But in 1905, when my connection with Mr. Elliott began, there were big changes for McKenzie County. It was organized, and when this happened the last of the romantic West was gone, voted out in favor of book law and order.

One holiday season during my time with Mr. Elliott was really memorable. I rode out to the HE headquarters to visit with Robert Cochran. On New Year's Day, on my way back to my camp, I went by the Schafer post office and got some mail. While I was answering two or three letters, a pain struck my back. I went out and got on my horse. It was twelve miles to camp and that pain got worse all the time. I had to ride in a slow walk.

When I got to camp after dark, I couldn't dismount. The boys came out and carried me in. In those days we didn't have first-aid kits or a dose of any kind of medicine; we weren't prepared for anything except snake bites. Sam Adams sat up all night heating salt as a poultice on my kidneys, but the pain didn't let up.

Next morning the boys went to the barn getting ready for their day's ride. Sam told them, "I'm scared we'll haul Billie out of here. It looks like we're too late to do much. There's a swelling in his kidneys and they're turning dark. They're full of poison, and the pain is so bad he can't stand it long."

While he was talking the old milk cow let go a dropping.

"There's my poultice!" Sam said.

He grabbed a feed bucket and got his poultice material into it while it was warm. Then he got a flour sack, made the poultice, and applied it over my kidneys. In less than two hours I was asleep. The cow kept Sam supplied with his remedy, and he kept me supplied with the applications for forty-eight hours. The third day I was up and going all right. A milk cow is good for more things than one.

I spent the winter of 1906–07 at the HE headquarters. In February Mr. Elliott came out. The herd was pared down and easy to handle. I talked it over with him, and in March I resigned. I traded my Cherry Creek camp to Fred Madison for horses. Fred wanted it for his sons, Nels and Andrew, and I wanted to get behind the Fort Berthold Indian Reservation fence with Frank Keogh.

XXII. THE CHANGING TIMES

WHEN I BECAME STRAW BOSS for Frank Keogh on April 1, 1907, I was just where I wanted to be. The admiration I'd had for Frank since the day I met him in 1902 had grown into affection. In those five years we'd built up a friendship that lasted for forty-eight years more till Frank died.

Although I can bring to memory a whole album of cherished friends, I still don't believe I ever had any other quite like him. He was older than I but nearer my age than any of the men I'd had close relations with up to this time.

Born in Benson, Minnesota, he'd come with his parents to western North Dakota in his boyhood and grew up there. Frank came as close to being a typical North Dakotan as anybody I knew, but he could hardly be called "typical." He was a man apart, extraordinary in every way.

He had plenty of Irish temper but he knew how to control it. He thought, moved, and acted with quickness and good judgment. His high standards didn't vary, whether he was in a cow camp, on shipping trips to Chicago or St. Paul, or in his own home. To me it was good just to be associated with him. His strength bolstered me many a time.

One of our first jobs together was to move four thousand head of cattle from Dickinson to the reservation. During the trip we saw how quickly the country was being settled now. The big shipping days for Dickinson were obviously at an end. For a distance of twenty miles there wasn't any place to stop and graze a herd. That was my last trip to the Dickinson stockyards.

At the ranch that spring and early summer we rounded up stock horses, branded colts, and then began calf-branding. It was a busy time. Georgia Townsend was proving up on her homestead and going back to her home in Cambridge, Wisconsin. She gave a farewell party, but we couldn't get away from our work to go.

Then when I could get away I had to make a business trip to Schafer, the county seat. When I left, Frank was having trouble with his appendix. He told me that when I got back we'd go to Sam Rhodes and buy some saddle horses.

When I got back nobody knew where he was. He'd been gone three days and I was worried. I'd seen him become so sick he had to get off his horse and lie on the ground for an hour or two until the pain in his side eased enough for him to ride again. Now I could imagine him at some vacant winter camp—or perhaps he'd made it to some creek or spring. He might even have made it to the shade of a tree—or maybe he was out on the bald prairie, suffering in the sun. I immediately started on a manhunt over a 212,000-acre pasture. Talk about looking for a needle!

I told some of the boys to ride the Little Missouri and look for tracks, and others to go to Clark's Creek camp and look along the creek. Others went to Bear Den and Boggy Creek camps. We'd ride every inch of the pasture, I said, and try to find Frank's horse, which would give us an idea where Frank was.

I rode to the west line of fence and went out to the ranches to see if anybody had seen him. Nobody seemed excited when I told them Frank was lost. Even his sisters, Sadie and Margaret, said, "Oh, he's just ridden off somewhere. He'll show up before long."

But this assurance didn't convince me. The next day at noon all the boys and I met at the Smith place, our headquarters. Nobody had seen Frank or his horse. The two men who'd covered the Little Missouri area had seen a horse's tracks in the sand at Manning Crossing, but the tracks didn't look recent, and the river was bank-to-bank full.

I told them that we'd eat dinner, catch fresh horses, and ride the range. We had to find Frank before we did anything else.

While we were eating, Frank and Sam Rhodes rode up with a bunch of young saddle horses. What had happened was that while I was gone he got to feeling a little better and rode across the Little Missouri to Bill Connolly's ranch to see Georgia Townsend and explain why we'd had to miss her party. When he got back to the river it was up. He then decided to go on to Sam's place and buy the horses. But he hadn't told anybody where he was going. Everybody gave me the horse laugh, but Frank didn't ride out again without letting somebody know where he was going.

About this time Frank Poe, the sheriff, got me to take the oath to be his deputy. The first thing Poe had me do was to look for any Indian that might have seen two men with six horses cross the Big Missouri somewhere. The horses had been stolen from Bill Day, a farmer near Watford City. We found six Indians who had helped cross the horses—Jim Baker, Spotted Horn, Bassett, and three others whose names I don't remember.

Jim Baker spoke pretty good English, so he was interpreter for the others. We went to the county seat, Schafer. Court was to open the next morning. Poe told me he had two suspects. He wanted me to take my six Indians to Hilderbrant's Hotel and let them look out of a front window while John Richardson, another deputy, walked the suspects down the street to see if the Indians could identify them. The Indians recognized them, and I recognized one of them, too. He was my old friend, Bob Miller, who'd shipped horses from Dickinson to Muskogee, Oklahoma, in October, 1900. At that time, as I've said, I visited his home and met his wife and two children, a boy and a girl. Miller was a man high in Masonry, and enjoyed a prominent place in his community. I'd heard that he was living in Williston, but I hadn't had a chance to meet him there.

Now we met Bob and another man, both suspected of horse stealing, and the Indians had identified them!

Bob seemed glad to see me and talked about the trip we'd made seven years before. But he was very sad, and I felt almost as bad as he did. What a price to pay for Mr. Day's horses—and Mr. Day got them back!

Court was delayed a few days. Bob and his partner were locked up in the little jail. I went to see him again.

Bob said to me, "Billie, you know I'm not guilty of this crime. I want to post bail and get out of this jail."

"I wish I did know you aren't guilty," I replied. "What do you think would help me prove you aren't guilty?"

"I can prove an alibi."

"Let me have it."

"I can't without involving somebody else I don't want to involve."

"If you've got somebody else you'd rather protect more than yourself, your wife, and children," I said, "you ought to go to the penitentiary."

"At any rate," Bob replied, "I want you to help me get out of here so I can work out my alibi. Get Poe to let you take me to see Frank Banks. He's a Mason. He'll go my bail."

I told Poe what Miller wanted. Poe said, "I don't believe it'll do any good, Billie, but get a buggy and team and take him out there."

Frank Banks and Bob Miller went out to the barn and stayed there for two hours. Finally Banks came out to where I was waiting in the buggy and said, "Billie, what do you think? Is he guilty or not?"

I told Banks what Bob had said about his alibi. "And I think he's guilty," I said. Banks replied that he thought so too.

Banks continued, "I took an oath that obligates me to see that a brother Mason has a fair and just trial, but it doesn't obligate me to protect a horse thief. Take him on back as soon as you can."

"I'll go get him," I said.

"Wait a little," Banks replied; "I left him sobbing. He'll come out soon."

He and Cox were tried, found guilty, and sent to the penitentiary for four years.

In August, 1907, we started the beef shipments from Hebron, North Dakota. We made three shipments, two trainloads in each. There were twelve hundred steers in the first shipment, fourteen hundred in the second, and fourteen hundred in the third. Frank and I had cut these four thousand beef steers out of the herd at the roundup. Frank's appendix again bothered him a lot, but he cut out as many steers as I did and took the jars of the cutting horse with the same sort of Irish grit he showed through all the hard work we did that fall.

When we were ready to make our first shipment the Little River was swimming deep, from bank to bank. We tied a log to the wheels on each side of the wagon to keep it afloat, and

201

everything went across without any mishap. There was plenty of room to graze the herd till we were within fifteen miles of the stockyard at Hebron. Then we had to do close herding because of the farms. The cattle were very wild and hard to check, especially when we got nearer the settlements where they heard barking dogs and the roaring and rumbling of trains.

On the last shipment we had fourteen hundred steers, twelve hundred of them from Texas. As we crossed Knife River they didn't water well. They made a run about eleven o'clock. A cloud had come up, with lots of thunder and lightning, and they stampeded. All hands were with them till we got them back on the bedding grounds. It was daybreak before they quited down enough for half the crew to go eat breakfast and change horses.

We got within two miles of the stockyards and camped for the night with a restless herd. We set up two guard shifts, one half of the crew till twelve o'clock and the other half till four. At four o'clock the day work commenced. As we had always done, we classed our cattle and shaped them up as they were to be sold. It was a hard job. Later, the system was changed so that the commission company you consigned your cattle to classed and shaped them in whatever way they thought would bring the best sale. This was a much better plan, for it could be done after the cattle reached market and were in the stockyards. But we couldn't do that then. The work had to be carried out close to the railroad, where the wild steers heard and smelled strange things—and they were already edgy.

Twelve hundred head of this particular herd were Arnett and Jefferies' steers that had been shipped in from Texas in 1904 as yearlings and turned loose on the Indian Reservation, where they hadn't heard any of the noises of civilization. Now, three years later, they had forgotten their earlier train ride. By nature they were wild and hard to handle in close, strange places and around unusual sounds. The other two hundred were our own 75 brand, much easier to work. We selected these quieter, more gentle animals to pen first, hoping they'd attract the wilder steers and make them easier to pen. We knew the next five hundred head—the Texas steers—would be hard to govern, and they more than lived up to our expectations.

202

We got them into the wings that flare out from each side of the gate entrance to the stockyards, but they balked at going in. We crowded the Texans but that didn't break down their resistance. They milled around and around in front of the gate, ignoring the gentle cattle already in the pen.

For the job we were on we needed a crew twice the size of the one we had—with some steer breaking back and a cowboy going after him, when we needed that cowhand somewhere else. The cattle still milled around, and Frank yelled across from the other side, "Billie, can you break this mill?"

I yelled back, "I think so, but everybody's going to have to crowd them from your side and from behind. If any of the steers break out from behind, let them go. Keep everybody with the main herd and push them hard."

Frank rode back and gave the orders.

I said to Jim Redy and Carl Sanders, who were just behind me, "I'm riding into that herd. Jim, keep close to me, Carl, stay close to Jim. We'll turn them the other way. Take your slickers and hit them in the face. Don't be scared—they won't hurt you. We're breaking this mill."

Finally the mill was broken, and they crowded into the gate. Jim, Carl, and I began loading, pushing them into the loading pens—also a difficult thing to do with stirred up cattle. It was late; time for dinner. Others came to help me while Jim and Carl went to eat. I'd forgotten about food, for the work had been going slow. With two trains to be loaded I knew it would be very late before the last train was ready to go.

J. E. Phelan—the 75 owner—was there, taking up Frank's time, which was why Frank forgot to relieve me. When the first five hundred Texas steers were loaded, the other seven hundred were brought in. The two hundred head of the 75 brand were left in the pen to attract them. All hands were with this last bunch and knew what to do, so it went much smoother. They milled at the gate but this was soon broken.

Frank and Mr. Phelan were going to Chicago with the shipment. They went downtown to make some preparations for the trip and got back just as the last car was loaded. I said to them, "My day's work is done. I think I'll go to the chuck wagon and have supper. I haven't eaten a bite since four o'clock this morning."

Frank looked surprised and said, "You haven't? You're too late for supper at the chuck wagon. Tom Burton has served supper, packed everything into the chuck wagon, and caught the train for Dickinson. He won't be back before tomorrow morning. You'll have to go to the hotel."

J. E. spoke up, "I'll go with you. I have a room there and I'll tell the hotel clerk you're going to use it tonight. Whatever you want, put it on my bill."

While I washed up for supper, J. E. found that the dining room was about to close, but he had them wait for me. I was nervous and tired, and he had a bottle of Scotch. He told me to take a drink of it, that it would make me feel better. I took a drink. Not being accustomed to it, I soon felt the effects.

As all this took place during the period of the 1907 bank holiday in President Teddy Roosevelt's administration, Frank didn't want to give checks to anybody. He'd told me that he'd given Tom Burton, the cook, a twenty-dollar check and told the others to see me for what they wanted. He said for me to hold everybody down to twenty dollars or less if it was possible.

I told Frank, "I'll tell them I have only $200 to take care of everybody, and then maybe they won't expect much. I'll write to Wilse Richards. He'll find a way to honor my checks for $200."

There was one barroom in town, and all of our boys were in it. None of them had more than a few dollars, but what they did have proved sufficient to get them started on a big drunk. When they found out I was in the dining room of the hotel next door, they flocked in. I invited all of them to have supper with me, as it was all on Mr. Phelan's tab.

He'd said to put anything I got on his bill, and fourteen more orders of ham and eggs wasn't much, one way or another.

The boys were in good spirits and all were calling Mr. Phelan "J. E." by now.

Then they wanted their checks. I told them about the bank holiday. When I told them I'd check on my own $200 it sounded good to them, for Jim Redy told them he'd put $150 in the little bank there in Hebron and couldn't get a dollar of it. Redy wanted to know how I could get that much money while Frank couldn't give his check on J. E. Phelan.

"Redy," I answered, "I just happen to have a good, strong banker."

When they got their checks they headed back to the barroom, the only place of amusement in town.

I found an easy chair in the lobby of the hotel and sat down, glancing through a newspaper and a magazine. Then I decided to go to bed. I'd been hearing loud talking and laughing from the direction of the barroom as I sat in the lobby, so I thought I'd take a look and see what was going on.

When I entered I saw Oscar Rhine, our horse wrangler, a kid barely sixteen years old. It looked like too rough a crowd for him. I told him to go to our wagon and see that there weren't any hobos around—it was close to the railroad—and then go to bed. I told him I'd get the rest of the boys out soon. Oscar left without complaining.

But it was easy to see that I was too late. Jim Redy and Jim Wilson were the leaders of the revelers, and they were going strong. Several bottles had been broken, and there was broken glass scattered over the floor. Nobody was paying any attention to the cash register, for the bartender had left his post and joined the boys. Anybody who had a mind to could take his turn as bartender. If he could set up the drinks fast enough he could stay—if he was too slow somebody else took over.

I got the bartender aside. "How long will this last?" I asked.

"My stock is low," he replied. "The way they're breaking it up, in two or three hours more there won't be anything left. It isn't what they're drinking; it's what they're breaking up and pouring out—that's their fun. They're not drinking much—just looking for excitement. This would be a bad time to cross them. Their good nature would change in a hurry and it would be hard to stop the trouble."

"I believe I can end this party without any trouble," I said. "There isn't a one of them I'm not in good standing with."

"Don't stop them," he begged. "Let them have their fun. I started it—I told them I was closing up tomorrow anyway—it's not legal to sell liquor in North Dakota now and Governor Burke is determined to close every saloon in the state.

"These glasses and bottles they're breaking up belong to the brewing company I bought beer from. The brewers won't need the glasses, and all their fixtures have been paid for several times over. Besides, I'm leaving Hebron on the westbound train tomorrow."

So the party continued until two o'clock in the morning, and when it ended there wasn't a glass to drink out of—or anything to put in one if there had been. Hebron was a saloonless, bone-dry town—the first and most successful dry town in the state, without the assistance of any law except the law of human nature.

Somehow our boys found the chuck wagon and got to bed before daylight. Tom Burton, our cook, didn't make it back from Dickinson that day, so we had to lay over till the next day for him to move the chuck wagon. The fellows got a chance to get a much-needed rest and to sweep up the glass off the bar-room floor and shovel it into a barrel that had contained beer.

We also got a chance to visit in Hebron. It was a small Western town, and I enjoyed meeting the people. Our boys seemed to be as famous there as Carrie Nation had been in other parts of the West, and the boys hadn't needed any hatchet.

The next day we moved thirty miles to Knife River where we began rounding up five hundred head of Mr. Phelan's stock cattle to move to the reservation. With shipping over, it gave me a little time to look after other interests. By this time the wide-open spaces of McKenzie County were entirely a thing of the past. There was a homesteader on every quarter section of land level enough to till.

Many of these homesteaders were young women from cities and farms of other states. They'd build their shacks at the corners where from two to four homesteads met—and thus they could visit each other, for they didn't have any way of getting around. A large number of cowboys around the country got the idea that they had need for a gentle extra horse that would insure for them a lady's company at picnics, dances, and other social events. I had watched how things were working, and I could see that the idea was paying dividends, for some of the cowboys were taking their saddle horses home and the young ladies home with them. You couldn't help but admire a plan that got you a housekeeper and an extra quarter-section of land.

I too had a young, gentle horse on a stake rope, as well as a new saddle and bridle. I was expecting that horse to do wonders for me, and I went to se him often. He stayed on that rope a year. But there was never a sign that anybody was coming home with him. I had expected too much. There are some things a horse can't do.

Each winter, in January, Frank and I started out riding the range looking for any cattle that might need feeding. When we found any, we'd take them to one of the feeding camps and stables scattered about over the range. The camp houses had a wood-burning stove, table, camp stools, and a bunk bed. We'd pack a bed and enough chuck to last several days and go to one of these camps. We'd ride that part of the range together, then go to the next camp and ride the range around it, till we had all the weak cattle on feed.

In January we rode every day in deep snow, with the thermometer ranging from 20 to 45 degrees below zero. We never saw how a camp looked during daylight, for we'd leave before daybreak and come in after dark. We also worked through in February and went over it again in March.

When a cowboy did that sort of work, he could look the boss in the eye when he received his pay check and feel, "I earned every cent of it."

In 1908 Frank and I went to Chicago with the last shipment. Going to market with the final cattle train each year was the usual thing. With us, as with most cowboys, it was vacation. After a year in the open, the sights of the bustling metropolis were an exciting change.

Every year the buildings got taller and the lights brighter. This time, after a few days in the windy city on Lake Michigan, I got my usual yearning to go to Wisconsin to see Georgia Townsend. Frank said he couldn't go, as he had business at home.

"Well, I've got business at Cambridge, Wisconsin," I told him. "I want another look at the stately trees and the shimmering lakes. And there's a good-looking young lady there. I want to see if she's changed her mind on anything that's important to me."

While I was in Wisconsin, Georgia's mother said, "I was so favorably impressed with your friend Mr. Keogh when he came here with you two years ago. He had such an open face and was so firm when he spoke. Then when I heard about that wild spree his outfit had in Hebron last fall, I decided there must be a weakness somewhere I hadn't noticed."

Western Union carries just what you send, and it is fast and sure. Grapevine is slower and it's just as certain to spread the news you don't want it to carry.

While Mrs. Townsend was talking, my thoughts were tumbling over each other they were coming so fast. But finally I said to myself, "I'm doomed and there's no way out of this one. I won't be welcome here anymore. This is my last trip. And I've heard an honest confession is good for the soul."

I answered, "Mrs. Townsend, you can depend on Frank's every act, look and word to tell you just what he is. He's honest with himself and everyone else. Everybody, and especially the men who work for him and know him best, respects him. Your first opinion of him was correct. Frank wasn't in Hebron when his crew had their wild spree. If he'd been there I don't doubt he'd have handled the situation different. I'm his straw boss. That leaves me in full charge when Frank's away. I decided it was best not to try to break up the spree. The blame's on me, not on him."

Everything was quiet till Mrs. Townsend said, "Good night. I think I'll go to bed." Georgia added, "You know where your room is, Billie. I believe I'll go to bed, too." I concluded that my stock was so low it was worthless.

But as she walked by she gave me a "Yankee dime," the first she ever gave me. I never needed a kiss more, for I was broke, as far as my stock in romance was concerned, and that revived me some. But my biggest worry was mostly what her mother might be thinking.

Next morning Mrs. Townsend was very pleasant, and the subject of the high jinks at Hebron wasn't brought up again. Still,

I felt it was time to leave, but to my surprise Mrs. Townsend insisted that I spend another day.

When I got back to the ranch I found a letter from Wilse Norrad asking me to come to visit him. He was in charge of his uncle Webb Arnett's ranch on Hance Creek, twenty-five miles away. He'd been there several months, but I hadn't had a chance to go over and see him.

Actually I hadn't seen him in several years, for he'd been up in Montana in charge of a ranch there. He'd married a beautiful girl of about nineteen. I'd heard about her and wanted to meet her and see if I could find out how an old cowboy like Wilse could get such a young lady.

There wasn't much I had to do about then, so I rode over to pay them a visit. Wilse met me and we went to the barn to put up my horse. He told me how he'd described me to his wife before I got there. She was lonesome, so he told her they could have lots of fun with me, that I was an old crippled fellow who hadn't ever done much, that he'd invite me over and I'd stay all winter. As we walked to the house we were talking. He opened the door and stepped back.

As I walked in, Wilse tripped me and I fell flat on the floor. While I was in this manly position he introduced me to his wife: "That's Bill, Grace," and "Bill, this is Grace. Just get up off the floor and have a chair."

I liked Grace. She was pretty and she was friendly. I still wondered how old Wilse got her and reasoned that girls must be easier to get in Montana and maybe I ought to go up there.

But the next day a pretty little pony-built girl in her teens came to visit Grace. She was Jude McLaughlin, whose folks had a ranch eight miles east. She'd met Grace at a dance but hadn't come to see her before—just decided now to visit her for a few days, so she'd saddled her horse and had ridden over.

What a coincidence, I thought. This may be the turning point in my life. She was a delight to look at—about 16 hands high, 110 pounds, dark-red hair and brown eyes, and fair skin. That red corduroy suit she was wearing just set her off. I'd never seen a prettier paint pony, or a pony of any other color that was prettier than Jude. I could tell it would be just as easy to fall in love with her as with any horse in my mount, and all my life I'd been falling in love with horses.

There was a kind of cuddly friendliness about Jude. She'd get close to me—like an old pal—and showed a great interest in anything I talked about. I was convinced I'd made a hit. I'd always heard of love at first sight, and this seemed to be it. The fourth day I said, "Jude, let's take a little horseback ride."

Wilse helped me saddle the horses and said, "Now be careful where you ride. You know Fred Voigt lives three miles north of here, and I hear he's been shining up to Jude."

Fred was an old friend who'd cooked for our chuck wagon. I felt confident that I had Fred bested, so after a pleasant hour of riding together I said, "Jude, let's ride by Fred Voigt's. I'd like to see him."

"I'd just love to do that," Jude replied. "I've been wanting to see Fred's place."

Jude seemed so happy about going it made my wings flop. Why hadn't I listened to Wilse? But it was too late now. I thought, "I'll play a bold hand. I'm losing, but I won't let old Wilse know it. He doesn't mind lying to me, so he won't know from me but what I've got Fred beat."

Fred had a comfortable little two-room house. Everything about it was neat and tidy. Jude kept squealing with delight over everything Fred had. She couldn't thank me enough for bringing her by. Fred thanked me for it, too, and asked Jude if he could take her to a dance; she said he could. We rode back and had a pleasant evening with Grace and Wilse. I never saw Jude again—or forgot her charms.

As I rode those lonely twenty-five miles back to our headquarters I had time to think: "Wilse got Grace because he could put up a good front—running a cattle ranch for his Uncle Webb, who had let him have a nice buggy and team—a sure sign of success. There's no point in me going to Montana. I don't have any Uncle Anybody up there, and I might not get anything but a sheepherder's job. I'll stay with Frank. North Dakota girls are just as pretty as Montana girls. Several of them are very nice to me, and very friendly too. One of them might change her mind.

210

Besides, my sorrel horse Hondo will be on a stake rope again when the green grass comes."

But my next tactic—of disagreeing with girls instead of giving them a lot of attention—wasn't any more successful.

I liked to go to Berg on the day the mail came in. This was always an event, and I'd meet most of the settlers, especially the lady homesteaders. At that time the subject of "woman suffrage" was a very lively one.

I'd heard my father say that the Constitution of the United States should give men and women equal rights in shaping our government. He thought a woman might make as good a President as a man and clinched his argument by saying, "Why not? Queen Victoria's been the best ruler England ever had."

One day there were several young women at the Berg post office waiting for the mail. They were all discussing the benefits of "woman suffrage." I knew if I agreed with them I wouldn't get a word in edgewise. So I decided to take the other side. I'd heard a lot of people argue against it, and thought I'd fire their ammunition.

With six champions of "woman suffrage" lined up against me the argument got so hot and heavy I wished I hadn't jumped in. Finally Emma Berg, about fourteen years old, said, "Don't pay any attention to what Billie says. He knows he's so old nobody'd have him anyway, so he doesn't care what he says."

I'd given some previous thought myself to the matter of growing old, but Emma's remark put the subject before me in a more personal way.

Neither Emma Berg nor I understood much about the mysterious workings of fate, and perhaps I didn't know my own mind about marriage. I saw girls who had great appeal to me, but there always seemed some good reason why marriage was out of the question. Usually money. After a while it became a habit to refer to myself as a rejected suitor, though I never had an offer rejected. If any of the girls ever gave me the air they did it so tactfully that I wasn't conscious of it. And my work usually kept me too busy to brood about it.

Frank Keogh and I kept on doing the same things as we had in the winters before, riding the range and gathering the cattle that needed feeding. Then in June, 1909, we received 2,500 two-year-old steers at White Earth, North Dakota. They'd come from Canada and all were red and red-roan Durhams. They came in three shipments, one train a day, so we were camped four days at White Earth. It was a small Western town, and we had a chance to get acquainted with its people and invite them to have a meal with us at the chuck wagon. Many of them did. Jess Wickham was the cook and he enjoyed feeding people.

The postmistress at White Earth was Miss Lillian Carney. Ed King, who had the feed barn, told me, "I made your boss Frank Keogh acquainted with Miss Carney. She's very good-looking, smart and friendly. Everybody here thinks the world of her. You want to meet her?"

"Yes," I said, "but let me do it my way. I'll go ask her for my mail and get acquainted that way. I'll find an opening to tell her something about Frank. She won't know that I know she's met him."

As a usual thing we got our mail at Berg, fifty miles from there. I didn't expect to get any at White Earth, but I went up to the window and asked. Lillian looked through the "Ts" and told me I didn't have any mail. I put on an act of great disappointment and said offhand that I was there with Frank Keogh's outfit and would be back. She invited me very sweetly to come back the next day and she'd try to find some mail for me.

Next day I was back again and went through the same act. After four days of this I was becoming well acquainted with the charming lady-postmaster and had told her all about Frank—that is, all I could without appearing to try to tell her anything about him. Then I didn't see her again till three years later—when Frank brought her to the ranch as Mrs. Keogh. (We remained good friends until Lillian died forty-five years later.)

From White Earth Creek to the Big Missouri we found new fields of wheat and flax. By now the Old West with its broad prairies and free grass was a thing of the past for sure. We were putting our last big herd on the Fort Berthold Indian Reservation.

October 25 of the following year—1910—was a memorable day for our outfit, and for the country—and for me. On that day the last trainload of the last big herd in western North Dakota was shipped out.

For four summers and three winters I'd been with Frank Keogh as a cowboy, and I'd enjoyed it to the hilt. He ran a smooth outfit and there wasn't any friction at any time. For eight more years I was associated with Frank and Lillian, their son Brooks, and their daughter Betty. Afterwards I had ranches of my own and a family of my own. When I returned to Texas after my cowboy days were over I met and married Lora Mae Boulden, a wonderful wife and wonderful mother of our two daughters, Lucille and Lillian.

But I still look back on that last day's work on October 25, 1910, with a bit of sadness. It was my last day as a working cowboy, though for the rest of my life I was not physically far away from the old ranch lands and never away from them in my heart. I'd covered a lot of ground since that day in another October—1892—when I went to work on Charles Goodnight's Cross J Ranch in Texas.

Though there'd been many rough places in my cowboy life, it had been easy to take because I'd been privileged to work for men like Charles Goodnight, W. G. Ray, Wilse Richards, Hiram Elliott, and Frank Keogh. All of them had some of the same traits of character. Each was honest in all dealings with all men —and demanded the same. In no other walk of life have I found their superiors—or even their equals.

I never worked for Mr. Goodnight again after I left him in 1896, but I never lost touch with him. And I visited him whenever I could. He told me once he thought I'd get along all right because I depended on myself. Like other men of his type, Mr. Goodnight had great compassion for the weak, but the men he wanted to deal with and to depend upon were men of self-reliance. He'd been a good example. Without preaching or teaching or many words at all he somehow taught others the value of depending upon themselves.

Perhaps more than anybody else in the risky cattle business he had his ups and downs, but he took them calmly and always went on to something bigger.

As the years went by, his physical appearance changed somewhat, of course, but the inner strength of the man never did. In later years, the hills on the Goodnight ranch didn't seem so high as they did in my youth. In fact, everything there had shrunk a little except Mr. Goodnight. The years couldn't change that personality.

Mrs. Goodnight, mother to the Texas Panhandle, died in 1926. Then one day in December, 1929, I stood on a windy hill a couple of miles north of the ranch headquarters, while Charles Goodnight was buried. Most of the men standing with me were of an aristocracy—former Goodnight cowhands. For all of us many memories came crowding. One thing we agreed on: Charles Goodnight had been a better cowboy than any of us, better than any other cowboy we'd ever known.

INDEX OF NAMES

221

222

TWILIGHT ON THE RANGE was composed in 11 point Caledonia, 2 points leaded, with Bodoni display and printed letterpress on 60-pound Adena Eggshell made by the Chillicothe Paper Company. Decorations for chapter divisions were drawn by Maxine Price. The book was manufactured by the Printing Division of the University of Texas.